Three Blind Mice

The Three Presidents Before Lincoln and the Decade of the 1850s

Darryl Murphy

Copyright © 2014 Darryl Murphy
All rights reserved.

ISBN-10: 1499245939
ISBN-13: 9781499245936
Library of Congress Control Number: 2014907727
CreateSpace Independent Publishing Platform
North Charleston, South Carolina

Table of Contents

Prologue ·v
Chapter 1 The Mice of Men, Fillmore, Pierce and Buchanan · · · · · ·1
Chapter 2 A Fragile America (and World) · · · · · · · · · · · · · · · · · · ·10
Chapter 3 Dred Scott and John Brown ·14
Chapter 4 Other Shit ·20
Chapter 5 Congresses and Cabinets of the 1850s · · · · · · · · · · · · ·25
Chapter 6 Post Presidencies of the Three Blind Mice · · · · · · · · · ·31
Chapter 7 Kansas Nebraska Act ·34
Chapter 8 Women in the 1850s ·36
Chapter 9 The Crimean War and Napoleon III · · · · · · · · · · · · · ·46
Chapter 10 The Impact of the Irish on America · · · · · · · · · · · · · · ·52
Chapter 11 The Pre Civil War Military ·56
Chapter 12 Nicaragua, Cuba and the Republic of
           Maryland (in Africa) ·82
Chapter 13 Native Americans and the 1850s · · · · · · · · · · · · · · · · ·91
Chapter 14 Utah, Brigham Young and the Mormons · · · · · · · · · · 101
Chapter 15 California, Minnesota and Oregon · · · · · · · · · · · · · · 110
Chapter 16 The United States Census and the Cotton Gin · · · · · · 125
Chapter 17 Art in the 1850s · 134
Chapter 18 F.L.O.T.U.S. · 156

Chapter 19 William Parker and the Christiana Riot · · · · · · · · · · · 167
Chapter 20 Literature in the 1850s · · · · · · · · · · · · · · · · · · · 174
Epilogue · 187
Bibliography · 193
Acknowledgements · 283
About the Author · 285

Prologue

Like other powerful institutions around the world America has had their historical brain farts as well. This writing will examine, well, the Three Blind Mice of the American presidency from 1850-1860. A Whig (Fillmore) and two Democrats, and how their indifference/sympathy toward slavery steered the United States directly into the American Civil War.

Millard Fillmore, Franklin Pierce and James Buchanan. Three men who were President, but hardly Presidential. Three men saddled with a Congress made up of individuals who weren't crafty enough in their own right to become President, but at the same time smart enough to make these three look like buffoons in perpetuity (by the way you know why they call it Congress? Because it's the opposite of PROgress, funny how that remains true even today).

Three men who slept walked through time, pissed off enough rich, white, male Northerners, to make them establish a new political party (the Republican Party) and get their guy (Lincoln) elected to the top job first time right out of the gate (not counting John Fremont's test run loss to Buchanan with an assist from Fillmore representing the, get this ("Know Nothing" Party)). See what I mean?

Talk about fucking shit up! They made Pol Pot look like Cincinnatus. These three were true human Slinky's. They weren't good for much but sure would put a smile on your face when pushed down the stairs! Anyway, mind you it will be a 21st Century look with no punches pulled. And yes, there is an air of brevity to my words. Don't take my sarcasm seriously while you discover the truth. So if you dare, read on.

For example, we all know that from the early period of the British monarchy (there's a reason Queen Victoria was called "The Grandmother of Europe" and it wasn't just because Prince Albert (her first cousin, by the way) found the best piece of ass in his life (I think all that fucking (nine kids) is what really killed him) and kept her womb full of royal brats.

Male royals, when looking for a permanent piece, pretty much stuck to the motto "no blood, no cock." And female royals pretty much stuck to the same mantra. At this point they're more inbred than a family of Tennessee hillbillies. It's no wonder the men went crazy and the women miscarried as much as the French surrendered over the course of time.

Sometimes it's all in the genes. All of this with absolute power and lackeys all around. As well as a groom of the stool (yes, the royal ass wiper, a, by nature, introvert that was the king's closest confidant and made sure Scott Tissue never went out of business). Imagine you had to explain that when meeting a girl at the bar and the "so what do you do" question comes up.

Don't fret it wasn't all bad. Being so close to power made him the envy of all other commoners. Its right up there with the guy who specializes in Oral Equine Urology (horse cocksucker) and the guy who produces midget porn (or is it dwarf porn these days, I don't know). But I digress;

Henry VIII is a good example. He fucked, divorced or beheaded his way through his reign until he got so fat and nasty he died from general disgust. At least Henry had the balls to tell the Catholic Church to go fuck themselves before he died. Even if Anne Boleyn (a cousin by the way) had to give them to him. But I liked the guy. Just sayin'.

And let's not forget the Papacy. Early popes displayed such traits as pedophilia, adultery, homosexuality, nepotism and fornication. From Leo to Adrian to Clement to Julius to Pius, just to name a few.

And the whole time brainwashing incestuous monarchs to kill each other, along with women and children, all in the name of God under the guise of the Holy Roman Empire (and we think the world has all gone to shit today). Along comes Martin Luther and John Calvin and say "Look we have a totally different line of brainwashing religious bullshit to get you through the day (and a newly invented printing press through which to spread the word)."

The Catholic Church would spend many unsuccessful years trying to let Europe know that manipulating the faithful is our fucking job. Thus, today we are left with Lutherans, Calvinists, Protestants, Baptists, Mormons, Moonies, etc. You get the idea.

The decade that was the 1850s was the pre fight weigh-in to the boxing match that would become the War Between the States. As much as we want to talk about the brilliance of our Founding Fathers, they were much more lucky than smart. Although smart enough to convince the bottom economic classes to fight for rights they had no intention of honoring.

version of history we were all taught).

A bunch of wealthy White men got pissed off that another group of wealthy white men four thousand miles away in Great Britain were fucking them over by taking too big a piece of the pie that they were fucking people out of here in the colonies. So they said to Georgie (King George III) and his message boy Robert Walpole (prime minister) "go fuck yourself."

So they put a few fancy phrases on paper. Like "all men are created equal", "no taxation without representation" and "life, liberty and the pursuit of happiness (although they forgot to tell you that you gotta catch it yourself). Of course, at the time, none of that bullshit applied to anyone else but themselves.

Then they convince the lower ten percent of society to fight for their newly stated rights and "bang," America is born. Thus was set in motion the core of the layered onion that is the United States today. The Articles of Confederation was sloppy and hastily done. The United States Constitution was much better.

The Constitution was, like the other three major state documents before it (The Continental Association, Declaration of Independence and The Articles of Confederation) were put in place to protect the wealthy. Only rich, White land owners could vote.

Three Blind Mice

Women were a social lower class and slavery was disgusting to some, tolerated by others and loved by yet others. I think George Carlin (a man way before his time, by the way) said it best about American capitalism, "rich people invented poor people to scare the shit out of the middle class and make them get up and go to work every day."

Washington takes office and one of the first things he does is tell the French (who have asked for assistance to help a revolution of their own) "thanks for the help you gave us but I'll be damned if we're gonna pay you back."

Jefferson comes up with "manifest destiny" which was political speak for White people are taking over this whole shit while we go from sea to shining sea. No condemnation here, what happened was inevitable, how it happened was shitty. Period.

James Monroe decided that he was sick of the Europeans fucking around in the Americas. He gets John Quincy Adams to write the new rule. This would become the Monroe Doctrine. It basically says to everybody and anybody if you fuck around in North or South America you are fucking with us and we ain't having it anymore. 'Nuff said.

That John Quincy wasn't done putting his stamp on the historical record. During the election of 1824 him and Henry Clay get together and fuck Andrew Jackson out of a well earned presidential election victory. He becomes the first (of four so far, Benjamin Harrison, Rutherford B. Hayes and George W. Bush being the others) United States Presidents to lose the general election popular vote and win the electoral college.

Darryl Murphy

George W. Bush would be the latest to do it (except he used the Supreme Court as his gangstas as opposed to Congress). Winning the Presidency of the United States is the BIG con, so anything goes. Like this:

Andrew Jackson was the big man on campus after kicking much ass in the Battle of New Orleans (who cares that a treaty ending the war had already been signed by the time the battle begun, we don't want that to get in the way of a good story).

The 1824 election comes around and it's a doozy. Today's presidential elections are debutante balls compared to Nineteenth Century machine politics. JQA's team accused his wife of being a bigamist/whore (which pissed AJ off to no end).

Despite the fact that Andrew Jackson won the popular vote and also won a majority of the electoral college votes (by the way, the Electoral College is the little yellow bus of political institutions and should be eradicated like polio), but not have the number needed to secure victory, he lost.

Without the number of electoral college votes needed to become President-Elect the election shifted to the House of Representatives. Henry Clay (who was Speaker of the House by the way and didn't think much of Mr. Jackson) was the Ross Perot of this election and shifted his support (and electoral votes) to JQA. Just like that, John Quincy Adams and his Elvis Presley style pork chop sideburns (all be them gray) win the election. Oh, and just for shits and giggles, good ole' Mr. Clay becomes Secretary of State for his generosity. Now that's a reach around! At least now you can see how Mr. Jackson would be quite peeved.

Three Blind Mice

Like our Three Blind Mice, John Quincy Adams would be a one term President as well. Karma is a bitch, isn't it? Jackson would have his victory in 1828. And he would have his challenges as well. He took bitterness into the White House as his wife died just after the election. He blamed the harsh attacks of his opponents for her death. He'd have to defend his wife (indirectly) once again. This time it was from the wives of the men in his cabinet. Known as the Petticoat Affair, what started out as a cat fight between a couple of uppity bitches eventually led to the resignation of most of his cabinet. All of this in the middle of his first term!

John Calhoun was President Jackson's Vice President. Mr. Calhoun's wife didn't think much of Mr. Eaton's wife. Mr. Eaton was President Jackson's Secretary of War. Soon, the Vice President's wife turned all the other cabinet wives against Mr. Eaton's wife and they refused to talk to her.

Jackson defended her and his Secretary of War and happily accepted the resignation of most of his cabinet. This scandal was truly a case where the women married to the men in the Executive Branch of the United States Government had half the power and all the pussy. Now, you would think there were more important tasks for the President to attend to. But, Jackson, still bitter over how his wife was treated made time to address this issue.

It was one of those occasions where a Presidency was significantly changed and it had nothing to do with politics. It would lead to Jackson being the first President to establish a "Kitchen Cabinet." This was an informal group of advisors (think of them as "Presidential Homies") that a President uses when he's seeking advice without agenda behind it. Personally, I think they were just a bunch of bitter bitches jealous that they weren't sleeping in the White House.

He would also, have to fight over the Second Bank of the United States (forerunner to the Federal Reserve, both financial pariahs that act as cold sores on a capitalist economy, Keynesian macroeconomic models have this theory all wrong in my opinion). What were Andrew Jackson's two biggest failings? As President, one was the forced migration of the Native Americans to what is today Oklahoma. Popularly known as the "Trail of Tears," many died brutally and unnecessarily because of this action.

An action he embarked on which was illegal and contrary to a Supreme Court decision. To this day there are many Native Americans who won't carry a twenty dollar bill because of their disgust of the man. I think if you asked a Native American today they would tell you that Andrew Jackson can kiss their ass with his tongue out. His second failing was nominating Roger Taney to the Supreme Court. Taney would later play a big role in stirring the pre Civil War pot with the Dred Scott decision (more on that later).

Martin Van Buren was Jackson's lap dog. He was good enough to continue Jackson's policies, appease the South and support slavery by tolerating it. He did invite the term "ok (okay)" into the American lexicon. Hailing from Kinderhook NY, he was known as "Old Kinderhook" during the election. The saying was Van Buren is "Ok". He was the first President born in the United States (although English was his second language, he spoke Dutch as his first language). The seven Presidents before him were born in what was then colonial America.

Three Blind Mice

Other highlights included William Henry Harrison (the Tippacanoe of "Tippacanoe and Tyler Too"), who died shortly after giving his inaugural address on one of the coldest days of the year. Dumbass! I mean really. It's cold and nasty out, your out there without a coat and hat and talk for two hours about some bullshit that you don't even believe. As a man in your late sixties do you really think you ain't gonna catch cold? Again. Dumbass!

So his Vice President, John Tyler, who ordinarily, like, every Vice President would have been the dingle berry hanging from a hair on the President's ass is all of a sudden something, but not everyone is sure what. Is he President? Acting President? What? To his detractors he becomes the original "His Accidency" (besides my Three Blind Mice). Much like Oedipus was the original Motherfucker in terms of level of originality (I don't want to imply he was fucking his Mom, please).

An ardent racist (much along the level of Woodrow Wilson, who routinely called Blacks "darkies" and purposely segregated the federal government and its facilities (a policy that would last well into the FDR administration nationwide)) he would have two unique American firsts. He was the first President not elected to the office. And he was the also the first President "not" to die a US citizen (he died in the Confederate States of America as a citizen of the Confederacy during the American Civil War).

After Tyler, James Polk came along and swept into office with his fists balled up. A true hawk, he was just about kicking ass. He threatened the British over the Oregon Territory and then turned around and bitch slapped the Mexicans (in the Mexican-American War), took away a bunch of their sand boxes and greatly expanded the United States.

Darryl Murphy

One of which would become California, today, the sixth largest economy in the world on its own. It's ironic that California would gain statehood under the first of our Three Blind Mice, Fillmore.

Chapter 1

The Mice of Men, Fillmore, Pierce and Buchanan

Now that you have some examples of the frailty of power let's have a look at the first of the Three Blind Mice.

Like Gerald Ford, he served a partial term, after the sudden death of Zachary Taylor (he of the cherries and milk, still a strange combination). He would piss off so many people in his own circle that come time to run for a full term in 1852 his own party wouldn't even nominate him. Imagine today a sitting President unable to secure his own party's mantle in the next election.

Born in the Finger Lakes region of New York his father tried to make him a haberdasher a la Harry Truman. He didn't think much of it and turned to the study of law. Admitted to the bar in the 1820s he set up shop, got married to a woman named Abigail and settled in Buffalo. He managed to be one of the founders of the University of Buffalo and served in the Mexican American War. So he wasn't a total dickhead. He was just not prepared to be President and frankly, never expected to be.

Darryl Murphy

Franklin Pierce was our most Shakespearean of US Presidents, a true combination of comedy, drama, tragedy and backstabbing. A native of the great state of New Hampshire he would become what the newsies of the day called a "doughface" (a northerner with southern sympathies). He got to Washington, D.C. in the 1830s. At the time the federal district was a real shithole. Most congressmen lived in boarding houses when in session. With his wife refusing to live in such a place, Frankie was alone most of the time. This allowed him to become an avid drunk. Legislatively, he towed the party line. During many of his binging sessions he befriended many southern Democrats who would later shape his presidency. Eventually he would go back to private practice and serve in the Mexican American War.

He also suffered true tragedy in his life. All of his children died in their youth. The most horrific being his son Benjamin. Benjamin Pierce died in a train accident right in front of his parents not long after his election to POTUS (President of the United States). As mentioned earlier, his Whig opponent in 1852 was General Winfield Scott (his boss during the Mexican ass fucking). Fillmore wanted in on the nomination, but was such an asshole politically within his own party they didn't even want him. Thus, he served as President without ever having been elected by anyone (thirteen was certainly unlucky for him).

During the election Pierce was kinda like Trent Dilfer when the Baltimore Ravens made a great playoff run and won the Super Bowl in 2000 with him at quarterback. Like Dilfer, Pierce was asked just not to fuck it up and let the veterans (senior party officials in this case) take care of it. So he made very few speeches or appearances and stayed out of the way.

Fortunately, for him, General Scott was throwing pick sixes (a "pick six" in football is when the quarterback throws an interception and the defender returns the ball for a touchdown) all over the place (politically speaking). Scott fucked up his speeches, bungled appearances, and generally made voters feel uncomfortable (Mitt Romney would use the same playbook in the 2012 election. The best being when he told Soledad O'Brien of CNN that the poor had a safety net and implied that under his administration poor people would remain very poor and very happy (in so many words). Again, politically speaking. General Scott was a great American military hero. He was just a shitty presidential nominee. The result was a landslide and Pierce got down to the political business of turning his back on his friends and leading the country to the doorstep of killing each other with passion and vigor in the American Civil War. He got plenty of help from his cabinet.

Ironically, one of his diplomats was James Buchanan, who would help fuck Pierce over with his compliance in the Ostend Manifesto (good friends are hard to find). In a bit of consistency, Pierce was the only President to select a cabinet and keep that cabinet intact for his entire term. His Vice President was one William Rufus King. The only federally elected official to take the oath of office outside the United States. He was a lunger (tuberculosis). A sickly man, he was rumored to be James Buchanan's long time fuck buddy. But more on that later.

The Ostend Manifesto; it was a diplomatic, literary piece of shit that would ruin America's (and Pierce's) reputation and expose her imperialists ways. Along with his Secretary of State, William Marcy and three of his foreign ambassadors (including future President James Buchanan), they would make a plan to eventually admit Cuba as another state that forced people to work against their will under the threat of violence (slavery).

The manifesto, (they met in Ostend Belgium, thus the name) recommended to Pierce that the United States should offer to buy the island of Cuban from the Spanish and if they refuse we should just take the motherfucker Don Corleone style. The American Mafia doesn't have shit on the United States Government. Crips and Bloods wish they could jack shit the way America does. Of course America would later put Hawaii, the Philippines (joke; what do you call a Filipino contortionist? A Manila folder!), Puerto Rico and Guam on an imperial dog leash. Again, with no reach around (or lube). Of course, the intention was to make Cuba a slave state and backdoor the free state/slave state conversation going on in the rest of the country. Northerners would be very pissed off and would make Pierce look foolish in the eyes of the nation. This was one of the events that would directly lead to the founding of the Republican Party in the mid 1850s.

It's interesting today that Democrats have the Black vote on total lockdown. Starting from 1865 up until Herbert Hoover fucked over Black voters with his failure to keep political assurances promised during the election, Republicans could always count on Black support. Even after that, from Ike (who declared racial discrimination a national security issue), to Nixon (who put the teeth in Affirmative Action), to Reagan, (who signed the Martin Luther King Jr holiday into law) the Republican Party had several instances where their interests and Black interest coincided.

Meanwhile, Democrats offered minorities social programs and a great place in the permanent underclass (historically speaking). How much have times really changed? Not taking a position, just food for thought. Remember Executive Order 9066? Executive Order 9066 put Japanese Americans in internment camps not long after the attack on Pearl Harbor. Franklin Roosevelt felt compelled to fuck over his fellow citizens, who, by all accounts, were just as appalled and shocked by the attack as every other American.

Imagine you're sitting at home, maybe reading a book, listening to a radio program or just bullshitting around YOUR house and some asshole shows up in a military uniform, armed, and tells you "don't pack a fucking thing, just grab a coat, your kids and get on the fucking bus." The United States Government would later ask some of these individuals to join the armed forces to prove their love for a country that just fucked them over for generations to come. Funny thing was the island of Oahu, Hawaii where Pearl Harbor is located was flooded with people of Japanese descent. And there was hardly a whisper about interment on the island. And even funnier is the fact that the United States went to war with Imperial Japan after they attacked an island that they themselves took by force and deposed its monarchy. In a later ironic twist, Japanese American military forces would become some of the most decorated units during World War Two. The most famous of those Japanese American units being the 442nd Regimental Combat Team affectionately known as the "Purple Heart Battalion." Like Black American military units they would have to prove themselves. And boy did they. Reagan would later offer surviving members and their families' beer and pizza money in the form of reparations to make up for his colleague's bad choice.

Another stain on America occurred with the Tuskegee Experiment which was a long term clinical study done by the United States Public

Health service. The government wanted to find out what would happen if you gave someone syphilis and not treat it (ever). Even though, you had the treatment right (penicillin) upstairs in a fucking cabinet. How this makes sense to a bunch of men sitting in a conference room in Washington, DC boggles the mind. Moreover, instead of using the uncle, who's always hitting on his little cousin at the family reunion, or the pedophile priest who, for some reason, just can't get his mind around the whole celibacy thing, or that crazy fucker who just likes raping and torturing women, they decided that poor, uneducated Black sharecroppers were great test subjects.

And yes, I think that rapists, pedophiles and repeat sexual offenders should have this idea meted out at their sentencing hearings. The judge's comments would be something like this, "I sentence you to a lifetime of syphilis as specified by the Federal Bureau of Prisons. You will be injected with the disease, not treated, and placed in a cell painted with pictures of penicillin dosages. In time you will go blind, lose your mind and die a horrible death. Have a nice life motherfucker." Violent sexual crime would go down to zero in no time.

Terms like "Bleeding Kansas" and "Missouri Ruffians" would enter into the American lexicon. Which would become the background for one of the greatest American Western films ever made. The Outlaw Josey Wales ("dying ain't much of a living boy"). Watch it if you haven't. You'll get it then.

President James Buchanan was actually an accomplished gentleman, another member of the "D.C. club" of the day. Please don't think just anyone can be President. You are either in the circle, or you are not in the circle. All three of these mice had previous Administration connections. Like the other two, Buchanan managed to stay just irrelevant enough to become a good candidate, an example of power being held in the hands of a few men in American history.

Another example of power in the hands of the few? There was a stretch starting with the Presidential election of 1952 until the 2008 election when, either, a Nixon, Humphrey, Dole, Clinton, or Bush was on every Presidential election (Republican or Democratic) party ticket. That's an incredible fact about real power in America.

That's a lot of wit, grit and bullshit. Mr. Obama broke that string in 2008. But with Mrs. Clinton's eye on the 2016 election, her daughter Chelsea potentially in waiting at some point, and a whole bunch of little Bushs' being groomed for senior politics you can tell your kids to forget about a shot at the White House anytime soon, unless they fuck or buy their way into one of those families. But I could be wrong. Just sayin'.

It was a similar scenario at the country's beginning. From 1788-1836 it was a Washington, Adams, Jefferson, Madison, Monroe or Jackson. In two hundred and twenty plus years of Presidential elections (1788-2008), ninety four of those years were in the hands of eleven rich, white men (eleven and half if you count Obama's White half). That's forty three percent of America's history boys and girls! And you think you really have "choice" with your vote? Hey, but back to Mr. Buchanan. He assumed the Presidency in March 1857. He was a Pennsylvania boy (from the Alabama part). The saying about Pennsylvania is "there's Philadelphia and Pittsburgh and Alabama in the middle."

He was ambassador to Russia and the United Kingdom, a Senator and Chairman of the House Judiciary Committee in the United States House of Representatives. So he wasn't a slouch, per se. However, like I said, if all politics are local he was just irrelevant enough to win the nomination. Helped by Fillmore and Pierce's incompetence he swept into the White House with ease. He was also a signatory to the Ostend Manifesto which helped to ruin Franklin Pierce. Whether or not this was by accident or not is a matter of opinion.

Whatever the case, he was a true dove as Commander in Chief when it came to preserving the Union. Yes, that's French for he was a pussy (and that could be because his asshole was anything but exit only). He was widely rumored to have been fucking his "special friend" William King (Franklin Pierce's Vice President) whom he shared a home (and bed) with. They could be found together everywhere in Washington, D.C. They would be chided as "Miss Nancy" and "Aunt Fancy." King died in 1853 and Buchanan was quite lonely after.

Makes you wonder as President if the White House butler ever asked him "Excuse me Mr. President, would you like a little shit on the dick before you go to bed tonight?" And Buchanan responding, "no George, but maybe tomorrow after the State of the Union." You think he was sneaking cock into the White House the way Kennedy snuck in pussy? He was so conciliatory to the South that when South Carolina said "fuck you" to the rest of the country he conceded that the federal government had no "legal" authority to interfere (he thought secession was illegal nonetheless, but the federal government had no basis to enforce it). Talk about serving french fries with mayonnaise. It just wasn't American.

Three Blind Mice

He basically said to Lincoln "this shit storm is yours." What a fucking lemon. He should have thought less about sucking William King's cock and more about governing. But, hey, he was an old man, presidentially speaking (65 years of age). So who could blame him for having a shriveled up speed bag for testicles.

Chapter 2

❦

A Fragile America (and World)

Besides happenings here in the United States, plenty of other shit was going down around the world. We'll examine a few just to make the point.

The British had just started sending convicts to Australia. Thus turning the continent into their personal Alcatraz on steroids. The very same British, who invented "oh, I think I'll stop in for tea and crumpets and while I'm here I think I'll take over the whole fucking country, or continent (whichever fits)." Why let the fact that there are already motherfuckers there get in the way? The Brits also blockaded, that year, Athens because they thought they had a bite at that apple as well but it didn't work. America, in a true version of "imitation is the best form of flattery" would take a few lessons from their friends later on in its history, fret not.

The Austrians take over Prussia and begin to lay the groundwork for what would become World War One. Fillmore takes office in the summer but what does he oath into? Meanwhile in Congress, Hank Clay has been pushing the Comprise of 1850 like Nancy Pelosi pushed universal healthcare. President Fillmore, who was against it during his stint as President Taylor's dingleberry (Vice President) suddenly changed his mind and was all for it. It would become moot when his fellow mouse, Franklin Pierce, backed the Kansas-Nebraska act.

The vigorish on the legislation was the Fugitive Slave Law of 1850. This law formally made the United States complicit sponsors of slavery. Remember, while the whole time the United States Constitution (which other peoples around the world, who also sought the right of self determination were adopting this document as their own political philosophy) still said "all men are created equal."

The United States was encumbered with the fact that those writing and interpreting the rules were still defining a very strict definition of "men." The Fugitive Slave Law of 1850 basically said to all Black people, free or otherwise, that White men drunk enough, nosy enough or just plain belligerent enough can accuse you of being not a person, but chattel and rounded up like a stray pet (except there ain't no SPCA for your ass).

The fringe behavior of slave chasers/catchers and common criminals would bring back the days of people like Patty Cannon. It was not unusual for free Blacks (including children) to be kidnapped, shipped to the Deep South and enslaved. Patty Cannon was a notorious figure from the early Nineteenth Century that ran a gang who specialized in kidnapping and stealing free blacks, especially children. From a criminal justice point of view this was an early version of human trafficking after the United States outlawed the importation of slaves in 1808.

It was the reverse Underground Railroad and the crime was simple. Steal a Black child off the street, ship the child south by boat and fence the child for whatever you could get. After the United States Congress ban the importation of slavery (but not slavery itself) slaves became three times more valuable than they were the day before the legislation was passed. Even in the early 1800s kidnapping was a crime in both the North and South.

However, no one was going to challenge a White person dragging a Black person through the street in leg irons. It was too common an occurrence and in the southern United States even more so. This set up well for Patty Cannon and her gang. This cunt lived on the Delmarva Peninsula close to the Maryland border counties of Caroline and Dorchester. Starting sometime after the end of the War of 1812 and continuing into the 1820s, the gang stole, beat and shipped many Blacks south and into slavery. Some died as a result of these beatings Patty Cannon was ultimately indicted for murder in 1829. She would die in her cell a month after being arrested.

So Fillmore, going all Neville Chamberlain, signs the bill and declares peace in our time, sort of. It's only a temporary patch as Pierce and Buchanan would have to deal with the shit that didn't flush. And it was dealt with very ineffectively. Neville Chamberlain would declare much the same prior to the start of World War Two. With a lot of appeasement help from Joseph Kennedy Sr. (who served as the senior diplomat to Great Britain before the war). It was during this time that we would learn the distinct difference between "The United States" and "These United States." As "states rights" was the Southern excuse to the Federal

Three Blind Mice

Government for everything. Which was French for "only we have the right to fuck over our own people and how dare you try to stop us."

Also in the 1850s, the Pinkerton's started their municipal version of today's Blackwater USA. Becoming local mercenaries to whoever would pay them. Their reputation would later be tarnished by their participation in labor union prevention later in the century.

California becomes a state in September, 1850. A place that, later, would bless America with some of the best wines in the world (by the way, I recommend an estate bottled Cabernet Franc from Amador County CA with this read). Fillmore would appoint Benjamin Curtis to the United States Supreme Court. Curtis was a principled man, and he would eventually resign from the court in disgust following the Dred Scott decision. Almost a decade later Curtis would make headlines again when he becomes one of the defense attorneys for President Andrew Johnson during his impeachment trial in the United States Senate.

In the meantime a young Abraham Lincoln was back working as a private lawyer after a stint in the House of Representatives. Although, that doesn't mean he wasn't stirring up a lot of shit. It wouldn't be long before he becomes the Michael Jordan of the Republican Party.

Chapter 3

Dred Scott and John Brown

Buchanan's greatest appeasement was the Dred Scott Supreme Court decision (1857). Prior to Dred Scott the Supreme Court's most important case to date was Marbury vs. Madison. This was a procedural case that would be popularly interpreted by Alexander Hamilton's Federalist Papers number seventy eight. Basically, John Adams, on his last day in office decided to hook all his rich buddies up and make them "somebody." One of his boys was William Marbury. A rich White boy from Maryland whom Adams made Justice of the Peace for the District of Columbia.

Thomas Jefferson, who wouldn't piss on Adams if his ass was on fire, said fuck you and your appointees. The argument eventually ended up in the Supreme Court. The Court, headed by John Marshall would side with the Jefferson Administration. However, the Court would get to define itself by declaring its rightful place in a three branch government. Although, it can be argued that to this day, the United States Supreme

Court remains the "sometimes stepchild" of the three branches of the United States Government. And are still manipulated by the Executive and Legislative branches of government for their own purposes.

Anyway another case was Dred Scott. Dred Scott was a slave who, through no fault of this own, found out he had a chance at freedom while on visit to a free state (Illinois and eventually, what is today Minnesota). This motherfucker sued his master and asked the government to declare him free. Why he wouldn't just Underground Railroad the whole process is beyond me. You gotta figure if he was smart enough to know he could take his plight to court he was smart enough to just run.

The bullshit ends up in the Supreme Court and Chief Justice Roger Taney's hands. Remember him from Andrew Jackson's administration? This guy definitely had judicial ADHD. Writing for the majority (dig that), he ruled that Black people were not citizens of the United States of America and therefore could not be afforded the privileges of citizenship (including suing some other motherfucker who had wronged them). Mind you, this was the mindset of the Court while the United States Constitution declared "all men are created equal." I never figured out why they didn't just add "when it fit our needs."

Fortunately, for everyone today, Northerners were steamed, as they took the decision as an abomination. Southerners took it as not far enough. The differing opinions would find its way, eventually to Fort Sumter in 1861. To be fair, all three of the Blind Mice would be pawns to the compromises of the original Founding Fathers. Getting the United States Constitution through the door was a bitch to begin with.

The North said slavery was a bullshit vice and to the South it was not only economically viable, but the lifestyle was the crack cocaine of the day. So, when the United States was formed the South delegates in Congress agreed, if the North would move the permanent National Capitol to the South (today's District of Columbia) and count the slaves as three fifths of a person we'll go along with this new country thing. You would think that, having elected, our first Black President in Barack Obama, there would be a movement to remove the "three fifth's of a person" language from the Constitution. But not a peep from the types that care about that kind of shit.

Further, it's incredibly ironic that this same man (Mr. Obama) has sworn to defend a document with his life that defines him as three fifths of a man. Most constitutional scholars will fluff off this argument by saying the Thirteenth Amendment (which outlawed slavery), the Fourteenth and Fifteenth Amendments, which gave citizenship to Blacks rendered the three fifths language moot.

But, like everything else in life, perception is reality. Sounds like lipstick on a pig to me. With all three of these Presidents there was an incredible lack of "political convexity" in their administrations. All of them acted like "holy shit, can you believe I'm in charge of this whole fucking country?"

The Panic of 1857 would be exacerbated by the Dred Scott decision and surely add fire to Reverend John Brown. Buchanan would lead from the back in both instances. The Panic was a global recession with the elephant in the room being an insurance company based in Ohio (that today would be deemed "too big to fail"). US exports plummeted,

Three Blind Mice

commodity prices dived and western United States real estate values went in the toilet. The subsequent run on the banks would be an epic illustration of the times. And all of this was happening to White people. So Blacks and other minorities really took it up the ass.

Mr. Buchanan decided the best course of action would be to decrease the money supply. This only made the problem worst as inflation took off like the Space Shuttle leaving the Kennedy Space Center. Eventually, matters of money would take a back seat to talk of secession.

In almost any Black neighborhood in American at some point, be it a bar, pool hall, elks lodge, whatever, you will hear someone say to someone else, "What's up John Brown?" In the same way someone would say "hello, how are you?" everywhere else. Why? It is a term of endearment and social commonality among Black folk. John Brown is that kind of figure to this day. He was the definition of the "Bleeding Kansas." A staunch abolitionist he saw slavery as an abomination to the soul of all men. But, he was not just about fiery oratory, he was a man of action. He banded a group together and raided an armory at Harper's Ferry, VA.

None of it worked out for Brown and his men. An ineffectual Colonel (sarcasm) named Robert E Lee squashed the whole fucking thing and they hanged his nigger loving ass along with all the others. By the way, Colonel Lee was Captain Lee when General Zachary Taylor was kicking Santa Anna's ass in Mexico during the Mexican American War. Man, the Union could have really used this guy. He was like Barry Sanders playing for the National Football League's Detroit Lions all those years. Great talent on a perpetually shitty team.

One could postulate that his leadership of the Army of the Potomac would have led to a quicker, much less bloody victory for the Union and would have put him in the White House after Lincoln finished his second term. Although, further postulation would foresee a much slower pace of Reconstruction with both men.

The Emancipation Proclamation allowed Lincoln an extra two hundred thousand men to fight and came at a great price for all involved (although the document only applied to Blacks who lived in states the Union didn't control). This is the beauty of war time decisions at the Commander-In-Chief level. The ineptitude of the Three Blind Mice made Lincoln the President and Lincoln the Man very complicated. He wasn't so much anti slavery as much as he was pro Union. Being anti slavery made being pro Union more palatable. Kind of like one being anti-abortion as opposed to being pro choice.

Because Fillmore, Pierce and Buchanan were sitting in Washington just sucking up oxygen on the question of slavery and everything else, Lincoln was forced to horse trade from the beginning of his administration. Lincoln offered several compromises on the question of slavery to preserve the nation. Everything from keeping it as it existed, to phasing it out, to outright mass relocation of Blacks to another part of the country South African township style.

So one could easily assume that had he lived the pace of Reconstruction would have been very slow and much less radical. Add to this the fact that he wanted to bring the South back into the national fold with much more appeasement than the Radical Republicans had in mind. Had Lee fought for the Union, Grant would have been working for him instead of overseeing his surrender. Basically, had Lincoln lived and Lee

Three Blind Mice

turned his back on the South, American history as we know it today would be very different. Lee was a tactical General, while Grant basically won the war through attrition. Grant's approach was "as long as I outnumber you I will eventually win." While this was true he needlessly sent countless numbers of men to their unnecessary death. Lee would have never conducted the war in this manner. He would have taken Winfield Scott's "snake strategy" and starved the Confederates out with much less loss of life. If for no other reason they were his peeps he was fighting against.

This, in turn meant we would have never heard of prison camps like Andersonville. The battles of Antietam, Gettysburg and Chickamauga would have never happened. And Sherman's "March to the Sea" would have never happened either. The war would have been shorter, less bloody, and still resulted in victory for the Union. Buchanan, is famous for saying to Lincoln, "If you are as happy entering office as I am leaving then you are truly a happy man." I think he knew the headache he left.

Chapter 4

Other Shit

Utah became a territory in the 1850s. They wouldn't achieve statehood until 1896. Mainly because Brigham Young and his minions wouldn't give up the idea that multiple pieces of permanent pussy (especially when the motto for these men was "the younger the pussy, the better") just wasn't kosher.

The Mormons were driven from the east coast of the United States all the way out west in part because the practice of polygamy presented a unique dilemma for the federal government. Plus, they were just a weird ass fucking group of people anyway. Although slavery was a major issue of the day that divided North and South, everyone agreed polygamy was just wrong. Utah will be discussed in more detail later. Nobody wanted to see a guy walk into the all you can eat buffet with six wives and 12 kids. Pap smear day in those households must have been a bitch.

Additionally, America was on the verge of switching their energy usage. In the history of the United States, on average, Americans change their forms of energy every one hundred and fifty years. From lumber, to coal, to oil, to whatever may come next. Solar, water, wind, nuclear, you pick. The industrial revolution was just underway and coal was the prince of warmth and cooking. Like any other time in America's history this would create a further gap in the economic classes. The South would be on the short end of the energy stick as well. Exacerbating an already bad social situation.

The Gadsden Purchase would take away Mexico's last piece of dignity it had left over from the Mexican American war. It was a land grab just like the one that started the war in the first place.

Probably no one piece of literature galvanized pre Civil War emotions more than Harriet Beecher's Stowe's Uncle Tom's Cabin. Written in 1852 the only book to outsell it in the Nineteenth Century was the Bible.

Harriet was born in Litchfield, Connecticut, in what today is the heart of the state's wine country, to an abolitionist family. She would follow those abolitionist beliefs as she became an adult. She lived in Hartford, Connecticut for 23 years where one of her neighbors was one Samuel Clemens (Mark Twain). She was also one of the founders of an arts school that would eventually become the University of Hartford. One of the original titles of the book was "Life Among the Lowly." In the first year after being published Uncle Tom's Cabin sold three hundred thousand copies. The book rallied the North against slavery and infuriated the South in the 1850s.

The story was about a slave named Uncle Tom. He was a long suffering "good Negro" that did his master's bidding even when he was getting dogged out. Uncle Tom's Cabin was inspired by the writing's of the slave Josiah Henson. Henson was a slave who worked on a plantation in Bethesda, Maryland just outside the District of Columbia.

He would ultimately escape and go to Canada (hooking up with descendants of Blacks who fought with the British Army during the American Revolution and those that got out during the War of 1812), become a writer, abolitionist and preacher. He would live until the age of ninety three, a long time for anybody during those days, much less a Black man. Canada would honor him as the first Black man to be featured on that country's postage stamp.

Although Harriet had good intentions for the book, its legacy remains a bad social footprint on Black America. Three major themes that arose from the book was the differences between light skinned and dark skinned Black Americans. As a result, dark skinned Blacks seemed to take on an inferior position within the sub culture of the race. The second was that of the lazy, shiftless Negro who won't work unless, it's under the threat of getting his or her ass beat. The tertiary result was that of Uncle Tom himself.

That sellout brotha who, not only looks out for himself, but, also will happily help Whitey keep another brotha down for his or her own benefit. Unfortunately, even today, there's a bunch of those motherfuckas still around.

The point here is that this was another event that gave those who wanted a reason to fight reason to do so. Also note it is not uncommon for President's to comment and offer leadership (of lack thereof) on social phenomena of the day. Although President's Millard Fillmore,

Franklin Pierce and James Buchanan had muted reactions to the book President Lincoln had plenty to say about it. Typical of his leadership, Millard Fillmore was acutely aware of the impact of Uncle's Tom's Cabin during his presidency but said nothing. Unlike, say, Woodrow Wilson, who commented on the impact of the D. W. Griffith's film Birth of a Nation.

His comments were taken as negative to Black Americans during the teens of the Twentieth Century and would expose Wilson's attitude towards Blacks at the same time. This was an example that the rest of the country would follow. Some White Americans basically said "if the President of the United States is a racist bastard, then why shouldn't I be?" The film, released in 1915, was so popular that it was the first movie ever to be screened at the White House. It also helped that Thomas Dixon Jr. (author of the book and play "The Clansman," on which the film was based) was a college classmate of W Squared (Woodrow Wilson) at Johns Hopkins University.

John F. Kennedy had to go on national television and speak to America about equality during the great unpleasantness happening in the South during early 1960s (one hundred years after the decade of the Three Blind Mice). George H. W. Bush had to go on television and tell motherfuckas to calm down after the Rodney King got his ass beat and Blacks had to make the point of enough is enough. Even Bill Clinton got into it with Sista Souljah during the 1992 Presidential Election.

Petroleum. From the Greek word "petra" and the Latin word "oleum" meaning "rock oil". The Chinese call it "shiypou," also meaning rock oil. The Chinese starting drilling for it as far back as the fourth century AD. Its relationship with man goes back thousands of years where it was used for medical purposes among the Persians. Later, in the Tenth Century, major finds occurred in what is today Iraq and Azerbaijan. In the 1850s the primary source of energy was coal. Oil was around but an afterthought.

Edwin Drake would be among the first to actually "drill" for the black gold when he did a Jed Clampett (of The Beverly Hillbillies fame) in the tiny town of Titusville, Pennsylvania in 1859. Once Drake made his find, others quickly followed. Pennsylvania became the America's leader in oil production. Texas and California would supplant Pennsylvania as national leaders in the production of oil and especially refining. Ironically, today, refining capacity (or the lack thereof) is a major component in the costs of gasoline at the pump. This discovery would lead to the world's dependence on oil as an energy source as we know it today. Although coal would keep its grip on the economy well into the Twentieth Century.

Today oil is a source of politics, war and religion. And still in the hands of the few. Dominated by a few Arab countries (Iraq, Iran, Saudi Arabia, Qatar, Kuwait and the United Arab Emirates), the United States of America and Russia primarily.

Chapter 5

Congresses and Cabinets of the 1850s

It's should be noted that the Legislative Branch of the United States Government had much more power than the Executive Branch between 1850-1860, specifically, the United States Senate. United States Congresses thirty one through thirty six would surely play a role in stirring the pre American Civil War shit storm.

The Senate had an all star cast of characters. They included; Hank Clay, Danny Webster, Jeff Davis, Will Seward, Sal Chase, Stevie Douglas, Johnny Calhoun, Sammy Houston and Lew Cass. In the House there was; well only one person of note (As far as this author is concerned). Johnny Breckinridge. If there was ever a time when America had a de-facto unicameral legislative form of government (a la Nebraska, the only state in the Union with one legislative body, God bless 'em), this was the decade.

There was a revolving door of men that made up the cabinets of the 1850s with President Franklin Pierce's cabinet being the exception.

Fillmore had two Secretary's of State, Secretary's of the Navy and Interior. He also had two Attorney and Postmaster Generals. His first Secretary of State was Daniel Webster. He was an ugly man with big ole' head and receding hairline. He thought his shit didn't stink and hated who he considered "common people". A great orator he talked a lot of shit. He served in the House and the Senate as well as Secretary of State for Presidents William Henry Harrison and subsequently John Tyler. He also ran for President three times (unsuccessfully obviously).

John J. Crittenden was Fillmore's second Attorney General. He was another member of the D.C. "boys club." He also served as Attorney General for Harrison and Tyler (briefly). Hailing from the Commonwealth of Kentucky, he served as Governor and represented the state in both the House and Senate. He was nominated to the United States Supreme Court by John Quincy Adams, but Andrew Jackson's boys in the Senate squashed that shit in a relished bit of payback for Jackson. He would also join Fillmore's Know Nothing party later in the decade. He authored several resolutions to keep the United States from breaking up in 1860. By that time however, all sides had their collective fists balled up and didn't want to hear anymore shit about "The" United States. It had become "These" United States. Pierce's cabinet would remain intact for his entire Presidency. The only time that has happened in our country's history to date. His cabinet was highlighted by William Marcy (Secretary of State). Who let the fiasco that became the Ostend Manifesto happen.

William R. King was his Vice President, and Jefferson Davis was his Secretary of War. Jeff Davis stands out because they would become lifelong friends and Davis would influence him for the rest of his life. King was unique because he was sick for most of his adult life, took the oath of office in Havana, Cuba (becoming the only federal official in American history to do so) and liked to suck cock (albeit only James Buchanan's).

Jefferson Davis was an individual that can best be described as a political conundrum. Born in Kentucky (the youngest of 10 siblings), raised in Mississippi and Louisiana, he was a true slave owning Southerner. At the same time he was a staunch American as well. A United States Military Academy graduate, he would serve in several American wars, including the Mexican American War. He would serve as a United States Senator, Secretary of War under President Pierce and, ultimately (and reluctantly) as President of the Confederate States of America.

He married President Zachary Taylor's daughter, whom he fell in love with while serving under his command at Fort Crawford. Zach didn't think much of JD trying to get in his daughter's panties. So Davis resigned his commission and they both went south to be with his brother. She would die from malaria while visiting Jefferson Davis' sister in Louisiana. Eventually he would marry the granddaughter of Richard Howell, at one time the Governor of New Jersey. They would have six children together. Her name was Varina Banks Howell Davis. She was the first and only First Lady of the Confederate States of America. Although she supported slavery and states' rights she was ambivalent about the Civil war. Later in life she would agree that the right side won.

Of their six children, four boys and two girls, only the two girls would live to an advanced age. The youngest Varina Anne "Winnie" Davis would become known as the "Daughter of the Confederacy." He ends up back in the military and under Zach Taylor's command would eventually gain some respect from Taylor and not have Taylor think of him as a little shit who use to fuck his daughter.

His military background would serve him well as Secretary of War. A position he got as reward for stumping in the South for Pierce during the election of 1852. Ironically, his military background would work against him as President of the Confederacy. He micro managed the Civil War as Commander In Chief. And failed miserably at the other duties a president has to contend with. I argue he should have moved the capitol from Richmond to Atlanta. It would have been much harder to capture and the Union would have had to spread out more of their resources, giving the CSA a better chance of fighting a numerically superior opponent. Anyway…

Buchanan appointed to his cabinet a bunch of men so self absorbed that all would exempt themselves from any blame for being responsible for the start of hostilities that became the Civil War. Five of them would serve in Lincoln's cabinet. He would have two Secretary's of State and War. Three Secretary's of Treasury and Postmaster General and two Attorneys General.

His most historically famous member was Edwin Stanton. Stanton served as Attorney General. He would go on to become Lincoln's Secretary of War. Stanton, having helped to win the war, he survived assassination from John Wilkes Booth's crew, lead the effort to hunt down those motherfuckers, hang them and end up as the centerpiece for Andrew Johnson's impeachment. Even after all of that shit, President Grant would nominate him (and he was confirmed by the United States Senate) to the United States Supreme Court. Fortunately or unfortunately he would never serve on the court as he would die four days after confirmation.

He was also unique, because, like most called to public service at that time in United States history he took a substantial pay cut and died in poor financial health. He was to Lincoln, as Commander in Chief what Vice President Dick Cheney was to President George W. Bush. Buchanan's Vice President was John C. Breckinridge. He was only thirty six years old when he became Vice President. Buchanan didn't think much of the kid as he was a "machine" choice. Such youth would not serve him well combined with Buchanan's elder status.

He was a man of varying positions on slavery. While he owned slaves, as a lawyer, he represented free slaves in court and even advocated for their relocation to Liberia. At the same time he supported the Fugitive Slave Act and the Dred Scott decision. If there was ever a "true" politician, this guy fit the bill. He would end up fighting for the Confederacy during the Civil War. Ironically he was a cousin of Mary Todd and was an actual friend of Lincoln's (although he obviously disagreed with his politics).

Another stand out character was his third Secretary of Treasury John Adams Dix. The United States Army post, Fort Dix in New Jersey was named after him. Dix made a name for himself when he arrested the Maryland legislature and prevented the border state from seceding. He also suppressed the draft riots in New York in 1863. Later he would serve as Minister to France and Governor of New York.

Buchanan's first Secretary of State was Lewis Cass. A veteran politician he served his country in several capacities for a very long time. In addition to being Secretary of State, he was a United States Marshal, territorial governor, senator, Secretary of War and presidential candidate. Not to mention he served in the War of 1812. To his credit he had the balls to tell Buchanan to go fuck himself when he figured out what a pussy he was for not standing up to the South and averting war.

Chapter 6

Post Presidencies of the Three Blind Mice

Each President takes a different path in his post presidency career. For four of them an assassins' bullet would take care of their exits. These were Presidents Lincoln, Garfield, McKinley and Kennedy. Thanks to four of the craziest fuckers known to man. Meaning you have to be a little throwed to the left in the first place to attempt to kill the fucking President of the United States! Smoking a joint and a bottle of whiskey isn't going to get you there. They were just nut jobs. Fuckheads one to four; John Wilkes Booth, Charles Guiteau, Leon Czolgosz and Lee Harvey Oswald. Yep, all crazy, in the "crazy" sense of the word.

Other's just wouldn't (or won't) go away. Jimmy Carter, for example, when he is not overseeing the delusion of fair elections in some third world country he's building houses for poor motherfuckers. Bill Clinton is making gobs of money talking shit disguised as speeches and keeping his wife in play for Presidential Election of 2016. Reagan just lost his fucking mind; Nixon went away and hoped nobody would notice the same with Ford, Bush Forty One and LBJ. Like these others, Millard Fillmore looked for ways to stay in the game. He could have kept himself busy with his work at the University of Buffalo, which he helped found. But it wasn't enough. But, mentioned earlier his own people didn't want him so he decided to hook up the Know Nothing Party. A different band of racist who hated the Mick-Kraut (Irish and German) crowd and Catholics in general.

They were also anti-immigration in ideology. They didn't make much noise nationally, but they did manage to hang around. They got a few mayors elected in the mid 1850s but were mostly kept in check by the GOP. Fillmore would run for President in 1856 under the Know Nothings with Andrew Jackson's son as his running mate. Of course it would amount to nothing and only make James Buchanan's win that much easier. He would actively be a pain in the ass to Lincoln during the Civil War. And actively support Andrew Johnson after. He did some travel to Europe, hung out with his second wife in a new big house and would eventually die in 1874.

Franklin Pierce would also go to Europe after his term was up. He would come back just in time for the start of the Civil War and, like Fillmore get down to the business of giving Lincoln shit. He was especially vocal of Lincoln's suspension of habeas corpus. Jefferson Davis was a great friend of his and Pierce maintained southern sympathies throughout the war (pissing of many in Lincoln's cabinet). He would die in 1869 from cirrhosis of the liver. All that drinking had taken its toll. He would have a bunch of schools and counties named after him.

James Buchanan would spend his post presidency defending his presidency. He had several opportunities to keep the slave loving assholes in check but, instead, continued to let them agitate. They (the

Confederates) finally said "fuck it, let's just go and start our own shit. This pussy in the White House ain't gonna do one fucking thing about it." And just like that the South told the North "you can kiss my ass." And they were right. Buchanan didn't do a fucking thing. Like Nixon's famous "I am not a crook" statement, he would analogously say "I am not a pussy."

Unlike the other two blind mice he would support Lincoln during the war. Not that it mattered. Most people blamed him for the whole mess anyway. He would die in 1868 with a legacy of having, well, just fucked up everything as president.

Chapter 7

Kansas Nebraska Act

Creating the territories of Kansas and Nebraska would be another catalyst in moving the United States to Civil War. The territory was rich farmland and the government was eager to have White men settle it. No problem, except some wanted it to be "free soil" others wanted it to be pro-slavery. And they were willing to fight and kill over who was right. In the Senate, Stevie Douglas and Davy Atchinson would end up being the major players in the legislative game to be played out. Senator Douglas, as Chairman of the Committee on Territories thought he had the answer by letting the issue of free or slave be settled by the locals. Atchinson, a devout "border ruffian" wanted all of the land to be worked by slaves (including the ones he owned).

Pierce would side with the pro slavery set eventually. Although, it would all be settled (like everything else that did and didn't happen between 1850 and 1860) by Lincoln and the Civil War. The act itself would set up boundaries and let the issue of slavery be decided by the locals. This was a total fucking cop out by the federal Executive and

Three Blind Mice

Legislative branches. Both the pro and anti-slavery types (the former called Jayhawkers and the latter called Ruffians) would set up territory governments. President Pierce would eventually send federal troops to Topeka (where the anti-slavery group had gotten together) and break that shit up. So you know where he stood.

This complete lack of leadership would lead to the downfall of the Whigs and concurrent rise of the Republican Party. This was typical of the leadership of the Three Blind Mice.

Chapter 8

※

Women in the 1850s

Even with the Three Blind Mice being the presidential equivalent of used toilet paper in a state fair porta potty, America was still very much controlled by rich, land owning White men. The women of the 1850s were the exact opposite of the Three Blind Mice. They were strong willed and, like all women of all eras, had to multi-task through society. They would create different challenges for the government while they battled the question of slavery.

They fought for equality, voting rights, the right to work, own property, an end to slavery and dignity. The powerful White men of the day had their hands full, to say the least. In addition to the first ladies of Millard Fillmore, Franklin Pierce and James Buchanan there were several other women who left their mark on society. Women's suffrage would take hold in the decade. And the fight would have headstrong soldiers to lead the way. Like the women of today's Gynocracies (a Gynocracy is a government led by a woman, Germany's Angela Merkel is probably today's best example), the female suffragists were intent to do double duty fighting gender indifference and also joining the fight to end slavery.

Women both black and white were in the fray. It was typical of the day that they fucked, cooked, cleaned and made babies. Took a nap and did the shit all over again. Black women had it especially hard as they were saddled with the debilitating trinity of bondage, gender and race.

White men chased them for pussy all day while they worked either in the fields or in the house as slaves. White women hated them because the White men wanted them. Black men beat them for fucking the White men and not resisting enough. On top of all of that, like all Blacks they were hated just for their Blackness! For Black women all of this was measured purely in epidermal dimensions. And yet they persevered through all of it and survived throughout the generations. Bad motherfucker's all the way around.

Women's suffrage took on many forms in different parts of the United States. In some states women lived under full suffrage. This meant that they couldn't vote for any fucking thing. In other places they could only vote in local elections. In yet other places they could vote in statewide elections. The Western United States was much more accommodating to women's rights than the Eastern United States. Part of the reason was statehood related.

Statehood in the Nineteenth Century was, in large part, a function of population. Many territories "recruited" citizens through offerings like land grants and rights. While many men, single and married jumped at the chance to start anew, only a few women took the chance to move west. Offering suffrage was a unique incentive. An example of this is Wyoming. By the time the Nineteenth Amendment to the United States Constitution was ratified by the states in 1920 women in Wyoming had been voting for nearly fifty years. On the subject of women's suffrage, by 1920 with the passage of the Nineteenth Amendment several western states afforded women the right to vote. These included the states of Wyoming, Utah, Washington, Colorado, Idaho, California, Oregon, Arizona and Montana. Montana voters would even elect the first woman to the United States House of Representatives in 1916. Her name was Jeannette Rankin. During her term in the Sixty-Fifth United States Congress she would participate in two memorable votes. The first would come just one month after she was sworn in. On April 5th, 1917 President Woodrow Wilson asked the Congress to declare war on Germany. She would vote "no."

On January 10th, 1917 a second vote (the first vote would be in 1915) would come to the floor of the United States House of Representatives concerning a women's right to vote. She would vote "yes." Although the bill would die in the United States Senate later in the year, Rankin became the first women to vote for a women's right to vote. Even individual counties and cities had their own laws regarding women and the vote. Female stars of the day included the likes of Lucy Stone, Elizabeth Cady Stanton, Sojourner Truth, Susan B. Anthony, Paulina Wright Davis, Harriet Tubman, Harriet Beecher Stowe and the tragic case of Margaret Garner.

Margaret Garner was one of these Black women I mentioned earlier. She was a slave who escaped from her master in Kentucky in 1856. She would make her way to Ohio and seek shelter with other runaways. Found by United States Marshals and slave catchers, who were enforcing the Fugitive Slave Law of 1850, they surrounded the house she had barricaded herself in.

Before they could remove her she killed her two year old daughter with a butcher knife rather than have the child returned to slavery. She wounded her other children trying to kill them and wanted to kill herself but was stopped by the Marshals. As if that wasn't fucked up enough, the Fugitive Slave Law made trial proceedings difficult. Should she be tried as a citizen of the United States for the murder or held as property under the Fugitive Slave Law of 1850?

Remember, the question of citizenship for Blacks would not be decided until the Dred Scott case (and the answer to said question of citizenship from the United States Supreme Court would be "fuck no"). Her attorney argued for the former, her slave masters, the latter citing that the Fugitive Slave Law had precedence as a federal statute. The judge would eventually agree with the slave masters and she was ultimately sent to the deep part of the South to die a slave.

In many ways, this was the Dred Scott case before Dred Scott. Had the presiding judge not ruled so quickly on the case the question of citizenship for Blacks would have had to be answered right then and there. It's interesting to note that slavery was such an ingrained part of life that, in American society, she could get away with murder but not her freedom.

Susan Brownell Anthony, like all of the women mentioned here was just incapable of bullshit. She derided the "aristocracy of sex" in America. She openly challenged the United States Government for equal rights for Blacks and women. In the 1850s the temperance movement was still in its infancy. Susan B. Anthony began participating in a series of meetings called the National Women's Rights Convention. It was here that she and others would demand the United States of America to stand up to the dictum "all government derives its just power from the consent of the governed."

She would go on to participate in every subsequent conference throughout the 1850s. Her cause célèbre would be the United States vs. Susan B. Anthony. Anthony was arrested in 1872 after voting in the 1872 Presidential Election. At trial she eloquently used the newly adopted Fourteenth Amendment as her defense. The presiding judge was United States Supreme Court Associate Justice Ward Hunt. Nominated by President Ulysses S. Grant and later confirmed by the United States Senate in 1873, Justice Hunt was nondescript and had little impact on the Court as Justice's go often siding with the majority in most cases.

Anyway, he would was a real asshole to Ms. Anthony. He refused to let her speak on her own behalf, ordered the jury to find her guilty, refused to poll the jury and wrote his opinion even before the trial had started! Talk about blind justice. He found her guilty and fined her one hundred dollars (which was a shitload of money back then).

Ms. Anthony basically said "I ain't payin' a fucking dime of that fine," and she didn't. Safe to say the United States government, made to look like the fuck faces they were, quietly let the case die with little fanfare and never bothered trying to collect the money from her. At the end of the day, these events did nothing but make her more famous. Shit, it even got her on the dollar coin. Even if the only place to find them these days is in subway vending machines in most major US cities. She would not live to see the passage of the Nineteenth Amendment to the United States Constitution. Ironic since she co-authored the draft of the amendment with Elizabeth Cady Stanton back in 1878.

An amendment that became necessary with the Missouri case of Minor vs. Happersett in 1875. In the 19th Century the White men who made up the United States Supreme Court spent a lot time being pimped by the other White men who ran the Executive and Legislative branches of government.
Case in point:

The Dred Scott decision in 1857 judicially said to Black people, "fuck you nigger, not only are you inferior to Whites you are not, and have never been a citizen of the United States, matter of fact you ain't even fucking human, you property motherfucker!" So go be a good slave, get back in the field and shut the fuck up.

Plessy vs. Ferguson in 1896. This was the case that famously established "separate but equal." The passage of the Thirteenth, Fourteenth and Fifteenth amendments to the United States Constitution had outlawed slavery, given Blacks citizenship and Black men the right to vote. Again, the White men of the United States Supreme Court judicially said, "Yea, Lincoln and the Radical Republicans did you a solid and gave you a bunch of shit we can't take back, so here is some new shit for yo ass."

The Court now said to Blacks "from now on you get the fuck up version of whatever we already have. Jobs, land, houses, schools, clothes, water fountains and whatever else we can think of." Yes, the United States would eventually pull their jurisprudent heads out of their asses in 1954 with Brown vs. Board of Education. Which, ironically enough was argued, and won on the strength of the Fourteenth Amendment to the United States Constitution. See how that shit comes full circle?

Like those two cases, the United States Supreme Court in Minor vs. Happersett ruled specifically that the United States Constitution did NOT grant women the right to vote. The Nineteenth Amendment to the United States Constitution would nullify the ruling in 1920. Judicially they said "Bitch, you want what?" "You better get your ass back to the kitchen and make me something to eat. And by the way, I want some pussy after dinner too."

In my opinion, women could have knocked out the suffrage movement in about a week. All they would have had to do was stage a National No Pussy strike. After about a week of masturbating men would have said "what is it you said you wanted?" Done and done.

Elizabeth Cady Stanton and Lucy Stone were two more women quite active during the administrations of the Three Blind Mice. Liz Stanton would be at the forefront of starting women's suffrage. She would fight hard for the vote but, her views would become parochial as time passed. Eventually she would side against the Fourteenth and Fifteenth amendments because they excluded the right of women to vote. This represented an unusual shift in position for a woman who started out as an abolitionist. Lucy Stone was also, all woman. She was known for using her maiden name even after she got married. This was not common at all in those

Three Blind Mice

days. Together with Elizabeth Cady Stanton and Susan B. Anthony they would become known as the "big three" of woman's suffrage.

When she married she insisted on going "dutch" with her husband on all matters concerning their relationship. Especially matters of finance. She focused on woman's rights as "human rights." The very simple, but, brilliant idea that as human beings women had the same rights as all other human beings. Imagine that? Or even further, imagine that men in power could not get their collective heads around that concept when it came to women and slaves.

Paulina Wright Davis was part of the same crew and her focus was on promoting the medical field as well as suffrage, abolition and education. She saw jobs as the answer to women's rights.

Harriet Tubman was an abolitionist, rescuer, nurse, Union spy and all around bad ass during the American Civil War. She was born a slave in Dorchester County on Maryland's Eastern Shore. She would escape to Philadelphia and eventually help over three hundred other slaves to freedom as well garnering the moniker "Moses." She took tremendous risks however and she showed tremendous courage despite those risks.

Even though she was deeply religious she also didn't take shit from anyone. She always carried a pistol with her and knew how to use it as well. If a slave she helped escape suddenly got the yips she calmed him down with a cock of that pistol. With Tubman you either got to freedom alive or you ended up a dead runaway who tried to escape. With all that was at stake she didn't give a fuck. She would continue to work on freedom for Black people her entire life. Despite frail health her entire life as a result of a severe head injury as a child she would live to be ninety three years of age.

Like Harriet Tubman, Sojourner Truth was a Black abolitionist and woman's rights advocate. She became famous for her "Ain't I a Woman" speech in 1851 at that year's Women's Rights Convention in Ohio. She also helped recruit Black soldiers for the union and tried, unsuccessfully to help Black folk get their forty acres and a mule. Born a slave in Upstate New York she grew up speaking Dutch. A fiery orator she was a woman well ahead of her time.

Another Black woman forgotten by history was Anna Murray Douglass. Whoever said, "behind every great man is a great woman" was talking about Anna Murray Douglass. She was Frederick Douglass' wife of forty four years. As famous as Frederick Douglass is historically he ain't shit without Anna. She was born a free Black. Frederick Douglass was a slave when she met him. So in addition to giving him some pussy she was the one who "taught" him what freedom was about. She was the one who encouraged him to escape slavery and gave him the fucking money to do it. While Frederick was out making speeches and doing the grip and grin with high society White folks she was making all the money, washing clothes for people to support the family and pay the bills. Oh, while doing all of this she turned her home into a major stop on the Underground Railroad and helped many Blacks make it to Canada. Her, not Frederick.

Anna went out of her way to maintain her public image even while Frederick was out fucking around on her (yep, like Martin Luther King Jr., John F. Kennedy, Bill Clinton, etc., he was getting so much pussy on the side like it was a supplemental vitamin). Frederick Douglass is still one of the most famous Black Americans in the history of the United States, but Anna Murray Douglass was the stuffing inside that turkey. Post 1850s two other women would stand out and make a case for suffrage through the manipulation of politics. Victoria Woodhull and Belva Lockwood would run for President of the United States.

As a suffragist Woodhull wanted to make the point that although women could not vote they were free to run for (and hold) public office. She was nominated by the Equal Rights Party to run in the 1872 United States Presidential Election. As an historical footnote her running mate for Vice President of the United States was none other than Frederick Douglass. This made her the first woman and him the first Black man to run for the Nation's highest political offices. Woodhull was also the first woman to own a brokerage firm on Wall Street.

Assisted by her sister and partially financed by Cornelius Vanderbilt she would open Woodhull, Claflin and Company in 1870. The firm was not some fly by night operation. The press called them the "Queens of Finance." The firm made a fortune from trading securities.

Belva Lockwood would run in the United States Presidential Elections of 1884 and 1888. An attorney, Lockwood would become the first female lawyer to argue a case before the United States Supreme Court.

Chapter 9

The Crimean War and Napoleon III

During the Franklin Pierce administration the Crimean War broke out. In 1853 the British, French and the Turks, with the Sardinians coming off the bench in a support role (go figure) got together and decided the Russians needed an ass kicking. Ironically, beside the Russians wanting better access to the Mediterranean Sea the Crimean War would become another of history's many religious wars. The Russians wouldn't fight the war completely alone. It was a sure bet that any war involving the Turks would bring the Greeks on the opposing side just for the fuck of it. Thus, the Russians got a Hellenistic assist from the men of Troy.

American didn't really have much of a role in the war. The United States was, however, sympathetic to Russia. Additionally, America did learn many things about military technology, communications, medicine (especially hospital sanitation through the likes of Florence Nightingale, "The Lady with the Lamp" as she would become to be known) and weaponry during the conflict. Franklin Pierce's point man in Russia was Thomas Seymour. A former governor of the State of Connecticut he

Three Blind Mice

made sure the Russian government knew we wished her well. As for the war itself, despite its limited role in Nineteenth Century world history, dead soldiers from the conflict had similar numbers to that of the American War Between the States. The Russians put up seven hundred troops against a million Allied troops.

Russia was the protector of Christians in the Ottoman Empire. This didn't sit well with the French and Napoleon III. This was especially true when it came to Catholic domination of the holy places of Palestine.

Napoleon III started the whole shit when he and the Catholic Church decided that they should be the defenders of the faith. An "evangelical" show of force and arms if you will. This was common manipulation by the Church for its own self interest. And how did the Catholic Church make their point in those days? Send the flock armed with rifles and warships and start fucking shit up. Soon the British (always looking for some new shit to take over) joined the fight. The Russians initially backed off, but the French and British said "fuck that, we're her now, let's get it on." The Russians would end up losing the war but would definitely get their licks in. Especially in the Battle of Balaclava where the British "Charge of the Light Brigade" would become famous for getting their asses kicked.

The war would end with the Treaty of Paris in 1856. It can be argued, however, that lingering animosities would eventually lead to World War One.

Whose lingering bullshit would lead to World War Two.

Whose lingering bullshit would lead to the Korean War.

Whose lingering bullshit would lead to the Vietnam War and the Cold War.

Whose lingering bullshit would lead to both, the Gulf War in 1991 and Iraq War as well as the current War on Terrorism.

The dots are very easy to connect here.

Napoleon III doesn't get half as much historical recognition as his uncle, the Little Corporal, Napoleon (the First) Bonaparte, however he surely left his mark on world history. But let's give credit where credit is due. Napoleon III was born into a crazy, fucked up, self centered, power hungry family. His father, Louis was Napoleon Bonaparte's brother. Oh, and just to close the loop Napoleon II was Napoleon the First's son. He was born Napoleon Francis Charles Joseph Bonaparte (in today's America that motherfucker would just be "Junior"). Known as the "Eaglet" to many, he was insignificant to any kind of history as his dad fucked up his future when he lost power.

Napoleon I did make him King of Rome for shits and giggles but it didn't mean shit. He did manage to be Emperor of France for about a week as well after his dad got the boot. Because of this many historians say he was the greatest French leader of all. He never started a war, never killed his own people and, most importantly, never presided over any surrender.

Napoleon III's father, Louis was always the little brother that could to his older brother Napoleon I. He could make due as long as he was helped and pushed a little. Louis was born with a pile of shit on top of his shoulders instead of a brain. A nebbish to his heart, Napoleon

Three Blind Mice

took care of him like an older brother should. He got him a job (first in Napoleon's army and then as King of Holland), got him some pussy (Napoleon's step daughter would turn out to be just fine) and basically made sure he stayed out of trouble. Turns out he wasn't very good at either one (being a king or husband). The Dutch people thought he was crazy (he did suffer from bouts of mental illness) and his wife found out he liked to suck cock as much as she did (yes, he was gay/bisexual).

As King of Holland (nepotism in politics is as old as time itself and this was no exception) he didn't know his ass from his elbow. Remember how John F. Kennedy brought in his brother Robert F. Kennedy to be Attorney General of the United States upon his election as President? In hindsight, compared to the Bonaparte family America's nepotism was pretty mild.

Napoleon III's mother was a woman named Hortense de Beauharnais. She was Napoleon Bonaparte's step daughter from his wife's, Josephine, first marriage. So, for a while, Josephine was Louis' sister-in-law and mother-in-law at the same time. In most cases having in-laws is already fucked up. In the nuclear family they are that piece of chicken that fell on the kitchen floor and the cook just places at the bottom of the plate hoping everyone will be full and not eat it. One can only imagine what multiple in-law titles in the same person might be like. That's getting fucked around in a whole new way. Yep, so Louis Bonaparte marries his brother's step daughter. Which now made Hortense not only Napoleon Bonarparte's stepdaughter, but her sister-in-law as well!

Who says the French don't know love (or the Corsicans, for that matter). Woody Allen wishes he could be that fucked up with his family.

Crazy fucking shit. But this is how you keep outsiders on the outside when it comes to power.

Hortense was, by all accounts, a wild bitch. A pretty blond, she knew her way around a pool hall and was quite the billiards player. In addition she never met a cock she didn't like to suck, was bisexual and into BDSM (bondage, dominance or discipline, sadism and masochism) Fifty Shades of Grey style. She loved getting that ass flogged. Her mother Josephine had that ho DNA as well. It wasn't all her fault though (her ho-ness that is). He first husband got his head cut off by the guillotine during the Reign of Terror. She slept around with a bunch of French elites until Napoleon came along. Six years her junior, all Napoleon knew was he that he found his freak in the bed.

She was a horny, older woman who was a widow. Fact was she was a little too horny. When Napoleon went off to war she promptly started fucking someone else. Ah, to be French! This was, genetically, where Hortense was spawn from.

Napoleon III was notorious womanizer (maybe because his mother was such a ho) and, in part because of this, his leadership was scattered, at best. Starting from his coup d'état in 1851, to building Paris' infrastructure, to his aims in the Crimean War and finishing up with his involvement in building the Suez Canal in Egypt. To fucking around in Hawaii (where Millard Fillmore had to tell him to fuck off). To fucking around with Italy to his involvement in Indochina (which would eventually lead to the French getting the shit beat out of them by Ho Chi Minh a century later (later Ho Chi Minh would give the United States same lesson). He even tried siding with the Confederate States of America at one point during the American Civil War to further French influence in the Western Hemisphere. When he figured out that no other European nation was going to join him he bailed on the CSA. All in Napoleon III was a poor man's Alexander the Great.

Chapter 10

The Impact of the Irish on America

The 1850s seen a huge influx of Irish immigrants to America. And, safe to say, they weren't always welcome. Outside of Native Americans, the Irish are the second most cited people to have the average American claim they have some of their blood in them. Ireland, in general, has a troubled history. Most of it at the expense of, guess who, the British. I think the only people that might challenge them as most conquered are all of Africa and the Sicilians. Starting with the Vikings and then the English they would endure centuries of ass fucking by various factions. British monarchs, Strongbow, Oliver Cromwell, etc. would all stake a claim to the Ireland we know today.

America has a long, and strong relationship with the people of Ireland. Several Presidents can claim some kind of Irish ancestry. Even Mr. Obama whose mother has Irish roots. Starting with Andrew Jackson, the list of Presidents is long and distinguished. After Jackson in Irish lineage, there's James Polk, James Buchanan, Andrew Johnson, Ulysses S. Grant, Chester Arthur, Grover Cleveland, the Harrisons, both

Three Blind Mice

William Henry and Benjamin, William McKinley, the Roosevelts, Teddy and Franklin, William Howard Taft, Woodrow Wilson, Warren Harding, Harry Truman, of course John F. Kennedy, Richard Milhous Nixon, Jimmy Carter, Ronald Reagan, George Herbert Walker Bush and George W. Bush, forty one and forty three, Bill Clinton and Barack Obama.

It could be argued that Ireland is the true birthplace of American Presidents. The Irish have had a say in just over half of the American Presidency. There is no doubt the Irish have had a significant impact on both American leadership and its leadership culture.

The biggest event on Irish immigration was the Irish Potato Famine in the Nineteenth Century. Lasting, roughly from 1845 through 1850, hundreds of thousands of Irish came to America just to find a decent fucking meal. As well as trying to escape persecution, bigotry and religious subjugation. Yet some of that is what they found in America when they got here. There were places in United States, especially the Northeast where they were just not wanted. Signs saying "No Blacks, no dogs, No Irish" were commonplace. But we'll come back to that.

First, the famine. Most Irish were already poor and Catholics were the "niggers" of the region as treated by the British. They lived under an English version of Jim Crow laws and were only allowed to own small tracts of land. Enough to grow a plant like the potato but not enough to graze cattle of any kind on. The lower classes paid rent back to the English aristocracy or their Uncle Tom Irish counterparts.

However, only enough harvest came to fruition to pay the rent leaving many mired in poverty. Sure as shit, in 1845, the crop failed. When it did many Irish were not only destitute, but starved. Many were jailed for begging, fishing, or simple trying to feed themselves. Starvation led to disease and disease forced many to get the fuck out. They left for America on floating shitholes disguised as ships. Upwards to a third died on the voyage (much like Africans during the Middle Passage). The British would send criminals as well. Just as they sent many other criminals to Australia at the same time.

Predictably, many ended up on the East Coast of the United States and stayed there. As once they got there they couldn't afford to go much further. Thusly, this is why so many American northeast and mid-Atlantic coastal cities have heavy Irish populations.

There is a similar apocryphal story about the Black migration from the South and the city of Newark. Many Blacks are in the city of Newark, New Jersey today because as they were going north hoping to get to New York City the conductor would yell Newark making it sound like "new work". Many Blacks got off thinking they were in New York City and ended up in Newark. Since they couldn't afford passage the rest of the way, they stayed.

Back to the Irish. Once in New York City they found, in many cases, they were just as fucked up as they were in Ireland. However, change would come. Many would find work in the local police and fire departments. So much so that that by the end of the 1850s their representation in these professions would be double that of the total population. Remnants of which can still be found today. They would also make their way in local politics as well. Mayors of many of America's biggest cities would elect Irish-American citizens.

Three Blind Mice

When JFK made it to the White House, it was "Danny Boy" (which was written by an Englishman, reputedly) until you couldn't stand it anymore. Which wasn't a bad thing. Danny Boy would go on to become one of the most popular songs of all time adopted by many other cultures.

Chapter 11

The Pre Civil War Military

So what was the military like in the decade before the Civil War? Like everything else let's look at the people involved.

Of the 60 or so major battles in the American Civil War each was led by a graduate of the United States Military Academy. And this was both on the Union and the Confederacy sides. West Point, founded at the start of the Nineteenth Century, had established itself not only as a training ground for future officers, but also as a first rate engineering school. Matter of fact, so much so that every engineering school founded after would follow their model. The United States Military Academy played a major role in the outcome of the Civil War (and many others after). The site itself has a unique story.

It was here where Benedict Arnold pulled a military Judas and attempted to fuck over the Continental Army. Situated along the Hudson River (by the way, can someone figure out if the Hudson is a fjord or an estuary), West Point was a perfect choke point to keep the British Navy at bay during the American Revolution.

Most of the Union and Confederate military leadership learned their craft at the United States Military Academy. Who were these Generals on both sides? Well, in no particular order (and this list is hardly complete) there was; Ulysses S. Grant, George McClellan, Thomas Jonathan "Stonewall" Jackson, Robert E. Lee, Joseph E. Johnston, George Meade, Herbert Haupt, Pierre Gustave Tutant (P.G.T.) Beauregard, Henry W. Halleck, William Tecumseh Sherman, Braxton Bragg, Jubal Anderson (J.A.) Early, William Rosecrans, Winfield Scott Hancock, Ambrose Burnside, Philip Sheridan, Ambrose Powell (A.P) Hill, George Pickett, James Ewell Brown (J.E.B.) Stuart, George Armstrong "where the fuck did all of these Indians come from" Custer and probably the craziest Union General of them all Daniel Sickles. While the South couldn't stop the ass kicking they were about to get, one has to admit their Generals had the coolest fucking names of the two sides, by far.

In the 1850s all of these men were simple soldiers, who, when given an order, they followed it, finished the mission or died trying. Because that's what a soldier does. We'll look into the details of a few of these men. However, it should be noted that what put the Confederate Army at a distinct military disadvantage from the outset of the war was a bad combination of good training, loyalty to the South and a severe lack of supplies.

Throughout his adult life and up until his election as President Abraham Lincoln really didn't give a shit about Black people or the question of slavery. Throughout the 1850s and right up to his inauguration his attitude to the "peculiar institution" was one of no interest. Yes, he thought the Southerners were backward in their thinking, but, so did most Northerners. But, like most Northerners he could tolerate it. As Jay-Z says would say in one of his songs "what you eat don't make me shit."

As it would be, right up until his first days in office, Lincoln's main focus was "I don't give a fuck what you do with them niggers but the Union will be preserved." When the South decided to establish the Confederate States of America knowing exactly where Abraham Lincoln stood on that shit two things psychologically and culturally happened for the military leadership on both sides.

For the Union Army, simple, Abraham Lincoln is Commander-In-Chief, he orders you to put foot-to-ass, and you do as so ordered. If you're an officer in the United States Army and you have sworn to uphold and defend the Constitution of the United States as per your commission, it is what it is. There's no opinion about politics, no debating the questions of the day, nobody gives a shit about what you like to drink or who you're fucking, just do your fucking job.

It was a little more complicated for Confederate Army officers. Remember, for the newly founded Confederate States of America there was no Confederate States Military Academy, no history of great leaders in famous battles or any history at all. All Confederate generals went to the same United States Military Academy that their Union counterparts attended. All of them stayed in the same barracks as their Union counterparts. Ate in the same mess hall, wore the same uniforms

Three Blind Mice

and complained about the same shit. All of them swore to uphold and defend the very same United States Constitution.

So when the South decided to go their own way, before these men (Confederate generals and their minions) could simply be given an order and follow it (as they have been trained), they had to get their minds around, politically, is this even right what we are doing? Make no mistake this was a psychological, involuntary reflex. Like your eyes blinking or your heart beating. This reality put the Confederate Army and its leadership a step behind the Union from the outset of the Civil War. Yes, I know the Union lost the First Battle of Manassas but the Rebels still got their asses kicked.

This was especially true for Confederate Army generals. They had to think politically, before they could think militarily. It's Cassius Clay versus Sonny Liston, only, one hundred years earlier. Because of all of the pre-fight bullshit Ali had already won three rounds before the fight ever started!

And all they wanted to do was be soldiers. So, as the 1850s evolves from a military standpoint, the Union had already won the war. When the actual killing started, Union soldiers had a defined mission; preserving the Union. Which would turn into "let's free the slaves too, fuck it." Confederate soldiers started killing basically under peer pressure. "I gotta fight so I don't look like a pussy to my neighbor."

The South lost because they lacked a moral imperative which is important to any fighting force at any time in world history. Look at the Allies in World Wars One and Two and the Vietnamese in Vietnam. Or, if you want to go backwards, look at the locals during the Siege of Vienna in the 1600s against the Ottomans.

What's interesting is the Southern states went through all of this just so they could keep intact the institution of slavery. Keep in mind, less than two percent of the southern population was even rich enough to own slaves! The few making decisions for the many and leaving hundreds of thousands dead in their wake. Its bullshit.

So let's look at some of the players.

There was no bigger fraud the General George McClellan. The "Philly Pholly." If there was ever an Anna Kournikova/Danica Patrick all hype, no substance, guy in the Civil War he was it. McClellan was a United States Military Academy graduate, Class of 1846. He was a classmate of George Pickett who would finish dead last in that same class by the way. McClellan would finish second. George McClellan, on the one hand was the accomplished man and, on the other an idiot in so many ways. He ran for President in the Presidential Election of 1864. He was even Governor of New Jersey at one time. He also fought in the Mexican-American and Civil War.

He was born in Philadelphia, Pennsylvania. His pops was an eye doctor. An ophthalmologist with much clout. His father was also one of the founders of Jefferson Medical College. In the 1850s, like most officers from West Point he handled various assignments related to engineering for the Army. He was stations in Delaware at one point, Arkansas and Texas at another.

Three Blind Mice

It's interesting to note that Pierce's Secretary of War, Jefferson Davis, would send him to Europe to scout out the Crimean War for the United States in 1855. He would come back to Philly and write about what he saw. Out of his report would come information on horse cavalry tactics and their effectiveness in battle. What he forgot to mention is that he copied that shit from the Russians who lost the fucking war. He would also design a horse saddle called the "McClellan Saddle" that would become very popular. It's still in use today. Ironically, during the Civil War his saddle would prove to be very practical to the Confederates because it wasn't as heavy as a traditional saddle.

This was important because it got to a point where the Confederate Army couldn't feed the fucking horses. They grew thin and weak and couldn't burden as much as a normal, healthy horse. He would go on to command the Union Army in the early stages of the Civil War only to be relieved by Lincoln because he was stupid and timid. Part of his hesitancy was that he thought he knew his counterparts every move. One of the reasons the Civil War lasted as long as it did was because these Generals knew each other so well from their days at West Point.

Just as President Abraham Lincoln suspended the writ of habeas corpus in the early days of the war (and was appropriately chastised for it), President James Buchanan before could have taken a similar tact and complicated efforts for the Southern states that ripped the country apart in the last days of his administration.

President Buchanan could have simple said to any officer thinking about leading troops against the United States "listen, if raise up arms against your country I will have you arrested and tried for treason." And the same for any elected official as well. His reasoning would have had some validity. He could have deduced that the United States Government spent good money educating, training and making you into a first rate engineer, "I'll be damned if you're gonna take all of that shit and turn around and use it against us." Fuck 'em all. Andrew Jackson wouldn't have thought twice about such a move. Early targeted arrest would have left no one to lead the Confederacy or Confederate troops and the idea of secession would have collapsed.

Ambrose Powell (A.P.) Hill was one of the first West Pointers who should have been arrested. He was a bit of a brat at West Point. He liked to party and chase women. So much so that, during one break in between classes he fucked around and got the clap (gonorrhea) so bad the shit made him miss so much time that he had to do a whole year all over again. I'm surprised his dick didn't fall off. Having graduated in 1847, like many other Generals he spent the 1850s during engineering work. Mostly up and down the Atlantic seaboard.

George Edward Pickett, he of the famous (as well as stupid and ill advised) "Pickett's Charge" at the Battle of Gettsyburg was another sub-par West Pointer. He graduated dead last in his class in 1846. Pickett had an interesting and tragic decade before his exploits in the Civil War. After graduation from the United States Military Academy, he got assignments in Texas and what is now the State of Washington.

While in Washington he was under orders to construct Fort Bellingham in what is now the city of Bellingham, Washington. Pickett would make headlines there for his role in what became known as the

Three Blind Mice

"Pig War of 1859." Pickett and his men were ordered to San Juan Island. A parcel of that land that was part of a small archipelago tucked in upper regions of the Pacific Northwest. Apparently there was trouble between the (who else, the fucking British, again) and a few American farmers.

One of these farmers was accused of killing a pig that wouldn't stay out of his garden. Problem was this pig belonged to the British Hudson Bay Company. The farmer offered to pay for the pig, but, that wasn't good enough. The company still wanted the farmer to go before a British magistrate. Pickett and his men said "fuck that" he ain't going nowhere and neither are we. In response the British sent a force of their own. However, when the British commander seen the determination of Pickett and his men to stand their ground, he pussied out and backed off. It seems that another Anglo-US war over a pig was not worth it.

Eventually the dispute was settled and the British left the island to the United States where today regular ferries go from the mainland to San Juan Island. Everyone should go visit sometime. He married twice in the 1850s and both of his wives died shortly after child birth. His first wife, Sally Harrison Minge, was a relative of President William Henry Harrison. She died during childbirth while they lived in Texas.

When he got to Washington Territory, he met and married a Native American woman known by the name of Morning Mist. She also died a few months after having a son, James Tilton Pickett. Sadly, Pickett's son would only live to be thirty two. He would die of tuberculosis. Soon the Civil War would breakout and he would opt to fight for his native Virginia. This, despite the fact that he really didn't care much for the institution of slavery. He just wanted to be a good soldier.

Confederate Army General James Ewell Brown (J.E.B.) Stuart was a great cavalry man for Robert E. Lee. Another Virginia boy, he didn't graduate from West Point until 1854. He was only thirty one when he died in battle during the Civil War. So he was very young for a General, but, well respected.

He spent the 1850s in Texas and Kansas during the "Bleeding Kansas" period. He was also part of the United States Army contingent that captured John Brown at Harper's Ferry. In 1859 Stuart developed a unique hook to better a soldier's saber. He received a patent and had it mass produced. He would be killed during the Civil War Battle of Yellow Tavern just outside Richmond in the Commonwealth of Virginia.

Thomas Jonathan "Stonewall" Jackson was another of the cool name having Confederate Generals. He has lasted into history with a reputation as very capable commander for the Confederate States Army. He earned the nickname "Stonewall" from the First Battle of Bull Run at the start of the Civil War. During the fighting another General, Barnard Bee is reported to have said "look at Jackson standing there like a stone wall." However he meant it, the nickname stuck and he became "Stonewall" Jackson forever.

Part of Jackson's story starts with his great grandparents on his father's side. Both came to America as convicted thieves on the British prison ship Litchfield in the mid seventeen hundreds, where they would meet and fall in love. Also, family related, Stonewall Jackson had a major falling out with his sister, Laura when the Civil War broke out. She was a staunch Unionist and hated the fact that Jackson decided to fight for the Confederacy. So this was a case where the Civil War truly broke up a family.

Three Blind Mice

Jackson's family grew up in what was then the western part of the Commonwealth of Virginia (what is now West Virginia). The folks that lived in the western part of the Commonwealth had very little in common with their eastern counterparts, especially when it came to Union versus Confederate. As a result, West Virginia is the only state granted statehood as a direct result of the Civil War.

Stonewall Jackson would graduate from the West Point in 1846. Since he hadn't gotten too much schooling as a child or a teen, at West Point he was a bit slow on the uptake. But the kid had plenty of street smarts and that was plenty enough to get him through. Like others he would spend part of the 1850s fighting the Seminole Wars. After that assignment he became a professor at the Virginia Military Institute. Because he was such a strict disciplinarian his students fucking hated him.

He didn't give a shit though as he broke balls every chance he got to educate those little fuckers. He didn't tolerate fools and was incapable of bullshit.

His first wife died after giving birth to a stillborn in the mid 1850s. After that shit he took a trip to Europe, came back, got married again, had a couple of girls (one who would die after her first month), bought a house and finished up the decade commanding a group of VMI cadets in Harper's Ferry supporting United States Army troops overseeing the hanging of John Brown. He was also very good to his slaves. As oxymoronic as that sounds. It's analogous to someone having sweet smelling shit (it's still shit). Even taught them to read and write, which was saying something since it was against the law in the Commonwealth of Virginia.

General Joseph E. Johnston stands out as one of the most senior General officers in the Confederate Army. He holds the distinction of being the highest ranking officer to leave the United States Army and become a Rebel. He also is recognized as the first United States Military Academy graduate to hold the rank of General in the United States Army. In the 1850s Johnston spent time in Kansas supporting government policy there and the Wyoming Territory fighting Native Americans. One of his junior officers was General George McClellan (a Captain then). He also put his engineering degree to good use helping to survey the Kansas border.

He was promoted to Brigadier General in 1860 and made Quartermaster General of the United States Army. He hated the post for several reasons. He wanted a field command, but most of all as the Civil War was looming he knew he was in charge of handling materials and supplies for the same United States Army he'd be fighting against.

This totally fucked his head up. Despite the fact that he was the first West Point graduate to have been promoted to General, Johnston always thought more of himself than others did. Jefferson Davis couldn't stand his ass. It was Jefferson Davis who tried to stifle his promotion to Brigadier General when the Quartermaster General came open. As President of the Confederate States of America this animosity would continue for the rest of the war. So when he offered his services to the Confederacy, in his mind, he thought it would be as the number one guy in the Confederate Army. Instead, the billet went to Robert E. Lee which pissed him off to no end. Johnston would soldier on and follow his orders as history would record.

Three Blind Mice

The Civil War could also be easily known as the "1860s War of the Engineers." One of the Generals on the Union side was General George Meade. He was a career army officer and another engineer from the United States Military Academy.

He is best known for kicking Lee's ass at Gettysburg. Although he had a chance to wipe him out during Lee's retreat and failed to do so it's still registered as an ass kicking. He was born in Spain (his father represented the United States Navy there at the time of this birth). His family came back to the United States with very little money and Meade was appointed to the United States Military Academy as a hardship case. But, he made the most of that shit and graduated in 1835.

In the 1850s he put his engineering degree to use building lighthouses and doing coastal surveying in the states of Florida and New Jersey. He designed the Barnegat, Absecon and Cape May lighthouses in New Jersey and the Jupiter and Sombrero Key lighthouses in Florida.

In the late 1850s he was sent to survey the Great Lakes. He would remain in the region until the start of the Civil War. After the Civil War, among other positions Meade would become Commissioner of Fairmount Park in Philadelphia. Today it is the largest inner city park in the United States.

Pierre Gustave Toutant (P.G.T.) Beauregard, a Confederate General, was a multi-faceted man who also graduated from the United States Military Academy. From Louisiana he was born to a French Creole family. English was a second language for him as he raised speaking French.

While a cadet at West Point, one of his instructors was a gentleman named Robert Anderson. Anderson would end up being the commander at Fort Sumter and would later surrender the Fort to his former student General Beauregard.

He spent much of the 1850s in his native Louisiana, Florida and Alabama doing engineering work along the Gulf Coast. He was unique among soldiers as he was quite active in politics. He campaigned with zeal for Franklin Pierce during the United States Presidential Election of 1852. He even ran for Mayor of New Orleans narrowing losing. He would also be appointed Superintendent of the United States Military Academy, eventually resigning after the state of Louisiana decided to leave the Union.

Henry W. Halleck was a Union General that was known by the derogatory name "Old Brains." A Southern sympathizer he was also known to be a great administrator which did dick for him in a time of war. He didn't put his engineering degree to much use. Halleck was much more an academic. He spent the 1850s mostly in the California Territory and was instrumental in its statehood process helping to draft that state's constitution.

He married the granddaughter of Alexander Hamilton, Elizabeth Hamilton. He would go on to become a partner in a law firm in Northern California and also speculate in real estate. Halleck would be a pallbearer at President Abraham Lincoln's funeral. He also would be credited with coining the name of the area known as "Russian America" as "Alaska."

Union General Philip Sheridan was one of the younger Generals of the American Civil War. Born in Albany, New York and raised in

Three Blind Mice

Ohio he was a short man, five feet, five inches tall. He didn't graduate from West Point until 1853. He did his engineering work in the Pacific Northwest surveying Oregon's Willamette Valley. Now a well regarded wine region of the United States known primarily for its production of the Pinot Noir grape.

A state of North Carolina born Confederate General, Braxton Bragg graduated from the United States Military Academy in 1837. Like Stonewall Jackson, he was known as a strict disciplinarian. Some would argue that he was even stricter than Stonewall Jackson. At one point, early on in his military career, when he was stationed at a frontier post, his subordinates tried to kill his ass. He served in the western theater during the Civil War and was a close advisor of Confederate President Jefferson Davis as well.

Always sharp at the mouth, Braxton Bragg moved to his own beat. He didn't care much for his superior officers and would often talk shit about them. At one point he was court-martialed, but, only received a slap on the wrist from then Secretary of War William Wilkins. He became quite popular for his bravery in the Mexican-American War serving under, then Colonel Jefferson Davis. He spent the early part of the 1850s stationed in what was then called Indian Territory (present day Oklahoma).

Later in the decade he would resign his commission and purchase a sugar plantation in Thibodeaux, Louisiana. While he used slaves to work the plantation, he was opposed to secession at this time. This opposition would not stop him from taking command of the Louisiana Militia at the outbreak of the Civil War. Today the United States Army installation in Fayetteville, North Carolina bears his name. It is the largest United States Army installation in the country and home to the well deserved and proud Eighty-Second Airborne Division as well as the secretive and deadly Special Forces unit known as Delta Force.

Jubal Anderson (J.A.) Early was a Confederate General that spent the entire American Civil War serving under Stonewall Jackson and Robert E. Lee. Born in the Commonwealth of Virginia he would graduate from the United States Military Academy in 1837. A Whig politically, he was against secession initially, but switched sides when President Lincoln started raising troops for the fight. He would spend the 1850s practicing law and doing quite well at it. He would go on to be a major player in the South's "Lost Cause" movement.

General William Starke Rosecrans was a Union soldier would gain fame for his ass kicking at the Battle of Chickamauga. Another "sharp at the mouth" General he often quarreled with General Ulysses S. Grant and Secretary of War Edwin M. Stanton. He would graduate from the United States Military Academy in 1842. Rosecrans would spend part of the 1850s teaching at West Point. He would apply for a teaching position at the Virginia Military Institute eventually losing the position to another graduate of West Point named Thomas Jackson (Stonewall).

Also in the 1850s he would put his engineering degree to use in Rhode Island, Massachusetts and the District of Columbia. Rosecrans was also an inventor. He designed the first kerosene lamp to successfully burn a round wick. He also helped build an oil refinery in the Allegheny Mountains and design locks along the Coal River in the state of West Virginia. He would spend most of the Civil War fighting Confederate General Braxton Bragg under Union General Halleck. After the war he would eventually move west to California and acquire land in Southern California's South Bay. Today Rosecrans Avenue is named after him.

Winfield Scott Hancock was born in Southeast Pennsylvania just outside of Philadelphia, Pennsylvania. A Union General during the Civil War he would distinguish himself at the Battle of Gettysburg. He was raised in Norristown, Pennsylvania. Which was, and remains, the county seat of Montgomery County, Pennsylvania. There he attended the Norristown Academy.

He was an 1844 graduate of the United States Military Academy accepted there after receiving a nomination from Congressman Joseph Fornance four years earlier. Fornance practiced law in Norristown and also served as Council President of the Borough of Norristown. Like other graduates at the time he would serve the early part of his military career in the Mexican-American War. Hancock would spend the 1850s in Southwest Florida on the back end of the Third Seminole War, in Kansas dealing with the military portion of that political fiasco and Utah straightening out those fucking polygamist. In 1858 he would finish the decade in Southern California. He became friendly with a number of future Confederate officers prior to the Civil War, but, would remain loyal to the Union. Wounded at Gettysburg, he would return to Norristown, Pennsylvania to recover. After the war, he would be put in charge of killing President Abraham Lincoln's assassins.

Eventually, he would be put in charge of the United States Army Fifth Military District covering Texas and Louisiana. In part, because he was a Democrat and had White Southern sympathies which met with then President Andrew Johnson's approval. General Hancock also stands out because he would run for President of the United States in the Election of 1880. He would lose the election James Garfield. Today, among other reminders Hancock Elementary School on Hancock Street in Norristown, Pennsylvania are named after him. He is buried in Montgomery Cemetery in West Norriton in the Commonwealth of Pennsylvania not far from his beloved Norristown.

Ambrose Everett Burnside was a multi-faceted man that served as a Union General during the Civil War. Additionally, he was an inventor, United States Senator and Governor of the State of Rhode Island. Born in the State of Indiana, his father was a slave owner from South Carolina. He had a big ole fucking head and because of his hairstyle the term "sideburns" became a part of American lexicon.

Having graduated from the United States Military Academy in 1847 he would also serve in the Mexican-American War. Near the end of the war, ironically, he would serve under, then Captain, Braxton Bragg. In the 1850s he would turn his attention to the making of firearms and would eventually receive a contract from President Buchanan's Secretary of War John Floyd. A fire at his factory would leave him broke and he would eventually end up working for the railroad under one of his future Civil War commanders, one General George McClellan.

Union General William Tecumseh Sherman made a name for himself with his famous "March to the Sea" during the Civil War. Born one of eleven children in the state of Ohio, he was the son of an Ohio State Supreme Court Justice who died when young William was just nine years old. With so many siblings Sherman was basically raised as a foster child by Thomas Ewing. Mr. Ewing was a prominent lawyer and Senator who was close to the Sherman family. It would be Senator Ewing would eventually secure Sherman's nomination to the United States Military Academy.

It's noteworthy that General Sherman was also a distant cousin of Roger Sherman. Roger Sherman was a prominent Eighteenth Century lawyer, politician and one of America's Founding Fathers. In fact, Roger Sherman is distinguishable in that he is the only man to have signed all four of America's significant "self determination" papers. They include the lesser known Continental Association, the Declaration of Independence, the Articles of Confederation and the United States Constitution.

Sherman graduated from West Point with the Class of 1840. Like many of the West Point graduates of the era, he would also have to fight those pesky Seminole Indians. Ironically, however, he saw no action in the Mexican-American War. He was "in the rear with the gear" doing administrative bullshit in Northern California. Among other duties he would put his engineering degree to use doing surveys for a tract of land that would one day become the city of Sacramento in the state of California. Today, that state's capital city.

General Sherman would spend the most of the 1850s working in the civilian sector as a banker in San Francisco. In 1859 he became Superintendent of the Louisiana State Seminary of Learning and Military Academy an institution that would later become Louisiana State University. Because of his time in the South, Sherman had no problem with slavery. But a breakup of the Union was just the type of bullshit he would not stand for and fight against.

Union General Daniel Sickles was as unique a character as there was in the 1850s. Sickles was one of the few Generals who did not attend the

United States Military Academy. In the American Civil War he made his name at the Battle of Gettysburg where he was gravely wounded, losing a leg. He would eventually be awarded the Medal of Honor for his actions there. In the 1850s his personal life made him famous for the scandalous way he lived. In 1852 he married a young gal named Teresa Bagioli. At the time he was thirty three and she was fifteen. Although almost no one approved of the marriage they did it anyway. There were actually two ceremonies, one civil and religious. It's interesting to note that the church ceremony was presided over by Archbishop John Hughes. Hughes, the first Catholic Archbishop of New York, became famous for being one of the founders of what is now Fordham University in the Bronx, New York and as well as leading the effort in getting New York's Saint Patrick's Cathedral built.

That was only the beginning with General Sickles. He was quite fond of new pussy and was an avid womanizer. He was most fond of a woman named Fanny White. Sickles loved Fanny because in many ways she was a lot like him. Fanny started her career out as a prostitute. She would eventually work her way up to madam managing the very brothel she worked in. Not only did she sell her flesh for money but she excelled at female pimpism. Sickles loved fucking her and they spent a lot of time together much to the chagrin of his wife Teresa. Eventually Teresa would find some new dick in the form of a gentleman named Philip Barton Key II. Philip Key was a man with serious connections in the Washington, D.C. metro. His father was Francis Scott Key of Star Spangled Banner fame and his uncle was the racist Chief Justice of the United States Supreme Court Roger Taney of Dred Scott fame. Key and Teresa Bagioli would start an affair that would eventually cost Key his life. Now that is some expensive pussy.

He would be killed by General Sickles who would find out about the affair sometime in 1859. Sickles attitude with Teresa was basically, "look, I can fuck whoever I want whenever I want, but you better not even think of giving your pussy away to another man, ever." And he meant that shit. When he found out that Philip Key and his wife were doing the nasty he flew into a rage and shot that motherfucker Casper the Friendly Ghost dead in broad fucking daylight. Of course he was arrested for that shit. And the trial was O.J. Simpson like at the time. It was a true sensation in the Nineteenth Century.

Among his attorneys was one Edwin Stanton who would direct Abraham Lincoln's war strategy as Secretary of War during the American Civil War. In a stroke of brilliance the defense would have Sickles plead not guilty by reason of temporary insanity and the jury would acquit his ass. This was the first time that such a defense was used in the United States. Sickles would live a long life dying at the age of ninety four in 1914. When he wasn't fucking or killing people he managed to become a rather diverse public servant. He served in both the New York State Assembly and New York State Senate. He also served in the United States House of Representatives representing the State of New York. Diplomatically, he served on James Buchanan's staff when Buchanan was Minister to Great Britain and he also served as United States Minister to Spain under the administration of Ulysses S. Grant.

Much has been written about both President Ulysses S. Grant and General Robert E. Lee. However, it is worth noting what they were up to in the 1850s. General Lee would become Superintendent of the United States Military Academy in 1852. One of the cadets under his charge was his son George Washington Custis Lee who would graduate in 1854. Lee also would spend time in the state of Texas making sure Apache Native Americans didn't scalp any of the White settlers there.

President Grant would spend the 1850s in Oregon and California on various assignments. It was during this time that he would become an excellent abuser of alcohol as well. Grant was also a horrible businessman and spent much of the decade broke as a motherfucker. These years greatly affected his prosecution of the American Civil War and his subsequent Presidency.

In the 1850s Commodore Matthew Perry was the face of the United States Navy. His exploits in Japan made him famous and was an early example of American global power being portrayed far away from home. Matthew Perry is considered the Father of the Steamship Navy. Born in Rhode Island he came out the womb with sea legs. His father was a Captain in the United States Navy and one of his brothers, Oliver Hazard Perry was a hero at the Battle of Lake Erie during the War of 1812.

Matthew would serve as a midshipman with Oliver during the Battle of Lake Erie aboard the flagship USS Niagara among other vessels. He also served on the USS President, USS United States and the USS Cyane in the years after the War of 1812. The United States Naval Academy was established in 1845. Commodore Perry would be instrumental in providing a matriculation curriculum that made sense for new midshipman. Those kids needed his help too. Nobody skated at the newly established naval school. It was hard to get in and real fucking hard to get out. By 1850 midshipman underwent a seven year program with four years on campus and three years at sea. The Academy wouldn't graduate its first class until 1854.

Three Blind Mice

Matthew Perry would provide important coastal support to General Winfield Scott during the Mexican-American War. He would personally lead attacks on the Mexican entities of Tabasco and San Juan Batista. Perry would become a much needed voice for naval modernization at the time as well. He would organize the first group of naval engineers and take command of the steam powered warship USS Fulton.

Perry would cement his name in naval lore with his historic Perry Expedition to Japan. It was a diplomatic and military mission to the Far East whose ramifications are still relevant to this day. The mission centered itself around establishing trade and diplomatic relations with the countries of the Far East, especially Japan. This was not to be an easy task. At the time the Japanese were a fiercely private people in those days (North Korea style). And as a country their attitude was basically, "don't fuck with us and we won't fuck with you." They treated other countries who came knocking at their door like Jehovah Witnesses. "Just get the fuck out of here."

Prior to Perry's expedition others tried to get some face time with the Japanese. In 1846 a group of American sailors from a whaling ship were taken hostage Somali pirate style in Nagasaki. The United States sent the USS Columbus and the USS Vincennes under the command of Commander James Biddle to go get them. The result was the Japanese smacked his ass around and sent him home with his tail between his legs.

Next up to bat was Captain James Glynn commanding the USS Preble. She arrived in April, 1849. Captain Glynn showed up with his fist balled up and made sure the Japanese knew it. After a minor test of his will and with some help from the Dutch, the Japanese released the prisoners. Not all of the captives made it out, however. A few died from the brutal conditions under which they were held and one sailor committed suicide. Of the survivors, by December, 1849 they were all back in the United States.

The story made headlines in the United States and Captain Glynn was the big man on campus for a moment. Big enough for him to recommend to the United States Government that America should try to open official relations with Japan. He cautioned that diplomacy was still the approach of choice, but, whoever goes should be prepared to put foot-to-ass if necessary. It was these events that set up Matthew Perry's famous expedition(s) starting in the early 1850s.

Commodore Perry set off from Norfolk in the Commonwealth of Virginia and arrived in Uraga Harbor (near present day Tokyo) in the summer of 1853. Under his command were the American naval warships, USS Mississippi, USS Saratoga, USS Plymouth and the USS Susquehanna. The Japanese attempted the same bullshit they had tried with Biddle and Glynn. Having heeded the advice of his predecessors however Perry was in no mood to be accommodating or fucked with.

In Perry's possession was a letter from President Millard Fillmore and he was going intent on delivering it. Perry threatened to shell the mainland to rubble and positioned the squadron's guns in a manner to show he meant what he said. However he said it the Japanese put down their chopsticks and decided to listen to the man. After delivering the letter Perry and his men left for some liberty (navy talk for vacation time) in China while those fuckers thought it over.

Commodore Perry returned to Japan in February, 1854 and, to his surprise the Japanese had accepted all of the terms President Fillmore stipulated in his letter. The result was the Convention of Kanagawa at which was signed the Japan-United States Treaty of Peace and Amity. So, once again in world history, two countries had to threaten to kick the shit out of each other to come up with peace. Perry signed for the United States and some Shogun motherfuckers signed for the Japanese. The treaty would open up the previously closed ports of Shimoda and Hakodate to United States shipping. This would end two centuries of isolation by the Japanese.

Everything after that was pretty much cool until the Japanese starting fucking with the Chinese, Koreans and the rest of Southeast Asia, including raping women and killing children in the 1930s and 1940s. Specifically horrible was the Rape of Nanking in 1937. Where an estimated twenty thousand woman, including infants and elderly females, were raped, mutilated and killed by Japanese soldiers. Some of these women had their pussies cut out after being gang raped.

There were also reports of Japanese soldiers making Chinese families commit incest. Sons fucking mothers, fathers fucking daughters, even monks, who swore to a life of celibacy, being forced to rape women. Look, war is one thing, but just being fucked up for fucked up sake is a whole other story entirely. The Japanese had just lost their fucking minds! And to what end? You decide.

But they really fucked up when they tried to butt fuck the United States at Pearl Harbor in 1941. It would take a minute for the United States to get their military shit together, but America would eventually make sure the Japanese got two nuclear bombs shoved up their asses in the summer of 1945. After that colonoscopy they got back in line real fucking quick. Haven't heard a military peep out of them since. In the Twenty-First Century the Chinese are the bullies in the region. You figure they would learn a lesson from the past, but motherfucker's don't learn shit. There's other ways to figure out the stove is hot other than putting your hand on it.

Anyway, Perry would also stop by the Island of Formosa (what is today Taiwan). He suggested to President Franklin Pierce that the United States make it a regional way station (and claim it as a United States territory) in the same way Spain had claimed Cuba as a possession. Perry basically said to his superiors "we're here now let's keep this fucker." Of course since it made WAY too much fucking sense the second of the Three Blind Mice, new President Franklin Pierce, passed on the idea. He feared it would be too costly to maintain so far away from the continental United States. Which is bullshit, because there was nobody around to tell them to get the fuck out. Plus the Americans had just got done bullying Japan to play political ball.

Of course none of that logic ever stopped the fucking Europeans in their conquest of the New World. It's a wonder someone didn't just say to President Pierce "have a little fucking balls every once in a while." This imperialistic hesitation would turn out to be another decision with long term ramifications. If the United States had taken possession of Taiwan the Pacific fighting in World War Two would have turned out completely different. Japanese belligerence in the region would have had to deal with an American military posture much closer to Japan than they would have wanted to. The United States, on the other hand, would have been perfectly placed to not only keep an eye on those fuckers but equally be prepared for any offensive action it deemed necessary.

Thusly, the attack on Pearl Harbor would have never happened. As a matter of fact, the whole Pacific Campaign of World War Two would have been conducted differently. In the Twenty-first Century Taiwan would have been a major island possession in an important part of the world and a significant military installation for the United States Navy. America would also have a much easier time containing Chinese aggression in the region today because they would never challenge the United States the way they bully the Taiwanese today.

Commodore Perry and his squadron finally made it back to the United States in 1855. Congress would give him twenty thousand dollars (a shitload of money back in the day) for his time. He would also be promoted to the rank of Rear Admiral.

Chapter 12

Nicaragua, Cuba and the Republic of Maryland (in Africa)

In the 1850s a "filibuster" was an individual who engaged in military activity in a foreign country, usually, for financial gain or power. The word originates from the Spanish word "filibuster" which, means to pirate or steal from.

So, filibustering is when some motherfucker decides on his own he's just gonna take over a fucking country because he can and nobody will stop him. Think imperialism, but the brutality is sponsored by an individual rather than a whole fucking country. Yes, the shit started before the 1850s and still goes on today (and not just in American politics). From Cecil Rhodes in Africa in the late eighteen hundreds to Hitler to Idi Amin, you get the picture. William the Conqueror was one the best early examples when he invaded England in Ten Sixty Six.

Three Blind Mice

Hollywood has made a killing on movies about filibusters. From the Island of Doctor Moreau to Francis Ford Coppola's Apocalypse Now to John Milius' Farewell to the King starring Nick Nolte the storytelling of filibustering is tried, true and profitable. Narciso Lopez and William Walker would two real life characters that would leave their marks on the 1850s. Lopez would try his bullshit in Cuba and Walker would try his bullshit in Nicaragua.

Narciso Lopez was born in Venezuela and get his military training from and eventually fight for the Spanish. By 1848 he got sick of fighting for those assholes and moved to the United States. His activities in the United States would become the forerunner to the 1960s Bay of Pigs. Lopez tried to recruit other Cubans in America to train, fight and take over Cuba. Ironically enough, like Formosa, the United States had several chances to take Cuba as a possession and always resisted. If they had Cuba wouldn't be the pain in the ass they became in the late 20th Century.

The United States Government was not pro filibustering at the time. Its attitude at the time was "if another country was going to be taken over it was going to be us fucking people over not some individual." Thusly Lopez had a hard time finding support. But he didn't give a shit and proceeded anyway. At one point he tried to recruit future President of the Confederate States of America Jefferson Davis and future General of the Army of Northern Virginia Robert E. Lee (who both considered the offer seriously) to lead his army.

Being pro slavery he figured if he could take over Cuba he could petition the United States for statehood and enter the Union as a slave state. He offered both Jefferson Davis and Robert E. Lee one hundred thousand dollars and a tobacco ranch as compensation for their time. They would both turn him down. Lopez would get financial support from, among others, the Governor of the State of Mississippi at the time, John Quitman. He would gather a small band of fighters and arrive in Cuba in 1850. Like the Bay of Pigs he failed to garner local support and would be forced to retreat back to Key West.

In 1851 he tried again and the same shit happened. Except this time Lopez would be caught and the Spanish executed his ass. His lasting legacy would be he designed and carried the flag that would become the Cuban national flag we see flying today. Had he been successful the United States would have been a major player in the Caribbean to this day. However, his exploits would inspire William Walker to start his bullshit in Nicaragua.

William Walker was the American version of Narciso Lopez. He would succeed in becoming President of Nicaragua for a minute in the mid 1850s. Born in Tennessee, one of his uncles was the founder of the Philadelphia Inquirer. Walker was a very smart man, graduating from the University of Tennessee at the age of fourteen. At age nineteen he would receive a medical degree from the Ivy League school the University of Pennsylvania. He would even practice law and journalism briefly. Ending up in San Francisco, he would come up with hair brained idea of establishing several slave states in Central America and controlling them himself.

In 1853 he succeeded in taking control of Baja California from the Mexicans. Having untenable control he renamed the area the Republic of Lower California and assumed control under the laws of the State

Three Blind Mice

of Louisiana. This made slavery legal. Because the Mexicans kept his ass on the run he had capital cities in Cabo San Lucas at one point and Ensenada at another. It wasn't long before they forced his ass out and he went back to California. He was put on trial for his arrogance, but since many people sided with his ideas, he was promptly acquitted. The acquittal would give Walker newfound confidence.

He would eventually turn his energy to Nicaragua. Before the Panama Canal, if you wanted to ship goods from the East Coast of the United States to the West Coast (say New York to San Francisco) the easiest way was to sail to Nicaragua, transverse Lake Nicaragua and hump your shit across a narrow strip of land near the Nicaraguan city of Rivas, get on another ship on the Pacific side of the isthmus and keep going.

The Nicaraguan government would grant control of the isthmus to a company controlled by American tycoon Cornelius Vanderbilt. Vanderbilt knew another greedy motherfucker when met one of which Walker was one. In 1855 Walker left San Francisco with a group of armed greedy motherfuckers and joined with the winning side of Nicaragua's then civil war (Don King style, you know, enter the ring with one motherfucker, but, always exit the ring with the winner). Walker, having command of the army took effective control of the entire county of Nicaragua by the autumn of that year. This was amazing enough.

Even more amazing was the fact that Mouse President Franklin Pierce recognized his government as the legitimate government of Nicaragua. At this point Walker probably could have gotten away with "jacking" a whole fucking country. But greedy motherfuckers don't think like that. He tried to go back on his deal with Vanderbilt, and since

Vandy was a greedier (and more powerful) motherfucker than Walker was he set about making sure he kept all the shit he owned down there.

He did this by collaborating with the Costa Ricans. Walker, in addition in underestimating Vanderbilt, starting talking shit about taking over other areas of Central America. So, the Costa Ricans got in that ass from the south and Hondurans got in that ass from the north. By late spring 1857 the United States Navy would have to bail him and his men out and take him back to the America. You would think he would have had enough fun at this point. But, not this guy. William Walker was the poster boy for the saying "a hard head makes for a soft ass." He would go back down to the region six months later and this time with thoughts of hooking up with some greedy British motherfuckers.

The British government (the ultimate global greedy motherfuckers of the day) had significant interest in the region in the form of the British Honduras (today known as Belize) and turned Walker over to the Hondurans. The Hondurans would promptly kill his ass by firing squad. Amazingly, Walker was only thirty six years of age at the time of his death.

William Walker was quite popular in the southern United States. Because of him many Southerners were of the opinion that any land south of Washington D.C. down to the tip of Argentina should be American slave territory. The City of Nashville recognizes him as the only native son to become a head of state. He even gets a mention in Margaret Mitchell's Gone with the Wind. In Costa Rica, the completion of his ass kicking (April 11), is recognized as a national holiday. The Costa Rican military leader, Juan Santamaria, who led the Costa Rican forces, is remembered as a national hero in that country.

Three Blind Mice

At its core, the Republic of Maryland was an independent nation that existed from 1854 through 1857. Ultimately, the Republic of Maryland would be annexed by the African nation of Liberia. The history of both countries have an intimate connection to the United States of America as both Liberia and the Republic of Maryland were founded by African Americans who were repatriated back to the African continent as part of the efforts of the American Colonization Society (the ACS) and its Maryland branch, the Maryland State Colonization Society (the MSCS).

The American Colonization Society was established because there was a group of rich, White, American men (on both sides of the slavery question) that realized the concept of "all men are created equal" and owning slaves (as well as marginalizing women) was ideological oil and vinegar.

This concept would continue throughout the history of the United States however. When the Administration of President George W. Bush, promoting democracy in the Middle East, saw that the Palestinians would democratically elect Hamas to power America's position would be "oh, we didn't mean those motherfuckers." They could only bullshit themselves and rest of the world for so long without losing legitimacy. So these guys got together and said "look, let's just send these motherfuckers back to where we got them from and history will remember slavery as a rental." Like everything else in America, some people loved the idea, others hated it.

Founded in Washington D.C. in 1816, its members were significant players of the time. They included; President James Monroe, future President Andrew Jackson, Francis Scott Key of Star Spangled Banner fame, Daniel Webster, Henry Clay and, later, even future President Abraham Lincoln. The organization's lasting legacy would be their role in founding the African country of Liberia, as well as the temporary states (later to be annexed) of the Republic of Maryland and Mississippi in Africa.

Some members were outright racists (but antislavery at the same time, if such a dichotomy can exist and it did). Some were elitist who considered Blacks inferior and even if free on a mass scale would never fit into a White dominated society. Others were separatists and wanted believed Blacks and Whites could not and should not live together. With the help of the ACS, freed American slaves starting arriving in what is now Liberia in the early 1820s. In the early years of the settlement the ACS always made sure that a White man was in charge. These Blacks must have been like "shit, we get all this way and these motherfuckers still in charge?"

And how do you get the masses to do any fucking thing you want them to? Ask Hitler, Mussolini, Stalin, you need propaganda. So the ACS started a publication to promote their ideas. It's ironic that, even though the ACS would fade over the rest of the eighteenth century, the publication would last well into the nineteen hundreds.

As mentioned earlier, even Lincoln thought it was a good idea to repatriate slaves to Liberia he did have slaves fight for the Union he when he needed more bodies for the war as the American Civil War dragged on. Anyway, eventually, the American Blacks would gain power in Liberia under minority rule. This would be a source of tension in Liberia throughout the country's history. They learned their lessons in unfairness well from their American White counterparts. The United States of American and Liberia continue to have a special relationship to this day.

The Republic of Maryland was unique was because it was founded by free American slaves specifically from the State of Maryland. Formed in 1854 it was sponsored by the Maryland State Colonization Society. This arrangement gave Maryland exclusive trading rights with the Republic of Maryland. The Republic of Maryland's first Black governor was John Brown Russwurm. Born in Jamaica to a White father and Black slave mother, his family first moved to Quebec, Canada and the settled in Portland, Maine.

He would end up graduating from Bowdoin College in 1826 becoming the first Black to graduate from that school. After college he became a staunch advocate of Black repatriation and colonization. This would lead him to put his money where his mouth was and he ended up going to Liberia in the 1830s. He would eventually become a leader in Liberia's education movement and this position would lead to his becoming the top guy in the newly founded Republic of Maryland. Its capital was Harper. A city in the southeast corner of what is today Liberia. It was named after ACS member Robert Harper.

The Republic of Maryland had a hard time staying independent. This was primarily because she couldn't defend herself from the local tribes who kept fucking with her. Eventually, the Republic of Maryland would seek military assistance from neighboring Liberia. After a while they would realize that they would need protection for the long term and agreed to annexation.

Mississippi-in-Africa would have the same problems. They would be founded by the Mississippi and Louisiana State Colonization Societies. They would succumb to annexation by Liberia for much the same reasons. Liberia's first President was John Jenkins Roberts. A free Black from Norfolk, Virginia he arrived in Liberia in 1829 and became President in 1847 upon Liberia's independence. Roberts' was crucial to the eventual declaration of Liberia's independence. As territory governor he encouraged the then legislature to vote on a referendum for self determination. It passed and he became President. He was, however, always mindful of keeping support of the ACS and, thusly, the United States.

He would also serve in the Liberian Army as a General, become a foreign minister to France and the United Kingdom as well as serve as President of Liberia College (where he was also a professor of law). Today, his birthday is a national holiday in Liberia. You can also find his mug on the country's ten dollar bill. Safe to say, he got a lot shit done.

Chapter 13

Native Americans and the 1850s

By the 1850s most of the Native Americans in the United States were well on their way to getting totally fucked over. Shit, before they ever pulled a knife, musket or canon the Europeans were already armed. The narrative went like this. The Europeans said, "Hi, we've been on this fucking boat for months and we are here to stay. We want clothing, shelter and natural resources. And we could use something to eat too. Oh, and by the way, we reserve the right to take any other shit we can think of later."

Native Americans said, "Nah, we'll take a pass. We think we will keep our shit, but thanks for coming by." The Europeans responded, "We wasn't asking motherfucker! But, before we stick some of these musket balls up your ass, here are a few diseases that should kill a bunch of you motherfuckers before any fighting even gets started.

Here's some small pox, a little measles, some typhoid fever for your ass. Hey, how about some tuberculosis and a little diphtheria so you can die a slow painful death of shallow breathing and bloody nasal discharge? Oh, and don't let us forget the chickenpox. And when you get enough of all that shit, we got some sexually transmitted diseases at the bottom of the kill bag. Our favorites are syphilis (you'll lose your mind, go blind and then die), gonorrhea (we call it "the clap"), you'll know you have it when deforestation occurs every time you take a piss, some chlamydia for the bitches and how about a dose of our industrial version of genital herpes?"

By 1850, whatever Native Americans were not killed by disease or weaponry lived west of the Mississippi River. Outmanned and outgunned by European Americans they were hardly ready to give up the fight, however. They would fight to keep everything from their lands, to their culture and in some cases, their very existence.

The sting of the Trail of Tears was still very fresh in the Native American mind. Now, fighting had become second nature. For some it was about protection, for others it was about revenge and for yet others it became sport to kill "paleface." The United States could see its greatness and, in order to satisfy its (manifest) destiny, like slavery, the question of the Native American had to be answered. The repercussions of that answer would be exposed in blood and disenfranchisement.

Some tribes would use negotiation, others would use the courts, many would just say "fuck it, let's fight." Some of these armed struggles would leave a lasting impression, and stain, on American history. Let's look at a few. The Seminole Wars is a good place to start. The Seminoles were a particularly pesky group for the United States Government. Maybe, in part, it was because the tribe was made up

Three Blind Mice

of both Native Americans and Blacks in what is today the State of Florida. Two peoples who were just fed up with the shit that was always being shoveled on top of them.

And, although the United States had to deal with them individually everywhere else in America, here they were together! The government was like "shit, each of these groups on their own are a bitch to deal with. Do we really want Florida that fucking bad?" The Seminole Wars would start in 1814 and be on, and off again, until the start of the Civil War. Most of the Civil War leadership made their bones fighting these motherfuckers and other tribes across the western half of the United States.

There were a total of three Seminole Wars. The First Seminole War had Andrew Jackson going into Florida and kicking the shit out the Native Americans in the area. These battles would sharply affect his Presidency years later. Jackson had had enough of Native Americans (and everybody else) for that matter after the Battle of New Orleans. Even though Florida was a Spanish possession he was determined to do what he saw fit.

Among his officers was a Brigadier General named Edmund Gaines (who Gainesville, Florida, among other places, is named after today). In later life Gaines would become an adversary of Jackson's and oppose Native American removal. The result of the First Seminole War was Spain giving Florida to the United States as they had neither the military or political will to defend her. Andrew Jackson became known historically as a national bully, but he was so popular in his day that nobody gave a fuck. After the First Seminole War, the United States decided to move the Seminole to the swamps of the Everglades. This was led by James Gadsden (yes, he of the Gadsden Purchase).

Darryl Murphy

Once Andrew Jackson was elected President or the United States the Indian Removal Act was passed and Jackson was determined to move all of those motherfuckers west of the Mississippi River. The Seminoles would hate their new living arrangements and once again begin to agitate. This time they were led by the warrior Osceola. The Seminoles didn't like the swamp but were determined they weren't going anywhere where relocation was concerned. So the Second Seminole War was underway.

The Second Seminole War was mostly an offensive action by the Seminoles. They were fed up with getting shit on by the United States Government and took the fight to them. The United States Government would spend forty million dollars and enlist forty thousand soldiers fighting the war. In between the Second and Third Seminole Wars there was an uneasy peace. Both sides kept fucking with each other. The solution for the United States was still determined to be moving all of the Seminoles west. This attitude would lead to the Third Seminole War. Mouse President Millard Fillmore even brought the Seminole chiefs to Washington and ass kiss them with medals and American city visits to appease them.

This did little to change their attitudes. When the chiefs got back to Florida they started their shit back up again. In 1855 the fighting started and would last until 1858 when the remaining Seminoles decided to go west. A few Seminoles would remain in Florida after the Civil War and beyond. But they would be effectively isolated by the post Florida Reconstruction Constitution of 1885.

Today the Florida State University mascot is named "Seminoles." This is a trivial recognition given the ass kicking taken by these noble people. In the 1850s the fighting between Native Americans and the United

Three Blind Mice

States would turn west. In what today makes up the states of California, Oregon, Washington, Utah, Texas and Arizona much blood would be shed. Texas, Oregon and Washington would see some of the bloodiest fighting during this period. White settlers looking for land, gold, silver and other natural resources first had to deal with Native Americans who had lived there for hundreds of years. And let's not forget the railroad. Shit had to be shipped somehow. So, on to other conflicts.

The Cayuse War was fought in and around present day Walla Walla in the state of Washington in the Pacific Northwest. It would put the Cayuse Indians against local settlers and the United States Army. The war started when the Cayuse demanded payment for any Whites crossing their land by stagecoach. The Whites looked at the Cayuse like "you must be crazy. You want money for me just sucking up oxygen in your neighbor? Fuck you."

The fighting started with an attack by the Cayuse on the Whitman Mission. Many Cayuse Indians had died from European diseases which they had no immunity for and blamed the newcomers. Since somebody had to take the blame for the Cayuse deaths they targeted Whitman and the settlers there. So the settlers got together and armed themselves with weapons provided by the Hudson Bay Company (yep, the same motherfuckers who would be the catalyst for the Pacific Northwest Pig War spoken of earlier). Eventually the militia would be supported by the United States Army. Even so the fighting would go on until 1855. The war was ended with the Cayuse ceding their lands and being forced to reservation life. However, the United States Government would decide to take a "negotiation first" approach with all Native Americans in the Pacific Northwest going forward.

While the Cayuse were getting fucked in the State of Washington, down south the Apaches decided they had had enough as well. The Jicarilla War started in 1849. It was fought between the Apaches and the United States Army in New Mexico. The Ute Native Americans would help out as well since them and the Apaches were homies. As was usual during the times, the war started when the Apaches, much like other Native Americans, started killing settlers feeling they were trying to take over their shit. And who could blame them?

Native Americans were of the belief, "here I am just minding my own fucking business and these other motherfuckers show up out of nowhere and want my shit!" How would you feel if some asshole showed up at your house and started going through your closet? Settlers and Apaches would continue to fuck with each other enough that by 1853 the United States Army would have to get involved. The apex of the Jicarilla was fought in the spring of 1854 when the Apaches were defeated at the Battle of Cieneguilla. Among the participants was one Kit Carson.

The Yuma War was fought between 1850 and 1853 in what is today Southwestern Arizona. The war was a struggle as to who has rights over the Gila and Colorado Rivers. The fighting was started by a band of outlaws led by John Glanton. They killed a bunch of Native Americans and in response the Yuman Native Americans killed them. After that California raised a militia and the war was on. This event almost bankrupted California. And all of this happened not long after California was granted statehood in September, 1850. Ironically enough the Yuma War would, in part be about the United Sates keeping the Arizona Native Americans from killing themselves. All of this was in the whole American self interest of progress.

Three Blind Mice

The Yakima War was fought between the United States Army and the Yakima Native Americans from 1855 and 1858. It was fought in present day Eastern Washington State and it is largely seen as a continuation of the Cayuse War. With the arrival of European-American settlers to the Pacific Northwest, the Native American was gradually squeezed out. Specifically in the states of Washington and Oregon.

Native Americans had tribal lands that numbered over four million acres. This would be reduced to ninety five thousand acres as time pasted. When gold was discovered in the area that's when the shit started. White settlers slowly started to encroach on the tribal lands. The United States Army would show up in 1856. Assisted by United States Marines and the United States Navy. These forces would turn back the Yakima tribe assisted by the Cascade and Klickitat tribes. It is noteworthy that after capture some Cascade Natives would be tried for treason and sentenced for murder. Unusual in that at the time they weren't event considered United States citizens.

The State of Texas would not be spared from the conflict between Native Americans and White settlers. The Battle of Little Robe Creek would be evidence of that. This was mainly a fight between the United States and the Comanche, Kiowa and Apache Native Americans. All of these tribes were a proud people who, for the most part, were also incapable of bullshit. Texas gained statehood in 1846. Statehood for Texas as a former Republic rather than a Territory complicated their relationship with both Native Americans and the United States Government.

Even after being granted statehood Texas would continue to see itself as an independent "place." Official United States Government policy specifically stated that conflict with Native Americans was to be avoided in every way. Texans said, "fuck that." Little Robe Creek was situated right on the border of western Oklahoma and the Texas Panhandle. The Comanche were vicious fighters that would be considered terrorists in the Twenty-first Century. Texas Rangers and militia would realize the only way to beat them was to become just as brutal. This brutality would be played out in the Battle of Little Robe Creek. Scalping and dismembering of limbs was a common ritual on both sides. And although Anglo-Texas would ultimately triumph, it would come at great cost to both sides. So the victory was pyrrhic at best.

This battle was an early example of all out warfare. Non-combatants (women and children) were considered targets. Advances in weaponry made a difference. Texas Rangers went from single shot to repeating fire rifles. This was also the first time a state had openly decided to defy federal law.

In 1855 there was a group known as the Rogue River Native Americans who resided along the Rogue River in what today is southern Oregon. This was another group of Native Americans that were just minding their own fucking business when settlers showed up wanting their shit. And, although the Rogue River Native Americans would eventually surrender in the spring of 1856 and be forced to reservations they too would make it hard on the settlers. The Native Americans would see victory at the Battle of Hungry Hill in October, 1855. Possessing the high ground they put an unexpected ass whipping on U.S. troops.

The Battle of Pease River was fought on December 18, 1860. It stands out because of Cynthia Ann Parker. Parker was an Anglo-Texan female kidnapped by the Comanche as a child. So, although, the battle would have similar Native American-settler overtones, it was really a rescue operation. The Comanche would keep and raise Parker in the fold into adulthood. She would end up marrying a Comanche chief, bearing him three children and forgetting all about her White life. Her family and the Texas Rangers put out an Amber Alert for her and never stopped looking for her. This was one of America's earliest cases of "a White girl is missing and we gotta find her at all costs."

While with the Comanche Cynthia Parker has become totally Comanche-ized. By the time she was rescued she could barely speak English. Her story became a national sensation. It is not clear why it is even called a battle. The Texas Rangers surprised the Comanche encampment and killed all of those motherfuckers.

After her rescue Cynthia Ann Parker didn't know where the fuck she was and only wanted to be reunited with her Comanche family. Who could blame her? It was all she knew her whole life up to that point. Her White family would keep her under de facto house arrest for the rest of her life. She would end up killing herself in despair.

The Walker War was a series of skirmishes between the Shoshone Native Americans and the Mormons under Brigham Young fought in 1853. This war boiled down to the fact that the Mormons had finally found a place where they could stop running in Utah and wanted all the land to themselves. So all the Ute tribes were in the way and had to be displaced. And, yes, the Mormons would get their way. For the United States the Native Wars were its version of trying to skin a raccoon in phone booth. You may skin it, but you ain't coming away unscathed from the experience.

Today, American's governmental relationship with Native Americans is administered and regulated by the Bureau of Indian Affairs, an agency within the Department of the Interior. It's the only federal agency of the United States Government whose perpetual mission is to give insufficient handouts to a group of people brutally fucked over just for sucking up oxygen on lands they were bequeathed at birth and have brutally taken away from them.

Chapter 14

Utah, Brigham Young and the Mormons

The State of Utah has one of America's most unique stories. Founded by the Mormons it is the most secular state in the United States. The state has a history of violence, sex, religion, racism, survival and, at the same time, tolerance. Much of their early progress to statehood was retarded by the Mormon's vice grip hold on the institution of polygamy. Organized as a Territory in 1850 they would not achieve statehood until 1896. The United States Government demanded a key provision denouncing polygamy be written in Utah's constitution before statehood would be granted.

Although much of the population of the United States is still mystified about exactly what Mormonism is, Utah remains a shining example of the right of American's to practice whatever fucking religion you want. Today over sixty percent of the population of Utah practices Mormonism. When the Mormons first settled out west they claimed a wide swath of land and called it "Deseret." In the Book of Mormon, the word means honeybee (thus the state moniker "the Beehive State").

Deseret would have been the largest in the country if it had maintained its boundaries. These boundaries included damn near all of present day Nevada and Utah as well as parts of present day Idaho, Colorado, California (including all of Southern California from the coast to the Arizona border), Arizona, New Mexico, Wyoming and Oregon. Basically, all of the land between the Rocky and Sierra Nevada Mountains south of the Oregon Territory to Mexico. It was not the craziest notion either. For example, much of Southern California was still undeveloped and most Californians lived in the north, which grew quickly because of the discovery of gold there.

Much of the land was uninhabited and it was harsh weather wise and shitty for growing anything. This meant no crops and no need for slaves, thus, they could avoid the burning issue of slavery and be left the fuck alone. When the Deseret request for statehood got to Washington D.C. however, the United States Congress said "that way too much land for these sex crazed motherfuckers" and stating whittling down that territory grab.

The Mormons were granted territory status instead as the Utah Territory which encompassed the northern portion of the then Deseret. This still contained present day Nevada, Utah and parts of present day Colorado and Wyoming. So it was still a big fucking piece of land. The capital of the new territory was established in the town of Fillmore. Brigham Young named it after then President Millard Fillmore. In a bit of ass kissing hoping it would accelerate statehood. Nope.

So how did the Mormons get there in the first place and who the fuck are they anyway? At the end of the day Mormons are a group of people who practice some version of religion just like everybody fucking else. They are no different, from Catholics, Baptists, Methodists, Lutherans, Muslims, Jews, etc. Well, maybe a little different. Led by Joseph Smith Mormonism was founded by a group of White men with hugh egos, a unique sense of the Bible's teachings and a crazy sex drive.

If Brigham Young was the Michael Jordan of the Latter Day Saints, Joseph Smith was Dr. James Naismith. He invented the fucking game. Which means he got to write the fucking rules too. Shit, Smith was only twenty four when he wrote the Book of Mormon. That's prime fucking age for any young man. So of course "plural marriage" made sense. Smith basically said "how do I brainwash a whole bunch of people, get them to follow my teachings and get laid all the time?" Snapped and his fingers and said amazingly, "I got it. I'll create a new religion and one of its basic tenants is that all the men can have as many ho's as they can handle."

It's like they were pimps and Johns at the same time. This was the greatest fucking scam ever. Are we sure Tiger Woods ain't a Latter Day Saint? We know Santa Claus wasn't. He only had three ho's. Smith taught that the highest level of exaltation could be achieved through plural marriage. Further, plural marriage allows an individual to transcend the angelic state and become a god, accelerating the expansion of one's heavenly kingdom. Highest level of exaltation? Transcending angelic states? Yep, that sounds just like the effect pussy has on every man.

For the men in the clan it was a stroke (pun intended) of fucking genius. I bet other religious leaders of the day were sitting around and saying "why didn't I think of some shit like that?" Can you imagine if

Viagra was around when these guys came up with this bullshit? Like everybody they have their own little set of rules and rituals that make their version of living comfortable for them. They just didn't have a place to practice their version of normal until they got to Utah.

But the Mormons weren't just about polygamy. And this wasn't the only issue that bothered other people. There was a cultish nature about the group. Many look upon Smith as a snake oil salesman. He had many "visions" and was always given instruction from angels who visited him personally. That shit sounds crazy today much less in the early 1800s. This led them to be driven out every town they tried to settle in. First Kirtland, Ohio, then Independence, Missouri. Joseph Smith's power and influence so enraged locals in Ohio they beat the shit out him and left him for dead.

Eventually, the Governor of Missouri would kick their asses out of Missouri and they would end up in Nauvoo, Illinois on the banks of the Mississippi River. In Nauvoo the Mormons gained religious, financial and political power. They even raised a militia called the Nauvoo Legion. By now Brigham Young was an influential member of the group and began asserting his influence. By the 1840s Smith was having many visions of theocratic rule over much of the entire planet.

In 1844 Smith's craziness would finally catch up to him. He kicked two of his advisers out of the group after they accused him of trying to fuck their wives. In turn they started a paper to expose all of Smith's and the church's bullshit and called for reform. Smith had the paper censored. Finally the Governor of Illinois, Thomas Ford had to get into the situation. He basically told Smith and his followers, "look I'll let you motherfuckers come in and get settled in the hopes that you would practice your weird bullshit quietly and contribute something to the state's economy. Now you're starting a whole bunch of shit with other people who were here before you and I can't have it."

Governor Ford would order them arrested and tried for inciting a riot and treason against the State of Illinois. Smith tried to run at first but would later surrender. It was a bad move. While in jail a mob ambushed the jail and shot both him and his brother. It was June 27, 1844. Joseph Smith was just thirty eight years old. Dude got into a lot of shit in a short period of time.

It is estimated that Smith had up to thirty wives. Ten of them were married to other men but "allowed" Smith to marry them anyway. So in addition to polygamy, they preached bigamy, trigamy and whatever other "igamy" you can come up with. One third of them were under twenty and some the others were widows well past fifty. He never met a piece of pussy he didn't like. Strangely, he would only have nine children and all by his first wife Emma. Ironically, those sons who would come to power within the church all opposed polygamy.

After all that shit went down Smith's followers knew they had fucked up another homestead and under Brigham Young's leadership headed west to Utah. Now, Brigham Young, when it came to fucking he was numero uno. He made Joseph Smith look like a celibate Tibetan Monk. This cat had fifty five wives (fifty four of them after he joined the church), fifty seven children and sixteen baby mamas!

He was clearly at the back of the baby names book. I'm not sure where he found time to find a state, lead a flock and establish a couple of universities. Half the fucking people in the state of Utah were related to him. Born in Vermont, he joined the church in 1832 after reading the Book of Mormon. He especially liked the all-you-can-fuck pussy part of the tome. He would become the next leader of the church upon the death of Joseph Smith. Once the group got to the Great Salt Lake they figured they had gone far enough. President Milliard Fillmore would name Young Governor of the Utah Territory and Superintendent of American Indian Affairs. Also, through his leadership, he got to building the states infrastructure. Other shit he got done:

Set up what would become the University of Utah.

Organized the Mormon Tabernacle Choir.

Purchased land in Provo, Utah and established what would become Brigham Young University.

He built several temples. He presided over the construction of the Salt Lake, Saint George, Manti and Logan Temples.

When he wasn't using his little head Brigham Young was using his big head to be a pain in the ass to the United States government at times. Although friends with Fillmore, he got on President Buchanan's last nerve. Brigham Young didn't care much for federal officials or the federal government. He constantly dismissed localized federal officials whenever a directive came in from Washington D.C. Eventually, President Buchanan had to send federal troops after his ass to unseat him and place a non-Mormon in power over the territory in what became known as the Utah War. Good news is not a drop of blood was shed in the conflict.

Three Blind Mice

Given their history of relocation Brigham Young briefly thought about having everybody pack up their shit and go to Mexico. But, having thought it over he decided to stay and give up the governorship. He also had varying opinions on Black in the Church. Brigham Young would die in August, 1877. He was seventy six years of age. Even in death his life was about pussy. His will left plenty to the sixteen surviving wives he was actively fucking. The six wives he had no carnal knowledge of, they didn't get shit.

Throughout the history of the Mormon Church from Joseph Smith to present day whenever and whoever if something didn't fit into their particular way of living they would "divine-intervention" their way out of it. In Washington D.C. it's called a bill. It's the perfect con. Maybe they should get one of their members to run for President of the United States of America. Oh, wait they already tried that. It didn't take.

There were Blacks in the church as they had a policy of accepting everyone and anyone. However, like all institutions of the day, racism and discrimination also had a place in the Mormon Church. Today five percent of the Mormon Church is made up of Blacks. These members are primarily from Africa and assorted Caribbean nations. One person who really pissed off Brigham Young was William McCary. A son of a slave he hooked up with the Mormons in Nauvoo, Illinois. He would eventually become a priest in Winter Quarters, Nebraska. It was here that he would claim to be a prophet and have the same powers as the white elders in the church.

This was very unsettling for senior church members and they would get to the point of kicking his ass out of the club. But, his real crime was when he starting practicing polygamy. That was a game only preserved for White men. The shit really hit the fan when he started taking White women as plural wives. Brigham Young and others thought this nigger had lost his fucking mind.

This would lead to a ban on Blacks being able to hold the priesthood within the church for many years until 1978. Again, by divine revelation. For the Mormon Church Blacks were castoffs of Cain and, generally bad people. As per the Mormon history their relations with Black people and slaves was a mixed bag. By the time Utah gained Territory status in 1850 the legislature (which was dominated by Mormons) would vote to allow slavery under the United States Government's "popular sovereignty" mandate which allowed states and territories to decide for themselves' how they wanted to live.

It should be noted that, while some politicians in Washington, DC thought this was a solution to the slave question this singular concept only hastened the pace to the Civil War. Support of popular sovereignty would also be a major leadership lapse of the Three Blind Mice. It was a decisive decision by any Executive Branch of the United States Government of the 1850s, either way, good or bad, opposition to it could have averted the American Civil War entirely.

Yes, even a decision to allow slavery. While this would have not been popular with Northern populist, abolitionist or slaves, they would have surely only addressed their grievances through the legal process and the courts of the day. Debates and oratory would have stifled freedom for Blacks for many, many years well past 1863 and the Emancipation Proclamation but there would have been no major violence.

Three Blind Mice

Utah would become the only area in the West that slavery was legal. The law was quirky however. It stated that slave owners could not have sex with their slaves and that slaves would become free if their owners were found guilty of general neglect. Mind you, one could not fuck their slaves but should feel free to have as many wives as their dicks could handle. The mindset behind this was church doctrine and practical reality. Without any agri-business to speak of in the territory there was no need for slave labor, but at the same time the language of the law was in keeping with what many people thought about slavery in the 1850s. The Mormons thought they were having their cake and eating it too.

There was other bullshit with Blacks and the Church as well. Brigham Young said that if Whites and Blacks married that this mean would immediate death, on the spot. The chosen seed should not be mixing with the seed of Cain, and all. According to Mormon teachings Blacks would only get "conditional" entrance into heaven. If they lived good lives they would be admitted as "servants." Ain't that a bitch? The result of all this was the State of Utah and events in the 1850s played a prominent role in making the United States what it is today.

Chapter 15

California, Minnesota and Oregon

There were three states admitted to the Union during the 1850s. Numbers thirty one, thirty two and thirty three were the states of California, Minnesota and Oregon respectively. Each of these states had to deal with the issues of the day. States rights and slavery were at the forefront of most conversations. The early governors played an important role in agenda setting.

The State of Minnesota sits in the upper mid-western portion of the United States of America. The majority of its population lives in the Minneapolis-Saint Paul corridor. This area is commonly known as the "Twin Cities." Early European settlers were of Scandinavian and German descent. Minnesota is a geographically diverse state with many water sources. This is why it is informally referred to as the "Land of Ten Thousand Lakes."

Minnesota became an official Territory in 1849. Statehood would not be achieved until May 11, 1858. It would become the thirty second of the eventual fifty states to make up the United States of America.

Three Blind Mice

Henry Hastings Sibley would serve as her first Governor. In addition to serving as Governor of Minnesota, he would also serve as Territory representative for the Territories of Minnesota and Wisconsin. Born in Detroit, Michigan, his parents were originally from Massachusetts. He would eventually settle in Mendota, Minnesota. Serving as congressional representative for the Wisconsin and Minnesota territories he worked hard in looking out for the interests of the people.

Wisconsin statehood would ultimately leave him representing only Minnesota. He would become the first Governor of Minnesota in 1858 based largely on the fact that he served as President of the Democratic Party at the first Minnesota Constitutional Convention held in 1857. One of the more serious issues he had to deal with was the railroads. At that time, the Minnesota State Legislature wanted to issue bonds to fund the railroad through the state as they deemed it good for business. Governor Sibley refused as he thought it a bad investment since the state would have no stake in the business after helping finance the venture.

The Minnesota State Supreme Court would order him to comply with the Legislature's wishes. Fortunately, Wall Street would bail him out after investors refused to buy the debt and repackage it to the secondary market. Post governorship he would serve in the Civil War locally, mostly fighting the Sioux Indians and other skirmishes in and around the state. He would eventually settle in Saint Paul and become a local businessman, ironically becoming president of several railroads.

Today, counties and cities in the states of Minnesota, North Dakota and Iowa are named after him. While Sibley would leave a legacy of hard work and dedication to the people of Minnesota, Alexander Ramsey (the man Sibley beat in the first governor's race), while probably working just as hard, had a little bit of motherfucker in him. Ramsey served as the second Governor of Minnesota. He also served as Mayor of the city of Saint Paul, Minnesota in 1855. Ramsey was a Washington, D.C. insider way before he ever got to the Minnesota Territory, however. Born in Pennsylvania, he represented the Commonwealth and served two terms in the United States House of Representatives as a Whig Party member in the mid 1840s. Figuring there was better political opportunity elsewhere after the end of the Mexican-American War, he headed west and would eventually end up as the first Governor of the newly formed Minnesota Territory in 1849. As State Governor he would become known for two specific efforts associated with his administration.

First he would become the first state governor to commit troops to the Union at the outbreak of the American Civil War. He would resign as governor shortly thereafter to serve as Senator representing the State of Minnesota as he felt he would be more effective serving the state with legs on the ground in Washington, D.C. during the war. He would also be remembered for his racist attitudes, especially, when it came to Native Americans. He thought like many White men of the day. He was quite vocal about not only removing Native Americans (mostly members of the Dakota and Sioux tribes regionally) from the state but, advocated just killing them if they refused to leave using words like "extermination."

He would also serve as United States Secretary of War under President Rutherford B. Hayes (it is of note that Ramsey would be replaced as Secretary of War by one Robert Todd Lincoln, son of Honest Abe). Today one of the largest parks in the state of Minnesota as well as counties and cities in Minnesota, North Dakota and Illinois are named after him.

The State of Oregon became the thirty third state on Valentine's Day (February 14th), 1859. The State of Oregon is situated in the upper Pacific Northwest portion of the United States of America just south of the State of Washington. The Spanish, French and the British got to the territory first between the Sixteenth and Eighteenth centuries. Lewis and Clark would show up in the early 1800s for the Americans. Moneyman John Jacob Astor would also send an expedition in 1811. Eventually, the British and Americans would almost come to blows for a third time over the territory in the mid 1800s. Oregon would officially become a territory in 1848 with the forced relocation of the area's Native American peoples.

The State of Oregon would also become notable for its handling of the slavery question. The state would be admitted to the Union as a free state. But, it was how they achieved such status that is interesting. The State's original constitution made the state a home only to White residents. No Blacks allowed, period.

The first Governor of the State of Oregon was John Whiteaker. Born in Indiana he would also represent Oregon in Washington, DC as member of the United States House of Representatives and serve as President of the Oregon State Senate and Speaker of the Oregon State House of Representatives. He also served in the Mexican-American War. He made a little dough in the California Gold Rush and moved his family to the Willamette Valley in the western part of the state. Running as a Democrat, he won a close election for Governor and assumed office in July, 1858.

His time as Governor was mainly consumed by solving land claims. Later in life he would serve as Oregon's Collector of Revenues for then President Grover Cleveland. The Whiteaker Neighborhood in downtown Eugene, Oregon is named after him.

California was admitted to the Union on September 9, 1850 as the thirty-first state. The State of California is unique on many fronts. For one it has got a bunch of fucking people living in the state rivaled only by all the fucking people that live between Boston and Washington, DC.

As a state California is one of the top ten economies in the world on its own merit. Making it a GDP (Gross Domestic Product) powerhouse. Outside of the states of Oregon and Washington California IS the West Coast. Half of the State gets three hundred days of sun and it hardly ever rains making living conditions ideal. California is a leading agriculture producer and produces ninety percent of the all the wine made in the United States. Not only do they make a lot of it, but, qualitatively, the gap between California and the other forty nine states is Marianas Trench deep. And it's everywhere in the state.

From Napa/Sonoma to Amador County and Placer County in the North. To San Joaquin County, south to Fresno in the Central Valley. To Monterrey County, Salinas and Soledad to Temecula and San Diego County in the south. God given perfect soil allows for every varietal of grape to be grown. From reds like Pinot Noir, Cabernet Sauvignon, Cabernet Franc, Tannat, Cinsault, Carignan, Red Zinfandel, Merlot, Nebbiolo, Tempranillo, Sangiovese Syrah, Petites (Syrah and Verdot) and Barbera. To whites like Chardonnay, Sauvignon Blanc, Viognier, Pinot (Grigio and Gris), Albarino and Reisling.

Three Blind Mice

So, today the State of California is a significant part of America's identity. Its beginnings weren't so pleasant however. The most important and culturally changing event for the state was the discovery of gold 1848 and the California Gold Rush. The California Gold Rush led to a massive surge in population (especially in Northern California), made some people very rich, made a lot more people very poor and would play a major part in the state being granted statehood.

There were also sociological casualties as well. As the gold became scarcer the quest for claims became more cutthroat. Native Americans followed by the Chinese would bear the brunt of hostilities for the sake of progress. Even today in recognition of the significance of the Gold Rush, California's state highway signs are in the shape of a miner's spade. By September, 1850 the United States Congress would admit California as the thirty-first state to the Union. At its first Constitutional Convention held in 1849 delegates met in Monterrey, California. Early capital cities included San Jose, Vallejo and Benicia, California before finally settling on Sacramento, California in 1854.

The only problem people had with California was getting there. It was a bitch of a ride from the East Coast of the United States to the other side of the country. Shit, even today, it's still a five hour ride by jumbo jet. So imagine making the journey by horse or wagon or even rail. If the weather or illness didn't get you, Native Americans sick of getting fucked with attacked whenever they could and even if you got past them there was still an assorted band of psychopathic, gun toting motherfuckers waiting to rob your fucking ass.

And let's not forget the various nefarious con men along the way. Or the fact that you just might turn on each other. See the Donner Party for an example of that kind of shit. So, as you can see just getting there was half the battle. Between 1850 and the start of the Civil War, California had a series of "characters" as Governors to lead the State. The State's first was Peter Hardeman Burnett. Of the men that led Oregon, Minnesota and California in the decade this motherfucker was a doozy.

Born in Tennessee and raised in Missouri he was another ugly motherfucker in appearance and temper. Maybe this is what made him such a son of a bitch. He would become both the first Governor of California and the first Governor of California to resign. He was self educated and would go on to learn the law after some time. He would one day represent Joseph Smith and those other fucking Mormon crazies that started all that bullshit it Nauvoo, Illinois in mid 1800s that I mentioned earlier in the reading. He never got to defend them because they would escape, surrender and ultimately be murdered by an angry mob.

In 1843 he would move him and his family to Oregon Country and join the provisional legislature in Oregon not long after arriving. An ardent racist, what was curious about his time in Oregon was that he was a leading proponent/advocate of, and, would successfully see passed a measure that would exclude Blacks from moving to the territory.

Even more curious was that additionally, if you were Black and decided to stay you could be arrested and flogged every six months until you got your Black ass out of the territory. This was, in effect a nasty mix of gentrification, apartheid and government sanctioned corporal punishment. All of this with the tacit approval of the United States Federal Government (if for no other reason by their lack of concern for allowing such a law). And to make the shit even more amazing, the State of Oregon would keep these exclusion laws on the books until 1926!

Three Blind Mice

Think about that for a moment, for over seventy five years, the law of the land in Oregon was that if you were Black keep the fuck out. And if you are already here, get the fuck out or we will send government officials to your house and beat your ass until you fucking leave. As an indignity that's just some cold blooded Nazi like shit. So, after making sure he made such a positive contribution to the Territory of Oregon, Burnett decided to head south in 1848 with his family and see if he could make some money while the Gold Rush was still hot.

He would end up in Sacramento as a real estate agent working for John Sutter Jr. selling plots to other Whites in the up and ever growing city. He was pretty fucking good at it too. The very next year he would find himself back in politics running as California's first Territorial Governor at the California Constitutional Convention in Monterrey, California. With his legislative background in Oregon he a won the election in a breeze. Just like in Oregon Burnett set out pass the same kind of exclusionary laws he got through the legislature there. Additionally, he wanted to impose taxes on other minority immigrants who wanted to work in the state.

Fortunately for everyone, Californians saw through this bullshit he was shoveling. He was widely ridiculed by everyone and especially the press. Seeing that he had no love around him he resigned in January, 1851. He never did much in politics after that. Serving as a judge for a minute and on the Sacramento City Council for another minute. Burnett never changed his racist attitudes towards Blacks, Chinese and Native Americans.

He would die in May, 1895 and be buried in Santa Clara, California. There has been no confirmation that, occasionally, a Black, Chinese or

Native American can be found leaving a bladder full of piss with a three inch head of foam on his grave.

John McDougall took over for Burnett in January, 1851. In addition to being the second Governor of California, he was also the first Lieutenant Governor of California. Born in Ohio he made his way to California via Indiana for the same reasons as everybody else at the time, the California Gold Rush. He got involved in politics shortly after arriving in the state. As a delegate to the California Constitutional Convention in Monterrey he was an original signer of the Constitution of California. At the Convention he was nominated on the ticket as Lieutenant Governor along with Peter Burnett.

One of his first acts as Governor was to move the capitol from San Jose, California to Vallejo, California. Having signed legislation sponsored by then State Senator (and former Mexican General) Mariano Vallejo who founded the city. It is interesting to note that later the capitol would be moved to Benicia, California, a city named after Vallejo's wife, Francisca Benicia Carillo de Vallejo. General Vallejo initially wanted the city to be called "Francisca," but changed his mind after the nearby city of Yerba Buena changed its named to San Francisco.

McDougall, like Burnett hated the fact that Native Americans wanted to stay on the lands where they were born and raised and actively encouraged settlers to harass and, in some cases, kill them to get them out of the way. McDougall also supported keeping Blacks out of the State. Unlike Burnett, however, McDougall thought the Chinese were a good source of cheap labor for the State and supported their rights to stay in California. The Chinese were free to work all fucking day, live in squalor and accept shit pay.

Three Blind Mice

McDougall's lack of political experience, fondness for the drink and gambling would lead to him being a one term governor. After leaving office he basically drank himself to death and died at the age of forty eight years old. After McDougall, California Democrats nominated California State Assembly Speaker John Bigler for Governor in 1852. He would win the election and become the third Governor of California by the slimmest margin in California history over Whig Party candidate Pierson Reading.

John Bigler and his brother William (Governor of Pennsylvania) stand out as the first of only two brothers to served as Governors of a U.S. State at the same time. The other set of brothers to serve as Governors at the same time were George W. (Texas) and Jeb Bush (Florida). It should be noted that Thomas Crittenden served as Governor of Missouri while his half brother General Eli Houston Murray was Governor of the Utah Territory in the 1880s.

John Bigler was born in Pennsylvania where he and his brother would later become newspaper men. John would later sell the newspaper to study law. When the California Gold Rush hit, he headed west. Not to mine for gold but to practice law. He would settle in California and find that nobody wanted his legal advice. After many odd jobs he decided to try his hand at politics when California announced its first general elections. He won a seat in the California State Assembly representing the Sacramento district rising quickly to Assembly Speaker.

Bigler would become the first post-statehood Governor elected by the people of the California. Unlike McDougall Bigler made times hard for the Chinese and other minorities and re-imposed taxes on them to

Darryl Murphy

work in the State. He also had to fight off pro slavery Democrats from Southern California. Despite this Bigler would win a second term in office (becoming the first Governor of California to do so and the last one to do so until 1914). It was during his second term that he would facilitate the move of the State's capitol to Sacramento in 1854.

He would run for a third term, but lose to J. Neely Johnson of the anti immigrant American Know Nothing Party. This made Bigler the first Governor of California to lose a general election in California's history. Bigler would later be appointed United States Minister to Chile by United States President James Buchanan with the help of his brother, the Governor of Pennsylvania (the state which President Buchanan hailed from). President Andrew Johnson would nominate Bigler as Sacramento's Federal Assessor of the Internal Revenue Service. But since Radical Republicans in the United States Senate could not stand his ass (President Andrew Johnson that is) Bigler's nomination was never confirmed. There was also an effort to name Lake Tahoe "Lake Bigler" in his honor. The name never stuck though and "Tahoe" was eventually adopted permanently.

In 1856 voters elected J. Neely Johnson as the fourth Governor of California. Johnson was one of only two California Governors to be elected from a third party. Born in Indiana he went to California to prospect during the California Gold Rush. Having studied the law in Iowa he settled in Sacramento and became the city attorney. In 1852 he was elected to the California Assembly representing Sacramento. Having secured the Know Nothing Party's nomination in 1855 he was elected Governor of California and took office in January, 1856 at the tender age of thirty years old. This would make him the youngest person to ever hold the office of Governor in California's history.

Three Blind Mice

Despite the fact that the Know Nothings controlled the legislature and most of the other statewide elected positions (his Attorney General, Treasurer, Controller and Lieutenant Governor were all Know Nothings) they couldn't get shit done. One major accomplishment was funding the building of the state capitol building. His term as Governor was dominated by the goings on of vigilantes in San Francisco.

In those days San Francisco was quite lawless. A band of self do-gooders (numbering some six thousand) decided to take the law into their own hands and start whooping ass where needed. Johnson tried several times to enforce law and order and failed each time. This was surprising considering he had the services of General William Tecumseh Sherman at his disposal. Eventually, these vigilantes would fight not only crime but political corruption as well. The vigilantes would ultimately take over the city of San Francisco and bring civility and prosperity to her, although not without controversy.

His failure to get make San Francisco civil led to his not being nominated for a second term. He lost the nomination to George Bowie who, in turn, lost the general election to Democrat John Weller. Johnson's failed nomination bid and Bowie's subsequent lost to Weller would spell the end of the American Know Nothing Party in California forever. Johnson would leave California for good after his term as Governor. He made his way to the Nevada side of the Utah Territory and would become a delegate to the 1863 Nevada Constitutional Convention in Carson City, Nevada.

The Governor of Nevada, Henry Blasdel, would appoint Johnson to the State of Nevada Supreme Court where he would serve for four years. Johnson left the Court in 1871 and moved to Salt Lake City, Utah where he died in 1872. He was forty seven years old.

1857 saw the election of the John Weller as the fifth Governor of California. Governor Weller was an Ohio boy and attended Miami (of Ohio) University. He studied law and served as attorney of Butler County, Ohio in the 1830s. Weller also served in the United States House of Representatives for the State of Ohio as well as serve in the Mexican-American War. He would also lose a close, hotly debated election for Governor of Ohio in the 1848 election. In 1849 President Zachary Taylor would appoint and then remove (because of scandal) Weller from a commission set up to form the post war boundary between the State of California and Mexico. Weller would stay in California and build his reputation enough that he would be elected to the United States Senate representing the State of California in 1851.

When his six year term expired he returned to California and won election as the fifth Governor of California beginning in 1858. Outside of threatening to make California an independent republic if the North and South broke apart (which he never did) he had a comparatively uneventful term as Governor. After his term expired James Buchanan would appoint him United States Minister to Mexico in 1860. He would eventually move to New Orleans, Louisiana after the Civil War and practice private law for the rest of his life. He died in New Orleans, Louisiana in 1875.

After John Weller, California would elect the ambitious Milton Slocum Latham as its next Governor. In addition to becoming Governor of California, he also served California in the United States House of Representatives and the United States Senate. Another Ohio boy (the State of California had this thing of electing young Ohioans as Governor in their earliest days after statehood was granted) he came to California via Pennsylvania and Alabama (where he learned the law) for the same reason every fucking body else did, the California Gold Rush.

He worked as a records clerk in San Francisco County and later became Sacramento District Attorney. In 1852 he won a seat in the United States House of Representatives representing Sacramento's district of California. While in Washington he made many connections that would benefit him later in life. He served only one term in the House and was appointed United States Customs Collector for the Port of San Francisco by President Franklin Pierce. Because of his days in Alabama and his friendship with the Southern leaning Mouse Franklin Pierce he was the perfect gubernatorial candidate for the pro slavery California Democrats.

The 1859 general election for Governor of California saw both, a pro slavery Democrat (Latham), an anti slavery Democrat (John Currey) and a newly organized Republican by the name of Leland Stanford. Stanford would not only go on to become the eighth Governor of California, he would also be a founder of Stanford University as well as become known as one of the "Big Four" that would form the Central Pacific Railroad (a group of businessmen that included Stanford, Collis Potter Huntington, Mark Hopkins and Charles Crocker).

Latham would beat them all and win sixty percent of the vote. He was only thirty three years old. Milton Latham would only serve five days as Governor of California before he quit. How? Why? On September 13, 1859 then California Senator David C. Broderick was killed in a duel by former California State Supreme Justice David Terry over the issue of slavery in the State. Latham knew he would have a much better chance of being selected as Senator to finish out Broderick's term as Governor-elect then not.

So this self serving motherfucker went about winning the election and the legislature fell in line. Thus he became the shortest serving Governor in California's history and the second to resign making California's run through the 1850s one of the most interesting in the history of the United States.

Chapter 16

The United States Census and the Cotton Gin

Here we will discuss the both the 1850 and 1860 Census and what it said about the United States during the decade. Right up front what came out of the Census was that Americans were doing a lot of fucking during the decade as the population exploded in the years after the Mexican-American War. The taking of census was mandated in the United States Constitution, Article One, Section Two. As it concerns the Census the Constitution reads, "representatives and direct taxes shall be apportioned among the several states which may be included within this Union, according to their respective numbers, which shall be determined by adding the whole number of free persons, including those bound to service for a term of years and excluding Indians not taxed three fifths of all other persons (read that as Blacks). The actual enumeration shall be made within every subsequent term of ten years, in such manner as they shall by laws direct."

The first Census post founding of the United States was taken in 1790. It's basically a head count so the United States Government knows how many motherfuckers are in the country and how many assholes should represent said motherfuckers. What information these nosy motherfuckers wanted changed dramatically between 1790 and 1850. By 1850 they wanted to know not only who you were and where you lived, but, what taxes you paid, what church you attended, your relative wealth or lack thereof and were you a criminal or not. The Censuses of 1850 and 1860 were distinctive in that they were the only two censuses that recorded slave schedules.

The Census was right in line with America's double talk/write. On the one hand the Founding Fathers insisted on an individual's right to privacy and on the other hand they insisted on knowing where the fuck you were at all times. They wanted to know who owned what people and how many. The Census Bureau acted as the National Security Agency of its day, whether by accident or on purpose. And there were times when the United States Government would use this supposedly "private" information for clandestine use. One instance that stands out was at the outbreak of America's involvement in World War Two then President Franklin Delano Roosevelt's Administration used Census Bureau data to assist it in rounding up Japanese Americans and relocate their fucking asses to internment camps.

As for Americans fucking each other, between 1840 and 1850 the population went from seventeen million people to twenty three million people. Between 1850 and 1860 the population went from twenty three million to thirty one million. Note that the 1850 Census was the first census that counted women, children and slaves. Yes, we should assume that if you didn't count socially, you didn't count actually prior to. In the 1860 Census the Bureau decided to count Native Americans, but, hold on, only those who had become "civilized." Meaning the United States Government only counted those Native Americans who had decided to take their inferior status like a man.

The Government found that there were four hundred thousand of these non willing capitulators. So, as you can see, the actual numbers of Americans were probably much higher given the criteria set at the time. The 1860 Census went even further in what it wanted to know about Americans. The 1860 Census revealed that, in addition to adding thirty five percent to the population thirteen percent of the population was a slave totaling some four million people.

What's interesting about the four million slaves is that according to the United States Constitution drafted back in the Eighteenth Century and up until the 1860 Census Blacks were still only counted as three fifths of a person for purposes of representation in Congress. Meaning forty percent of the Black population didn't even fucking exist!

Two things came out of this. One, this demonstrates how the South had a disproportionate amount of power compared to the North in the United States Congress. The fuzzy math said the North had one population and the South had the same population plus their property also counted as a portion of population! Second, while slaves got to be counted as property and population the slaves themselves got no rights at all. So Blacks served not only as physical labor but, also as political labor through their physiology.

Imagine, today if you could count your house, car, laptop, tablet, couch, golf clubs, etc. as a percentage of the population for purposes of representation in the United States House of Representatives. Sounds fucking crazy, right? But this was the law of the land in those days. And all legitimized by the Census. Thank God for the Senate. But, let's not suck their dicks to full ejaculation just yet. As Voltaire said, "I rather be ruled by one King than one hundred rats."

From the 1850s to today the Senate is full of guys holding onto power like a baby suckling from his or hers mother's tit because they realized a long time ago they blew their shot at the top spot (President of the United States). Even today the senior membership of the United States Senate is full of old men (and women) playing out the eighteenth hole of their lives who are nothing more than solution-less agitators who seek relevance through slick sound bites and personal attacks much to the detriment of their constituents and the citizens of the United States of America.

While both parties are guilty of this, whoever is in the minority at any given time is better at it than his or her majority brethren. That said, don't hate the player, hate the game. The people elected these greasy motherfuckers. It's safe to say, regarding the Founding Fathers and the ratifying language of the United States Constitution, those good 'ole country boys from down South got one over on those Northern intellectuals. The South may have lost the physical Civil War in the 1860s, but it surely won the mental and political Civil War in 1787 at Independence Hall in Philadelphia, Pennsylvania.

Ironically enough, in financial circles, it was this same kind of arrogant thinking from the North that led to Charlotte, North Carolina becoming a banking powerhouse in the 1980s. Hugh McColl and his cronies at NationsBank (formerly NCNB and ultimately Bank of America) brought that "twang" from the South and talked those Ivy League assholes in New York and Boston and San Francisco right out of their underwear. Before you knew it Wall Streeters were trading in knishes with mustard, oysters on the half shell and sourdough bread for chicken and waffles.

The head of the Census Bureau in 1850 and 1860 was Joseph C.G. Kennedy. Born in the Commonwealth of Pennsylvania he graduated from Allegheny College, in Meadville, Pennsylvania. In 1848 he would move to Washington, DC to oversee the Census of 1850. He was widely responsible for the changes in criteria, data points and gathering methods used in the 1850 and 1860 censuses. The release of data for the 1860 Census was truncated by the outbreak of the Civil War. He would die after being stabbed by John Dailey in 1887, a gentleman who believed Kennedy fucked him over on a business deal. Sarcastically speaking, Kennedy would not be counted in the 1890 Census.

Another player of the 1850s who used the Census to stir the slavery pot was Hinton Rowan Helper. This was a guy born and raised in the South who was an actual CRITIC of slavery! Go figure that shit. Helper was born in the state of North Carolina to a slave owning family in 1829. As an adult he also got the fever and went to California during the Gold Rush hoping to strike it rich. Alas, like most he didn't find shit and came back to North Carolina wondering "why the fuck did I do that?"

In a show of sour grapes he would write a book about how fucked up he thought the state of California was called the Land of Gold Versus Fiction. He accuses Californians of lacking morals, calls them some of the dumbest motherfuckers he has ever met and basically shits all over everything about the State. It is interesting that he was fond of the San Francisco Vigilantes. It was his second book that would really raise eyebrows around the country. Published in 1857 the book, titled The Impending Crisis of the South is a stinging criticism of Southern culture and slavery. It argues that slavery had restrained economic prosperity. He used the Census to make his point statistically about land values, literacy rates and the lack of a manufacturing base compared to their Northern counterparts. Maybe some Black woman put some of that pussy on him, whatever it was he hated the South, slavery and what it stood for. Either way, the book was a hit.

People in the North loved it and used to it rabble rouse the abolitionists. People in the South hated it. Nobody hated it more than slave owners. They thought it might incite slaves (those who could read and were more than willing to tell the illiterates) to escape on the one hand. And, on the other hand they thought lower class Southern Whites might want to rethink their economic status, violently or otherwise. No matter what side someone was on the matter, hate it or love it, everybody bought the fucking thing. By the start of the Civil War the book had sold one hundred and fifty thousand copies.

Authorities in the South banned the book and handed out punishment if you got caught with it. It was to the South what Salman Rushdie's Satanic Verses was to the Muslim community. For Radical Republicans they not only endorsed the book it was fucking campaign material. Crazy thing was it would turn out that Helper hated slavery, but he also hated Black people as well. He was all about the "now that you are free, get the fuck out movement."

During the Civil War President Lincoln made him a diplomat to Buenos Aires, Argentina. While there he came up with the dickhead

Three Blind Mice

idea of building a train from North America to South America so that Whites could replace Black people down there. When he got back to Washington, he realized himself how crazy he was and committed suicide by turning on the gas in his apartment. Was he a kind of literary Van Gogh? You make the call.

There was probably no greater contribution to the breakdown of America's social fabric than the combination of man and machine in the form of Eli Whitney and the cotton gin. At the same time the cotton gin as a forerunner to future cotton production is still very evident to present day. Eli Whitney could not have foreseen either of these two realities. The cotton gin was agriculture's atomic bomb. It had both destructive and positive influences on the future of society globally.

The cotton gin was to the agricultural South what Henry Ford's assembly line techniques were to Detroit's auto industry. It transformed the South into an economic powerhouse and, later, an arrogant belligerent in the American Civil War. The machine's goal was simple. Make more cotton by separating the fiber from the seeds. Prior to the cotton gin the crop was picked by hand. The process was laborious and took many man hours to complete. The average slave took about ten hours to produce one pound of cotton separating fiber from seeds by hand. This was partly because it was hard fucking work in hard fucking working conditions. The other reason was because the average slave was in no fucking rush to get the shit done. They worked from "can't see to can't see." Meaning they couldn't see the sun when they started and couldn't see the sun when they finished

The field Negro was fed only enough to let him know he was hungry and under constant threat of a whip had no attitude to be overly cooperative. There was no OSHA in those days. With the cotton gin two slaves could do fifty pounds in the same time span. The cotton gin led to the expansion of slavery and the greed of White plantation owners.

This greed would eventually lead directly to the Civil War. The North was equally culpable as much of the cotton produced in the South was exported out of northern ports. Why cotton? Humans have been planting, cultivating and domesticating cotton since the time of the fifth millennium BC. It is a versatile plant with many uses. Today, it's in everything from dress shirts to bath towels and robes to socks to bed sheets to tee shirts and under garments. In the Twenty First Century the world's leading producers of the crop are China, India and the United States. Within the United States of America the states of Texas and California lead national production. Approximately three percent of the Earth's agriculturally feasible land is used to plant cotton. So, as you can see, its popularity has not waned over time.

In the southern part of the New World cotton became a preferable planting crop because the climate and soil was ideal for growing it. Eli Whitney's cotton gin, patented in 1794, led to a cotton "gold rush" of sorts in the southern United States. The need for manpower (slaves) was greatly expanded by the cotton gin. So much so, that by the 1860 United States Census one out of every three people in the South was Black. Remember, as mentioned earlier, that because of the Three Fifths Compromise agreed to in the United States Constitution this greatly over inflated the South's political power in Washington, DC. I'm surprised the Confederate States of America didn't have a picture of the cotton gin on their currency during their short existence or, at least, a picture of Eli Whitney on one of its bills. For the South, the cotton gin's invention was on par with the invention of fire, gunpowder and the wheel.

Three Blind Mice

In the Nineteenth Century the economic life blood of the Southern states was king cotton. By 1860 the South was producing sixty five percent of the world's supply of cotton. Eighty percent of the cotton the British got their hands on came out of the southern United States. For all he left as a legacy Eli Whitney was, for the most part, a very unassuming man. Born in the Commonwealth of Massachusetts he initially set out to study law. Educated at Yale University in New Haven, Connecticut he would spend much of his adult life in the State of Georgia.

Without knowing it he would be on both sides of the Civil War. The cotton gin for the South and the advocacy of interchangeable parts as it related to machinery in the North. Whitney also made muskets for the United States Army. The cotton gin was his real baby however. He never became rich off the cotton gin. Whitney spent most of his profits suing others who copied his work. It would make him famous though. It's ironic that before the invention of the cotton gin slavery was on the decline nationwide. Whitney would die of prostate cancer at fifty nine years of age in 1825.

Chapter 17

Art in the 1850s

Art is the one true aspect of the human condition that really is like no other. It allows us to not only think outside of the box, but it also allows us to throw away the box and truly think free. In music some modern day examples include Bob Dylan, Jimi Hendrix, Bob Marley, George Clinton of Parliament Funkadelic fame, Louis Armstrong, Johnny Cash, Stevie Ray Vaughan, Duke Ellington, Charlie "Bird" Parker, Miles Davis, Thelonious Monk, the Philadelphia Sound, anything Motown and yes the Sugar Hill Gang. Elvis Presley, The Beatles and Michael Jackson were, and still are, very popular and sold a lot of records, but they weren't the underbelly of their genres like the above were.

Other originators include the Blue Eyed Soul masters; Tower of Power, Average White Band, Hall and Oates, Wild Cherry, Teena Marie and Three Dog Night just to name a few. Then there was Mandrill, The Ohio Players, AC/DC, Queen, Aerosmith, Issac Hayes, Ella Fitzgerald (the Queen of Jazz), The Eagles, Carlos Santana, James Brown (the hardest working man in show business) and Aretha Franklin (the Queen of Soul). It should be noted that Ella Fitzgerald originally wanted to be a dancer. When she got her chance to perform at the famed Apollo Theater in Harlem, New York, where she intended to dance, she backed out at the last minute because she was intimidated by the other dancers she had seen go before her. The master of ceremonies asked her if there was anything else she could do and Ella offered to sing. And the rest was history.

Like any other period art played a major role in the daily lives of the people of the 1850s. And there were many players of the day. Whether it was music, paintings or photography that whole thing about "soothing the savage beast" really meant something during the decade. In the 1850s people sang, painted and took pictures of every aspect of life just like today. Be it slavery, politics (both local and national), economics, social life, ethnicity, war, love and so on. It was almost as if people were in a rush to be creative as war was pending and no one knew of what would happen to the free mind and the human instinct to expound reality. So, let's check out what was happening in the 1850s creatively.

One of the biggest stars of the 1850s was Johanna Maria Lind. Known as Jenny Lind she was an opera singer. She was Luciano Pavarotti with tits. A Swedish soprano she could blow like nobody's business. At the invitation of the ultimate hustler of the day, P.T. Barnum, she embarked on an American concert tour in 1850 that would last through the spring of 1852. Barnum was in Europe at the end of the 1840s and although he had never heard her sing and admittedly didn't know shit about music he knew a good act when saw one. And Jenny was the goods. She was selling out everywhere in Europe.

As well as a phenomenal singer Jenny Lind was also a very smart businesswoman. She agreed to do the concerts but wanted a substantial payment of money up front plus one thousand dollars per concert. P.T. Barnum never paid upfront money for anybody but he knew he had to have her. And she didn't just want pizza and beer money either. She demanded one hundred eighty five thousand dollars. To get the money Barnum mortgaged all of his property.

Once the deal was done P.T. Barnum got down to doing what he does best. He went Don King on the promotion of Ms. Lind. He hyped the shit out of her leaning heavily on her charitable efforts as well as her voice. By the time he got done with his bullshit everyone in America knew who she was. So popular was Lind thanks to Barnum's shenanigans, when her ship arrived in New York there was forty thousand people at the piers to greet and get a glimpse of her. This certainly caught her off guard but she loved it.

Like any good American athlete of today. When she realized (from the size of the crowds) how much money was going to be made off the concerts she went back to Barnum and said, "hold on motherfucker, I want to renegotiate my motherfucking contract." Barnum was to make five thousand five hundred dollars from each gig. Ms. Lind got him to additionally agree to pay her all of the proceeds above and beyond his fee. Barnum had to agree, she had him by the balls at this point. She cut a better deal than Floyd "Money" Mayweather could ever get from a network.

How good a deal was it for Ms. Lind? The first concert she did in New York had ticket sales of twenty five thousand dollars. You do the math. It was like that everywhere she went. If she lived in the Twenty First Century she would have had to do her concerts at stadiums that could hold six figure crowds. Like the home of the Dallas Cowboys, AT&T Stadium in Arlington, Texas or the University of Michigan's Big House or the Rose Bowl in Pasadena, California.

After New York she toured up and down the East Coast of the United States. In Washington, D.C., First Lady of the United States Abigail Fillmore attended one of her concerts and invited her back to the White House afterwards for refreshments. When she hit New Orleans the shit really hit the fan. People clamored so much to see her that not only did the promoters auction off the tickets to her concerts to the highest bidder, they charged a fee to get into the auction! Ain't that some shit?

New Orleans being what it is, gave an opportunity for all kinds of people to make a buck selling Jenny Lind shit on the street. From trinkets to street food, it was all for sale. Of course, Ms. Lind didn't see a dime of that shit. But imagine if she did. She would continue the tour up the Mississippi River doing the cities of Natchez, Mississippi, Memphis, Tennessee, Saint Louis, Missouri and Nashville, Tennessee. She would finish up her tour in Louisville, Kentucky, Cincinnati, Ohio and Pittsburgh, Pennsylvania.

After that her business with P.T. Barnum was concluded. Barnum made out like a fat cat from the deal. He netted over half a million dollars from the hustle. To put that in perspective five hundred thousand dollars in 1851 would be worth fifteen million dollars in 2014. Not bad for nine months work. She gave ninety concerts under her agreement with Mr. Barnum and after that contract expired she stayed in the States for another year and just kept on singing.

It worked too. All told she would earn over three hundred and fifty thousand dollars! This was a shitload of money for any fucking day. And I'm talking about those days, these days or any other day. That's just about ten million five hundred thousand dollars in 2014. True to her nature she gave most of the money away to Swedish charities. She left such an impact with her visit to the United States the city of Jenny Lind, California was named after her and she didn't even fucking visit the state. From a marketing perspective she was Tiger Woods, Michael Jordan, Phil Mickelson and Peyton Manning all wrapped up in one.

The Luca family would become the 1850s version of the Winans family today. A black family from New Haven, Connecticut they consisted of father Alexander Luca, his sons Alexander Jr., Simon, John and Cleveland. They sang and played instruments mostly throughout the northern United States. They were also active abolitionist. In 1850 the Slippery Noodle opens in Indianapolis, Indiana. The Noodle is still open today and it is one of the oldest blues factories still operating in the state. The blues is a uniquely Black form of music that originated in the South and takes on many forms. Cleveland, Ohio and San Francisco, California become the first cities in America to introduce music as part of its public school matriculation in the early 1850s. This development would lead directly to the formation of America's music industry.

The Black version of Jenny Lind was a woman named Elizabeth Greenfield. She was known as the "Black Swan." Born a slave she was adopted by Philadelphia Quakers as an infant. She would grow up to be blessed with a booming voice. She would sing in front of audiences throughout the United States and would even give a performance before the British Royal, Queen Victoria in 1854. She was the first Black

American to perform before any kind of royalty. She died in Philadelphia, Pennsylvania in 1876.

In 1857 Edmund Dede would become the first Black from North America to graduate from the prestigious Paris Conservatory. He would ultimately serve twenty years as conductor of the orchestra at the Theatre L'Alcazar in Paris.

The Confederate States of America rally song "Dixie" would be written in 1859 by a Northerner, Daniel Decatur Emmett. Emmett was an Irishman born in Mount Vernon, Ohio. In addition to writing "Dixie" Emmett would also be a founder of the first blackface minstrel troupe. Blackface minstrel shows had been around for some time. They were first introduced by Thomas Rice with the character "Jim Crow." Emmett's group was the first to have an entire band in blackface. Regarding Dixie, when it first came out, like Michael Jackson's "Thriller" it was an instant hit. The South especially took to the tune and it spread very quickly. Emmett is quoted as having said that if he knew the Rebels would have loved it so much he would have never written the shit. After the Civil War, Abraham Lincoln noted that he had always like the song Dixie and was glad that the Union had captured it back.

The thing about being a painter is the deader you are the better your shit is. When it comes to painters, the 1850s (known as Realists) were, like the Civil War, a precursor of sorts to the great revolution in art that would start with the Impressionist and move forward to present day. Works done after the 1850s would be done by some of the greatest art minds known to man. This includes (in no particular order) the Impressionists, the American dominated Tonalists, Surrealists, Fauvists, Cubists and Modernists. These artists included Monet, Van Gogh, Gaugin, Renior, Rousseau, Matisse, the Alsatian Hans Arp, Miro, Picasso, Dali, Braque, Morisot, Sisley, Cezanne, Ernst, Duchamp, Modigliani, Soutine, Utrillo and Pissaro. We will examine some the great works and artists of the 1850s.

For Americans the most recognizable work to come out of the 1850s was Emanuel Leutze's Washington Crossing the Delaware. The piece is currently on display at the Metropolitan Museum of Art in New York City. It depicts General George Washington's crossing of the Delaware to go whip some Hessian ass Christmas night 1776 during the American Revolution War. The Hessians were hunkered down in Trenton, New Jersey and the crossing would be the beginning phase of the American Revolutionary War Battle of Trenton. There were a couple of versions painted by Leutze. The original, finished in 1850 was damaged by fire, although eventually restored Leutze made a replica that was first shown in 1851.

Note that the original (post restoration) was hanging at the Kunsthalle Bremen Museum in Germany. In an ironic twist of fate it was destroyed in a World War Two bombing raid by, who else, the fucking British. An accidental or purposeful final fuck you to the Americans perhaps? Either way the second version is the one that now hangs at the Metropolitan Museum of Art.

Close examination of the painting reveals that Leutze represents a unique image of the American colonies through the men on the boat. On the boat is a man wearing a Scottish bonnet, a Black man, a Native American, a Western Frontiersman and a couple of farmers. The man holding the flag is future President of the United States Lieutenant James Monroe. General Washington is standing tall in the boat with a "I don't take no shit" look.

Three Blind Mice

The piece has been copied by others many times and today the image is on the back of New Jersey's State Quarter. Leutze would make a companion piece entitled Washington Rallying the Troops at Monmouth which is at the Doe Library on the campus of the University of California, Berkeley. Some American textbooks have altered the painting because George Washington's watch fob dangling from his thigh makes it look like his dick is hanging out. Emanuel Leutze was a German born American who learned how to paint in Philadelphia, Pennsylvania. He traveled back to Germany and other parts of Europe to study and work on perfecting his art.

It was while in Germany that he would paint Washington Crossing the Delaware to inspire reform minded European leaders. He would come back to America and settle in New York City in 1859. He would also commute to Washington, D.C. frequently. There were two other works of note completed by Leutze that are standouts as well. The first is a portrait of United States Supreme Court Chief Justice Roger Taney completed after the conclusion of the Dred Scott case. Today this piece hangs in the Harvard Law School (hopefully they are avoiding teaching his brand of law).

The second is a mural painted behind the western staircase in the United States House of Representatives chamber of the United States Capitol. It is titled Westward the Course of Empire Takes Its Way or shortened to Westward Ho. It pays homage to the idea of Manifest Destiny and the fact that the United States, in their own mind should exists from the Atlantic Ocean to the Pacific Ocean by any means necessary.

Another noted artist of the 1850s was the Englishman William Holman Hunt. He painted mainly devotional and religious themed works. He was greatly influenced during his travels to the Holy Land. He initially began traveling because of love. His first wife was a woman named Fanny Waugh. When she died Hunt turned around and married her sister Edith. Only problem with that was at the time marrying your wife's sister was against the law in England so he was forced to leave the country to get hitched.

Some of his noted 1850s work include A Converted British Family Sheltering a Christian Missionary from the Persecution of the Druids. Up until his death Hunt considered it one of his best pieces. Today it can be seen at the Ashmolean Museum in Oxford, England. In 1853 Hunt painted The Awakening Conscience. This piece shows a woman in the process of getting out of a man's lap while they sit at a piano.

The impression one gets when viewing the work is that this motherfucker done said something real fucking stupid and she is like "I don't know what I thought I ever saw in your fucking ass anyway, I'm out." It's pretty fucking funny if you ask me. The piece is part of the Tate Collection in London, England. In 1854 he completes The Light of the World. The painting represents Hunt's visual interpretation of the Bible's Book of Revelation, chapter three, verse twenty. "Behold, I stand at the door and knock; if any man hear My voice and open the door, I will come in to him, and sup with him, and he with Me."

It's worth noting that the door on the painting has no handle and can only be opened from the inside. One might conclude that Hunt insinuates that even though Jesus is the Man, he ain't gonna force himself on nobody and you have to take his love in voluntarily. While at the same time Hunt leaves you with the impression that Jesus says, "but, don't take too long to answer the door." It's a very compelling piece for both experienced and neo-enthusiasts as well. It is hanging in the chapel at Kebel College, Oxford, England. There is also a life sized version hanging in Saint Paul's Cathedral, London, England.

Between 1854 and 1856 Hunt would complete two versions of The Scapegoat. This was a visual interpretive of the "scapegoat" as described in the Bible Book of Leviticus. On the Day of Atonement a goat would have its horns wrapped with a red cloth, representing the sins of the community, and be driven off. Hunt started working on the piece at the shore of the Dead Sea. One version shows a dark haired goat and a rainbow. The other (larger) version shows a much more sublime light haired goat.

The great thing about art is that there are three levels of the thought process. One; what the artist envisions before he or she ever makes a stroke. Two; what the artists defines the piece to mean when he or she completes it. And three; what the non participating viewer sees and interprets after the fact. Hunt's The Scapegoat captures all of these processes. What he had in mind before he starting painting was one thing. What he defined it as when he finished was another thing. What others saw it to be was completely different.

Hunt tells the story of what happened when he showed the piece to the Belgian born art dealer Ernest Gambart who lived in France. Hunt would explain that the painting was based on a book called the Bible and asked Gambart if he knew of this book (sarcastically). Sarcastically back, Gambart says I have never heard of this book to which Holman replies, "I forgot the book is not known in France but we English read it from time to time."

It was as if to say the French are a bunch of fucking ignorant heathens. In the end Hunt felt that the general public didn't have a high enough intelligence quotient to understand the work. Today the dark haired goat is at the Manchester Art Gallery, Manchester, England and the light haired goat is at the Lady Lever Art Gallery in the village of Port Sunlight, Merseyside, England. You can also find his works in the Uffizi Gallery, Florence, Italy and the Museum of Fine Arts, Boston, Massachusetts.

Jean Desire Gustave Courbet would come make a mark of his own during the 1850s. Some of his works during the decade include the A Burial At Ornans. This piece records the funeral of his uncle, who died in September, 1848. The style stands out because he didn't use models to paint rather he used the actual townspeople that attended the funeral. Measuring ten feet by twenty two feet A Burial At Ornans ushered in the period known as Realism. A new genre that was not very respected at first but gained widespread admiration over time by many in the art world.

Ironically enough, later in his life, Courbet would to hate this piece. The piece is part of the permanent collection at the Musee d'Orsay, Paris, France. In 1850 he would also complete Farmers of Flagey on the Return from the Market. It hangs in the Museum of Fine Arts and Archeology in Besancon, France. The Museum itself is interesting because predates the Louve by over one hundred years. The city of Besancon lies in the northeast corner of France about two hundred miles from Paris in one direction and seventy miles from Lausanne, Switzerland in the other.

In 1855 Courbet would paint his good friend and avid Courbet collector Alfred Bruyas. Bruyas also collected many other artist of the day. He would eventually donate his collection to the Musee Fabre in

Montpellier. Montpellier is on the southern coast of France along the Mediterranean Sea not far from Marseille and Nice. Also at the Musee Fabre is Courbet's The Meeting finished in 1855. This painting was based on the Wandering Jew who taunted Jesus on his way to the Crucifixion and was then cursed to walk the Earth until the Second Coming of Christ. One of his last works of the 1850s was a portrait of the French opera singer Louis Gueymard. Courbet paints Geuymard in his title role of Robert le Diable (Robert the Devil). It was a five act opera composed by Giacomo Meyerbeer. This piece is hanging at the Metropolitan Museum of Art in New York City.

Although he would not complete it until 1866 by far everybody's favorite Courbet work is his Origin of the World. It is an erotic themed close up of a woman's hairy pussy with her legs wide open. For effect the painting is mostly torso omitting the limbs and head and making visible the right breast complete with a stiffened nipple. For Courbet this was the very definition of Realism. Today it can be seen at the Musee d'Orsay, Paris, France.

Jean Francois Millet was another French painter that influenced the period of Realism as well as Naturalism. He did several pieces during the decade. One of his standout works was The Gleaners finished in 1857. Millet became fascinated with the women and children going through the process of gleaning. This was when the poor would go through various fields and collect bits of grain that was left over from that season's harvest.

Explaining this condition through art became a driving force for Millet. In the painting one can see these women scavenging in the foreground just in eyesight of full stacks of grain. Like other artist of the day, the piece was not well received. Today it can be seen at the Musee d'Orsay in Paris, France. In 1857 Millet painted The Angelus. This painting was important because it lead to the invention of Droit de suite. Droit de suite is French for "right to follow." It was a right granted to artists or their heirs to receive a fee on the resale of their works of art. Millet sold the painting for one thousand francs. The owner of the painting later sold the painting for five hundred fifty thousand francs while Millet's family continued to live in poverty. So this fucking led to the rule. The painting is in the Musee d' Orsay, Paris, France.

In the 1850s he would also paint The Sheepfold. One of the last pieces he would do in the decade. This piece is in the Kelvingrove Art Gallery and Museum, Glasgow, Scotland. Jean Francios Millet would influence many other later artists. These include Vincent Van Gogh, Claude Monet, George Seurat and Salvador Dali. Millet would also be immortalized in Mark Twain's 1898 play Is He Dead?.

Two other important paintings of the 1850s were completed by the famed artist Edgar Degas. One of the founders of Impressionism and a self described Realist, Degas was gifted early on. The two paintings were Achille De Gas in the Uniform of a Cadet and The Bellelli Family. The former at the National Gallery of Art, Washington, D.C. and the latter at the Musee d'Orsay, Paris, France. Achille was Degas' younger brother. The spelling "De Gas" was first used by Degas' father, Auguste, to make the family seem more regal than they really were. Edgar would revert back to the family's original spelling when he became an adult.

The Bellilli Family is an art piece depicting his aunt Laura, his uncle Gennaro and his two nieces Giulia and Giovanna. Also in the painting is a portrait of Laura's father who had died recently. Degas was influenced by many portraitists in completing The Bellelli Family. These included Anthony van Dyck, Giorgione, Sandro Botticelli, Hans Holbein, Jean Auguste Dominique Ingres, Diego Velasquez, Francisco Goya, Gustave Courbet and Honore Doumier.

Degas starting painting at an early age in life. Born in Paris he graduated from the Lycee Louis Le Grand. He would become one of the few artists to actually make money from selling his work while he was alive. He was also known for his sculptures, especially of dancers. Later in life he was a known and active anti Semite and disassociated from all of his Jewish friends. His 1879 painting At the Bourse effectively conveyed his feelings on this in art.

Degas was greatly influenced by Edouard Manet. In the 1850s Manet would paint both The Boy with Cherries and The Absinthe Drinker. The Boy with Cherries is part of the collection at the Meseu Calouste Gulbenkian, Lisbon, Portugal. The Absinthe Drinker was another period piece not held in high regard when put on display. It is a painting of a drunk who use to hang around the Louvre dressed up to look respectable. On the one hand Manet attempts to make the man look respectable with a cloak and hat. On the other hand there is an empty bottle on the ground and a half full glass of absinthe. The wino's elevated right foot shows the viewer how fucked up he appears to be (and rightfully so, a whole bottle of absinthe will get one very fucked up). The painting is part of the permanent collection of the Ny Carlsberg Glyptotek, Copenhagen, Denmark. Manet would die from syphilis in 1883. He wife was a woman named Suzanne Leenhoff. She was interesting because she was fucking Manet's father at some point in life.

Darryl Murphy

One of the most prolific artists of the 1850s was Eugene Delacroix. His works included Apollo slaying Python, Desdemona Cursed by Her Father, Christ on the Sea of Galilee, Moroccan Saddles His Horse, Jerusalem Delivered/Clorinda Rescues Olindo and Sophronia, the Bride of Abydos, The Death of Desdemona, The Justice of Trajan and Ovid Among the Scythians. Apollo Slaying Python was painted by Delacroix for the ceiling of the Galerie d' Apollon in the Louvre. The work is a great example of good over evil and genius over stupidity.

Desdemona Cursed by Her Father was inspired from William Shakespeare and hangs in the Brooklyn Museum of Art, Brooklyn, New York. Christ on the Sea of Galilee was painted during the time when biblical art was popular among French Catholics during the reign of Napoleon III. The piece is part of the collection at the Walters Museum of Art, Baltimore, Maryland.

Moroccan Saddles His Horse was inspired by Delacroix's travels around North Africa. Delacroix saw the North Africans as regal people in the sense of the Greeks and Romans. It hangs in the Hermitage Museum, Saint Petersburg, Russia. Another piece he did, Jerusalem Delivered, is based on the poem by the Italian poet Torquato Tasso. It is the hyped version of the First Crusade where Catholic knights battled the Muslims to take back the city. The painting is at the Neue Pinakothek, Munich, Germany. Delacroix's Bride of Abydos is based on the 1813 poem by Lord Byron. It can be seen at the Louvre, Paris, France. Death of Desdemona was also based on Othello. The whereabouts of the painting are unknown.

Justice of Trajan is based on an episode in the life of Roman Emperor Trajan. Trajan, who ruled from ninety eight to one hundred seventy AD was known as an even handed Emperor. Delacroix attempts to capture the spirit of this ruler. The painting is part of the collection at the Honolulu Museum of Art.

There were actually two versions of Ovid Among the Scythians (the first completed in 1859). Ovid was a Roman poet who was kicked out of Rome by Augustus and sent to live with the Scythians. The Scythians were an ancient Persian tribe who were thought of as uncivilized by Roman standards. Delacroix paints a scene where Ovid is taken in by the Scythians and treated kindly. The first painting is at the National Gallery, London, England. The second version, completed in 1862, is at the Metropolitan Museum of Art, New York, New York. The second version is painted with much brighter colors than the first.

Delacroix died in 1863 so much of his work in the decade that was the 1850s was near the end of his life. It seemed like he was almost rushing to get those last pieces finished. He was born in France and also attended the Lycee Louis Le Grand. He was an artist right from the moment he popped out of his mother's pussy. His travels to Spain and North Africa inspired him greatly and Napoleon III held him in high regard. When he died he was buried at the famed Pere Lachaise Cemetery.

Three other great works of the 1850s came from the artist Jean Baptiste Camille Corot. The works were painted late in his life. They include Une Matinee, La Danse des Nymphes or A Morning, The Dance of the Nymphes. It is housed in the Musee d'Orsay, Paris, France. The work was important because it would influence many future Impressionists.

Some interpret that Corot was visualizing his love of the opera by having the foreground being a stage and the surrounding trees acting as a curtain of sorts. Corot's Le Concert Champetre or Woodland Music Makers echoes many of the same themes. This was shown in the Salon of 1857 and shows three women in the foreground (one with a cello). It hangs in the Musee Conde, situated in the Paris suburb of Chantilly, France.

In 1859 Corot exhibited Macbeth and the Witches. The piece is taken from the Shakespeare play Macbeth. It visualizes the scene where Macbeth comes along three witches who foretell his rise to the crown of Scotland. Macbeth and the Witches is part of the Wallace Collection, London, England. This was one of two Shakespearian canvases that Corot would do. In 1874 he completed Hamlet and the Gravedigger. Hamlet and the Gravedigger can be seen at the Ordrupgaard Museum, just north of Copenhagen, Denmark.

Corot was born in Paris and didn't really take to painting seriously until his mid twenties. Like most French artists of the day Corot would make a pilgrimage to Italy to study the masters of the Italian Renaissance. Leonardo da Vinci would leave the biggest impression on him. He was also smitten by the women of Italy describing them as the most beautiful in the world and the difficulty of picking one was what kept him from marriage. Corot was a complete "mama's boy." He remained very close to both his mother and father right up until their deaths. Only after their passing did he really start to come into his own.

His first submission to the Salon was in 1827. The Salon was important to all artists of the day. It was where you not only exhibited your work but sold your work and cemented your reputation. It was the Olympics of art in the Eighteenth and Nineteenth Centuries (note that the Salon would lose its panache starting in the 1870s as many Impressionists formed their own exhibitions after being rejected by the Salon). The Salon still exists to this day.

By the 1850s Corot was a well respected artist and would become a leading figure of the Barbizon School along with Theodore Rousseau, Jean Francios Millet and others. The Barbizon School wasn't an actual school but a gathering of like minded artists in the town of Barbizon, France. Many young Impressionist of the era visited Barbizon. Among them were Claude Monet, Pierre Auguste Renior, Alfred Sisley and Frederic Bazille.

Corot's work was very successful commercially. As a result he was quite generous with his profits. He bought Honore Daumier a house and gave ten thousand francs to Millet's widow to help her take care of her children. He also supported a children's center in Paris. Corot was so fucking good, and, so fucking respected his mentees included Camille Pissaro, Eugene Boudin (who subsequently mentored Claude Monet) and Berthe Morisot among other. Claude Monet described him as "THE" master. Today he is known as one of the six greatest landscape painters of all time.

Corot would end up painting over three thousand pieces. The saying "imitation is the best form of flattery" truly applied to Corot. Many artists simply repainted Corot's work and sold it as authentic. This would prompt French writer Rene Huyghe to comically quip "Corot painted three thousand canvases, ten thousand of which were sold in America."

He never bothered to care, however and took it as a compliment. Corot died in 1875 and was also buried at Pere Lachaise Cemetery.

William Powell Firth was a celebrated English painter during the mid-Nineteenth Century. His 1850s works include Life at the Seaside, The Derby Day and The Crossing Sweeper. Life at the Seaside shows a good time being had by all at a seaside resort. What is interesting is the attire of the subjects in the painting. They all look so fucking hot. The Derby Day had been described as Firth's best work. Completed in 1858 it shows a day at the Epsom Derby.

Named after the First Earl of Derby the Epsom Derby is an annual thoroughbred horse race run in Surrey, England. First contested in 1780 the Epsom Derby is the granddaddy of them all. Even America's Kentucky Derby takes a back seat to the Epsom Derby. Firth does masterful work in showcasing the event as much more than a horse race. Viewing the painting one can see gambling going on, pickpockets at work, prostitutes plying their trade and beggars begging. It was quite a sensation when first exhibited at the Royal Academy in 1858. It is part of the collection at the Tate Gallery, London, England. Its popularity spurred Firth to do a second version that is on display at the Manchester City Art Gallery, Manchester, England.

For William Firth painting The Crossing Sweeper showed a picture with themes of various societal ills. In the 1850s a crossing sweeper was an individual who used a broom to clear a path for another individual who wanted to cross the street. They were like those aggravating motherfuckers who want to give your windshield an unsolicited cleaning while you are stopped at a traffic light. Except in this case

Three Blind Mice

most crossing sweepers were sweeping up horse shit. So it was a nasty fucking job.

In the painting Firth captures the grittiness of the job showing a little boy in ragged clothes assisting a woman as she begins crossing a street. It noteworthy that the woman in the painting is looking away from the boy dismissively as if to say she is way to noble to even acknowledge his existence. It is also a statement about social status and economic hierarchy. These are two repercussions of society prevalent to this day. The Crossing Sweeper is at the Museum of London, London, England.

William Firth was born in Alfield, a small community in northeastern England. His father got him into art and he would eventually befriend and become greatly influenced by Charles Dickens. Firth was noted for his private life. He was married and had twelve children with his wife while at the same time, just down the road, he was fucking his former domestic and had seven more kids with that bitch. Near the end of his life he would paint his only nude portrait named After the Bath. It was ironic because he was damn near eighty years old when he did it. He was a horny motherfucker right up to his death.

George Inness was to American landscape painting what Corot was to, well, landscape painting. Two of his 1850s works include Milton, New York and Lake Nemi. Both held by the Yale University Art Gallery in New Haven, Connecticut. Inness was born in the Hudson Valley region in the state of New York. As a youngster he started out as a map engraver. He would travel to Europe and end up training at the Barbizon School which would greatly influenced his landscape painting. He was as to be commissioned for a series of paintings by the Delaware,

Lackawanna and Western Railroad. Later in his career theology would play a role in his work. He died in 1894 in Scotland.

French artist Edouard Dubufe gets mention for his beautiful painting of Rosa Bonheur with Bull completed in 1857. It is at the Palace of Versailles.

Rosa Bonheur was probably the most famous female artist of the Nineteenth Century. Her most famous 1850s work is The Horse Fair which currently hangs in the Metropolitan Museum of Art, New York, New York. Bonheur began painting The Horse Fair from a series of sketching she made while attending the Paris horse market. To keep a low profile she would dress like a man whenever she attended the fair. The piece would was first exhibited at the Salon in 1853 and travelled throughout Europe under wide acclaim. It would end up in hands of Cornelius Vanderbilt II and he would subsequently gift it to the Metropolitan Museum of Art in 1887.

Rosa was born in Bordeaux, France to a family of artists who would all go on to become well known within the art world. Her father and siblings were all painters and they all could bring it. So much so that pioneering eugenicist Francis Galton used the Bonheurs as an example of "hereditary genius." A term used to describe pattern behavior within nuclear family units among other things. Rosa also became famous for her lifestyle. She liked wearing men's clothes, smoking cigarettes and licking pussy (yes, she was a lesbian).

Albert Bierstadt would finish two significant pieces in the 1850s, among others. These were Gosnold at Cuttyhunk in 1858 and The

Three Blind Mice

Marina Piccdola, Capri in 1859. The former at the New Bedford Whaling Museum, New Bedford, Massachusetts and the latter at the Albright-Knox Art Gallery, Buffalo, New York. In the 1850s he would also do The Old Mill, The Portico of Octavia, Westphalia and The Wolf River, Kansas hanging at the Detroit Institute of Arts, Detroit, Michigan.

Bierstadt was born in Germany and his family moved to Massachusetts when he was one year of age. As an adult he spent much of the 1850s traveling west and studying landscapes across the United States. During the Civil War he was one of the pussies that paid for another person to serve in his place. He did manage to complete over five hundred pieces during his lifetime.

So, like every aspect of life in the 1850s artists and their paintings would show the way of what was to come. As a sign of what was to come the world would be blessed with the birth of American painter John Singer Sargent. Sargent was a leading portrait painter of his day. He would also be prolific. During his lifetime he would complete over nine hundred oils and two thousand watercolors. Singer's greatness was that he was a Realist who painted during the Impressionist, Fauvist and Cubist eras and resisted it all.

Chapter 18

F.L.O.T.U.S.

FLOTUS stands for First Lady of the United States. You can't apply for it. If a teacher asks a little girl what she wants to be when she grows up she does not respond, "I want to be First Lady of the United States." No, in most cases you fuck your way into it. At its core, the First Lady of the United States is the permanent piece of some dude that, by a bunch of different circumstances, and a lot of luck became President of the United States (P.O.T.U.S).

It's not inconceivable that most First Ladies have strolled through the White House thinking about all those times she was gonna leave his fucking ass. But then thought, hey, it didn't work out too bad. It's the carnal knowledge version of Powerball or Mega Millions. Becoming First Lady is like becoming a boxer. You just wake up one day and that's what you are.

A mother doesn't sit around asking her daughter, "How are your First Lady studies coming along?" You don't go to school for it, there's no degree conferred upon you and you don't practice it like a doctor practices medicine or a lawyer practices law. At the same time it is also like a judgeship or a tenured college professor. Once you become First Lady that's what you are for life.

Today the First Lady of the United States is the official hostess of the White House. She is one of the most influential and recognizable pieces of pussy on the planet. Because she is married to the President of the United States, pillow talk becomes another fucking cabinet meeting. It's called pussy control. Except in this case the things he has to do to get "make up" sex affects a whole fucking country. Maybe they should put her pussy in a briefcase to be carried around by an aide like they do the nation's nuclear weapons codes (the football). The world would be a much safer place.

First Ladies can be trendsetters like Jackie Kennedy who brought a sense of fashion and elegance to the White House during the Kennedy Administration. Betty Ford was a firebrand for such issues as equal rights for women and substance abuse. Nancy Reagan gave all Americans "Just Say No" and made drug awareness a theme of the day. Michelle Obama championed childhood obesity so that Twenty First Century children don't turn into a bunch of internet using, lazy fat shits.

Florence "Flossie" Harding, Eleanor Roosevelt, Hilary Clinton and most of all Jackie Kennedy had to deal with their husbands fucking around on them and everybody knowing it. All of these First Ladies would stand by their men. These women would seek their own agendas and take a "the fleas come with the dog" attitude. This is versus adding a little "First Lady piss" to the President's morning coffee.

Then there was Edith Wilson. She was the second wife of President Woodrow Wilson, who, for the last year and half of his presidency controlled who and what issues of national importance got to the President after he had suffered a stroke and was bedridden most of the time. Because of this most historians consider her to be the first female President of the United States. Although she downplayed this role she truly controlled the administration of the Administration.

This would make for many chapped asses among the powerbrokers in the Legislative Branch of the United States Government. But she didn't give a fuck. She blamed it all President Wilson's doctors who she said told her to take over. There is no doubt that the stoke President Wilson suffered fucked him up real good. Physically, he was paralyzed on his left side. This also means that the thrombotic nature of his stroke surely diminished his deductive reasoning capacity.

The debilitating effect of President Wilson's stroke is what his doctors should have explained to Mrs. Wilson as well as his Cabinet and the Congressional Leadership (forcefully and publicly). Hey, but doctors are like every fucking body else, there's good ones, bad ones, smart ones and dumb ones. Simple everyday activities were an enormous challenge for President Wilson. It had to be almost impossible for anyone to dutifully attend to the affairs of any fucking country. He was in no shape to deal with the shit Edith was bringing him even after she screened it.

In retrospect, at a minimum, this was a clear case where the Vice President of the United States should have become the Acting President of the United States. The Vice President of the United States at the time was Indiana born Thomas R. Marshall. But Marshall himself was one

Three Blind Mice

of the reasons he didn't become Acting President. Marshall had a jovial nature and liked to tell jokes. This personality trait led President Wilson to view him as a simple motherfucker not to be taken seriously.

Woodrow Wilson didn't think much of the Vice President and as a result he marginalized him during much of his presidency. Vice President Marshall also disagreed with the President on several positions as well. Additionally, it didn't help Marshall's cause that he thought the Vice President's constitutional role as President of the United States Senate was more important than being Vice President of the United States.

Mrs. Wilson and other Administration insiders effectively kept the severity of President Wilson's stroke from Vice President Marshall. Although he knew of Mrs. Wilson's power grab he never challenged it. The result of this scenario led directly to the United States Senate deciding not to join the League of Nations. This was a gap in both Presidential and Executive Branch leadership.

So, over time the First Lady of the United States has evolved into being many things. Abigail Fillmore, Jane Pierce and Harriet Rebecca Lane Johnston were all very different women as First Ladies and handled the duties of First Lady in very different ways.

Abigail Powers Fillmore was born in upstate New York not far from Saratoga, New York in a town named Stillwater. She was the youngest of seven children. She had six brothers, Cyrus, David, John, Royal and Lemuel Powers. She also had a sister named Mary Powers. Her father, Lemuel Leland Powers, was a Baptist minister who helped to start a church in Stillwater. By the late seventeen hundreds he had over four hundred members in the flock. He died in 1800 in Stillwater.

Upon his death Abigail's mother moved to the western part of the state of New York. There are rumors that the reason she moved was because her husband was giving a little extra tending to some of the females in the flock. Her mother was Abigail Newland Powers Strong. After her first husband (Abigail Fillmore's birth father) died Abigail Newland Powers got remarried to Captain Benjah Strong.

Strong was a widower who fought in both the French and Indian War and the American Revolutionary War. He was a first cousin of Revolutionary War hero Nathan Hale. Hale became famous for the quote "I only regret that I have but one life to give for my country" right before the British hung his ass. He brought nine children to the marriage. Abigail Fillmore's step siblings included six step brothers and three step sisters

As a young adult she became a teacher. This was an unusual thing for a woman in the Nineteenth Century. As life would have it one of her students was a gentleman named Millard Fillmore. Young Millard would get the hots for his teacher and eventually his feelings would not go unrequited by Abigail. Now, it wasn't quite Mary Kay Letourneau and Vili Fualaau as they were only a year apart in age, but, it was a student-teacher relationship.

They would marry in 1826 and have two children. The children were named Millard Powers Fillmore and Mary Abigail Fillmore. Millard Powers Fillmore or "Powers" was a definite mama's boy who loved Abigail deeply. He didn't take kindly to President Fillmore's second wife nor think much of his father for marrying the bitch.

Three Blind Mice

Mary Abigail or "Abby" was a bright young lady and quite cultured. She spoke French (fluently), German, Spanish and Italian (conversationally). She was also a versatile musician. She played the piano, harp and guitar. When Abigail Fillmore was ill she even filled in as First Lady per her father's request. Tragically, she died suddenly at age twenty two from cholera.

Having been mostly home schooled Abigail was a voracious reader and very intelligent as well. She was not pretentious and preferred Washington's cultural attractions versus anything high society. She attended official ceremonies with the President often times as the only woman present. She opposed the fugitive slave law and convinced the President to get the United States Navy to discontinue the practice of flogging. She was not over the top, but very much had the President's ear when it needed to be had.

Abigail Fillmore will best be remembered for establishing the first White House library. Her best times were she entertained herself with the readings of her favorite writers. This included Charles Dickens, Washington Irving and William Thackeray. She died in March, 1853 not long after catching pneumonia from attending President Pierce's inauguration.

President Franklin Pierce was married to Jane Pierce. Jane Means Appleton Pierce was born in Hampton, New Hampshire in 1806. She was the third child of six children. Her other five siblings were Mary, Frances, William, Robert and John. Her father was Jesse Appleton, the second President of Bowdoin College. Jesse presided over the school right before three of its most famous students arrived one of which would be his son-in-law, Franklin Pierce. The other two were Nathaniel Hawthorne and Henry Wadsworth Longfellow.

Her mother's name was Elizabeth Means Appleton. By all accounts she was a dedicated mother and dutiful wife. She spent most of her time taking care of her children at home. Jane was home schooled but suffered throughout her life from bad penmanship. As an adult Jane spent the better part of life all fucked up in the head. This was due in part because she experienced so much tragedy in her life. It also didn't help that she hated her husband's drinking, hated Washington, D.C. and hated being first lady.

Matter of fact when she found out her husband had secured the Democratic Party's nomination for President of the United States she fainted. That was the depth of her despair. What really kept her emotionally distraught were the events of her children's lives. The Pierce's had three children, Franklin Pierce, Jr., Franklin "Frank" Robert Pierce and Benjamin Pierce.

None of the three children lived past the age of twelve. Franklin Jr. died three day after birth. Franklin Robert Pierce died as a result of an 1843 typhus epidemic in Concord, New Hampshire. In January 1853 President-Elect Franklin Pierce, Jane and surviving son Benjamin boarded a train for Washington, D.C. to get settled in and prepare for the transition from President-Elect to actual President of the United States in March, 1853. On the way they stopped off in Andover, Massachusetts to see family and friends.

Three Blind Mice

On January 6, 1853 a few minutes after train pulled out of Andover the train wrecked and the Presidents car rolled down an embankment. Everyone survived except Benjamin who was thrown from the train and nearly decapitated as his skull was crushed right in front of Franklin and Jane Pierce. He was twelve years old. That was it for Jane. Who could blame her? Losing a child is difficult enough, but losing a child like that it's almost impossible to be considered "normal" ever again. In the meantime President Pierce turned to the bottle. Neither of them was fit for the task ahead.

She refused to continue on to Washington, D.C. and did not attend the inauguration. In many ways she blamed Franklin's ambition as the reason Benjamin died. When she did finally get to Washington she didn't give a shit about being First Lady. On many occasions her aunt Abigail Kent Means acted as First Lady. When Ms. Means was not around future unpopular First Lady of the Confederacy Varina Banks Howell Davis would officiate. Varina was the second wife of Jefferson Davis (remember, Davis' first wife was the daughter of President Zachary Taylor), who, at the time was Secretary of War in the Pierce Administration.

Mrs. Pierce spent most of her time writing letters to Benjamin and then tossing them into the fireplace, letter, after letter, after letter. It would be two years (1855) before she would do anything official as it pertained to being First Lady. Even then her effort in anything other than mourning was, at best, half ass. She died in Andover, Massachusetts in December 1863. The diagnosis was tuberculosis but she also died of a broken heart only a mother that outlived all of her children could know.

Since President James Buchanan was a lifelong bachelor Harriet Rebecca Lane Johnston filled the role of First Lady during his term. Harriet was the daughter of President Buchanan's sister Jane Ann Buchanan Lane. Harriet had six siblings. There were five brothers and one sister. Their names were James Buchanan Lane, Thomas N. Lane, Joseph Stark Lane, Elliot Eskridge Lane, Mary Elizabeth Speer Lane Baker and William Edward Lane. She would outlive them all. In chronological order she was the sixth of seven children or what some would prefer to as the "knee" baby. This meaning she was the baby before the baby with the last child representing the foot of the sibling tree.

Both of her parents died when she was very young leaving her an orphan. She ended up living with her Uncle Jimmy (President James Buchanan) who at that time was a United States Senator representing the Commonwealth of Pennsylvania. By all accounts President Buchanan was a very effective guardian to the young Harriet. He enrolled her and her sister in boarding schools. First, he sent them to a school in the city of Charleston, West Virginia.

Sometime after James Buchanan became the seventeenth United States Secretary of State under President James Polk he enrolled the girls in a Catholic school located in the Georgetown section of Washington, D.C. This would have a great impact on Harriet's religious views during her lifetime. She would follow James Buchanan to London when he was appointed United States Minister to the United Kingdom. Queen Victoria would give her the rank of an ambassador's wife and she proved to be quite popular.

When James Buchanan took office as President of the United States in March, 1857 he designated Harriet as White House hostess. In her day

Three Blind Mice

she had the same kind of popularity as Jackie Kennedy would almost one hundred years later. During social events she was caring in arranging seating so that Southerners always sat with other Southerners and Northerners always sat with other Northerners. For being only in her late twenties this showed an incredible maturity and keen grasp of the political sentiments of the day.

President Buchanan was very protective when it came to men courting young Harriett. She would finally marry in her late thirties. The man she married was a banker from Baltimore, Maryland named Henry Elliott Johnston. They would have two children, James Buchanan Johnston and Henry Elliott Johnston. Both would die young and within two years of each other.

The deaths of her children would set in motion a series of philanthropic events that would stay in place well into the Twenty First Century. One would be a pediatric home for children at Johns Hopkins Hospital called the Harriet Lane Clinic which is still serving children today. This would be the first pediatric specific medical facility in the United States. She also would insist it serve all children without regard to race or creed, a highly unusual demand of the day.

Also, in honor of her sons she set aside money and land to found what is today known as Saint Albans School in Washington, D.C. Still around today its alumni is a who's who of sons of America's political elite and well collected.

She donated her sizable art collection to the Smithsonian Institution. Thus, she would become known as the "First Lady of the National

Collection of Fine Arts." The United States Coast Guard would even name a ship after her. It would be called the United States Coast Guard Cutter Harriett Lane and it is still in active service as of 2014. Throughout her post White House days she was friendly with most of her succeeding First Ladies and often attended social events held there. She became a sort of First Lady Emeritus for these women.

These women included Martha Johnson, President Andrew Johnson's daughter who filled in as hostess because her mother Eliza was too ill at the time. Julia Grant, wife of President Ulysses S. Grant. Lucy Hayes, wife of President Rutherford B. Hayes. Lucretia Garfield, wife of President James Garfield. Mary Arthur Mcelroy, sister of President Chester A. Arthur (President Arthur's first wife had died before he took office). Francis Cleveland, second wife of President Grover Cleveland and the youngest First Lady in the history of the United States. She also mentored Ida McKinley, wife of President William McKinley.

She would die in 1903 at the age of seventy three. Ironically she would die in the town of Narragansett, State of Rhode Island and Providence Plantations. This was the same place that Jefferson Davis' daughter Winnie would die only five years earlier.

Chapter 19

William Parker and the Christiana Riot

William Parker was a slave raised in Anne Arundel County, Maryland. It is the area that surrounds the state's capitol of Annapolis and a major commercial outlet for the slave trade at the time. He would become a central figure in the 1851 Christiana Riot. The Christiana Riot and the resulting repercussions would expose the failings of the Fugitive Slave Law of 1850. Christiana, Pennsylvania is located in Lancaster County. The county lies just north of the Maryland border. The border line was established one hundred years earlier by the Mason-Dixon Line.

The establishment of the Mason-Dixon was an important decision because it thusly settled an ongoing land dispute between the State of Maryland and the Commonwealth of Pennsylvania. The Calvert Family (which controlled Maryland) and the Penn Family (which controlled Pennsylvania) feuded bitterly over exactly how big their states were. In the early 1700s the Calvert family insisted that Maryland's northern border extended to the fortieth parallel. This meant that Maryland's border extended far enough to the north to include the City of Philadelphia.

The Penn family insisted that their southern border extended at least twenty miles further south of Philadelphia per the original grant to William Penn. The dispute was finally settled when Charles II would rule that Northern Maryland and Southern Pennsylvania would begin and end at what became known as the Mason-Dixon Line. This was defined as fifteen miles south of the southernmost house in Philadelphia.

So this is the backdrop through which Lancaster County would become embroiled in what was the Christiana Riot. Pennsylvania would become a free state which would abolish slavery and Maryland would remain a slave state well into the 1850s. Because of its location in the Commonwealth of Pennsylvania Lancaster County became an important "depot" on the Underground Railroad, especially in the 1850s.

William Parker would escape from slavery in his late teens and find his way to Christiana, Pennsylvania where he would not only settle but raise a family as well. Parker was greatly influenced by abolitionists William Lloyd Garrison and Frederick Douglass. He actively recruited members to arm and protect themselves "by any means necessary." He felt if his government was not going to protect him and his property then he was going to do it himself.

He would form the Lancaster Black Protection Society. It wasn't just a catchy name. They were not to be fucked with. This was a bold position for even a free Black to take in the 1850s, much less, a young runaway slave now in his twenties. Yes, William Parker was truly the Malcolm X of his day. Slave catching was a nasty, but, viable, sustainable and profitable business after the passage of the Fugitive Slave Law in 1850. He knew that living so close to the border of Maryland slave catchers would snatch any Black man regardless of their social standing, free or runaway.

Both Whites and Blacks were keenly aware of Parker's reputation for violence with purpose to protect himself and his family. This resolve mixed with his hatred for slavery had several effects on the neighbors. First they rallied around him for mutual benefit. Secondly, his farm became a great place to go for slaves who would escape from plantations in Maryland and other slave states.

Word got out that he would never give a runaway back to slave catchers if they could make it to his place. Lastly, his farm became a major stop on the Underground Railroad as Parker would help many get to parts of Ohio, Philadelphia, Pennsylvania and Canada. Part of the Christiana Riot was started because of the notion that slave owners in Maryland treated their slaves better than those assholes further down the slave owning trough in the deep southern United States. That's bull fucking shit of course. Slavery was slavery and not one motherfucker that was owned wanted to be or was happy about it. Analogously anyone who thinks that should ask themselves, "would you want a mild case of herpes?" 'Nuff said.

This was the case of Edward Gorsuch, a slaveholder that thought because he didn't beat his slaves they were actually happy. Nope. Four of his slaves would escape over the issue of some stolen wheat and end up at Parker's place in the Commonwealth of Pennsylvania. This "nice" slave owner wasn't so kind as to let these motherfuckers get away. His kindness led him to gather a posse of slave catchers and a United States Federal Marshal, cross into Lancaster County and confront Mr. Parker armed to the teeth.

Both sides were determined to have their way and Gorsuch knew the kind of man he was dealing with in Parker. On September 11th, 1851 the shit hit the fan. When it was finished Gorsuch was dead, two others were wounded and the fucking United States Marine Corps had to be called in to quiet things down. And they still didn't get their fucking slaves back.

Of the group that fought with Parker four of them got away including William Parker and Gorsuch's four slaves. The others were captured by the Marines, placed under the custody of the United States Marshal present and sent to Moyamensing Prison in Philadelphia. Moyanmensing Prison was a fairly new facility having been completed in 1835. Situated in South Philadelphia it was designed by a Philadelphia architect named Thomas Walter. As the fourth Architect of the Capitol, Walter would later be responsible for designing the central dome of the United States Capitol and the north and south wings of the building to house the United States Senate and the United States House of Representatives respectively.

Eventually all thirty eight men would be charged with treason. Among the indicted was four White Quakers. If convicted all would be held sentenced and sent to Eastern State Penitentiary, also in Philadelphia. You can believe they were all a bunch of shivering bitches because they knew Eastern State Penitentiary was no fucking joke. One has to think that maybe William Parker knew this before he got the fuck out of town.

The Quakers were a religious sect that arrived in America in the late Seventeenth Century. Like the Mormons people thought that they were a little fucking crazy. If the Mormons were the steroids version of religious craziness the Quakers were more like a sleeping pill. Anyway, the only places they could find to live in those days was (what today we know as) the State of Rhode Island and Providence Plantations and the Commonwealth of Pennsylvania. The latter because William Penn (who owned all of Pennsylvania) was a Quaker himself so Pennsylvania became, well, a Quaker state. A Quaker participating in the raid was unusual because while being opposed to slavery as well as excessive drinking, they abhorred violence.

Many people in the South wanted justice for the murder of a White man, especially a plantation owner. To many Southerners a message needed to be sent other enslaved Blacks not to try the same shit Gorsuch's slaves did. In late September, 1851 there were thirty eight indictments handed down by a grand jury. On November 15th, 1851 the first (and only) of the men to be tried was a gentleman named Castner Hanway. He was one of the White Quakers. He was charged with liberating slaves, conspiracy, resisting arrest and treason.

The prosecution gambled that if they could convict the White Hanway from the giddyup, convicting the others would be a walk in the park. It was a mistake. One of the attorneys for the defense was Thaddeus Stevens. Why would Thaddeus Stevens, approaching sixty years old at the time want to get involved in this mess? A few reasons quite frankly. He had moved to Lancaster in 1842 so these were "his" people. It was from Lancaster that Stevens would represent the Commonwealth of Pennsylvania in the United States House of Representatives.

It is of note that one of his fellow attorneys in Lancaster at the time was future President of the United States James Buchanan who was about to named President of the Board of Trustees at Franklin and Marshall College in Lancaster County, Pennsylvania. It is also of note that Stevens would employ the services of Lydia Hamilton Smith when he moved to Lancaster. A mulatto, she would work with him for the rest of his life and become known to many as his common law wife.

He was a staunch opponent of slavery and an equally proponent for Black American rights. Part of the reason for this was because had been born with a club foot and was ridiculed mercilessly as a child and labeled a cripple. He also saw the case as a chance to upstage his fellow Congressmen who supported the Compromise of 1850 and the Fugitive Slave Law of 1850. So, with the zealous representation of Congressman Stevens the jury would acquit Castner Hanway in fifteen minutes.

After that the authorities has no choice but to release the others involved. It was a major fuck you to the pro slavery types in the Southern United States. From a jurisprudence standpoint the case also represented one of the earliest examples of one side's legal resources being just flat out better than the other side. In the Twentieth Century four more well publicized trials would expose the same fact.

These include:

1. The 19991 William Kennedy Smith trial where he was accused of raping a woman after a night of drinking and partying with the late United States Senator Ted Kennedy and his cousin Patrick Kennedy. He was acquitted. Miami, Florida based attorney Roy Black kicked much ass for the defense.

2. The 1992 trial of the Los Angeles Police Officers accused of beating the shit out Rodney King. Defense attorneys Michael

Stone, Darryl Mounger, Paul DePasquale and John Barnett ran circles around chief prosecuting attorney Terry White. Their acquittal would be one of the key factors that led to the infamous Los Angeles riots of 1992 that left fifty three people dead.

3. The Mike Tyson rape trial of 1992. In this case the State of Indiana would be ones with the better legal resources hiring special prosecutor Gregory Garrison. Vincent Fuller was capable and although he had represented John Hinckley Jr. and Jimmy Hoffa on separate occasions, by this time he was simply known as boxing promoter Don King's "tax" attorney. So, for some, it was as if Mike Tyson brought a knife to a gun fight.

4. The O.J. Simpson murder trial concluded in 1995. Everyone knows what happened there.

So, the lesson here is if you ever get jammed up, forget about guilt, innocence, negligence, culpability or even right and wrong. Just make sure your legal representation is flat out better than the other side's.

As for William Parker he would use the same Underground Railroad network that had assisted so many others and get him and his family to Canada with the assistance of one Frederick Douglass. Once in Canada he didn't have to walk around with his fists balled up anymore. He would live a somewhat quiet life while at the same time still being involved in anti-slavery activism. He would become a writer for Frederick Douglass' newspaper the North Star.

Chapter 20

Literature in the 1850s

Besides Harriet Beecher Stowe's century best selling Uncle Tom's Cabin and Solomon Northup's Twelve Years a Slave there were many other famous writers and works penned during the decade. Some of the 1850 writings would end up in American classrooms and as "yeah, I read that a long time ago" bar talk well into the Twenty First Century.

In 1850 a novel is written as historical fiction about a woman accused of adultery and shamed in front of the whole town as punishment. The woman would end up pregnant from the affair and have a baby girl. As the story unfolds readers find out the father of the little girl is a clergyman. Set in Seventeenth Century Boston, Massachusetts the book is titled The Scarlet Letter. For those of you who don't know (or don't remember the actual letter referred to in the book was an "A").

Its author was Nathaniel Hawthorne. The Scarlet Letter would be his masterpiece. It became an instant best seller. It was one of the first books to be mass produced. The first twenty five hundred copies sold out in ten days. Today, one of those originals can fetch upwards of twenty thousand dollars. Hawthorne wrote the book in while he lived in Salem, Massachusetts. He didn't get rich off of the book however. It's estimated that in fifteen years he only made fifteen hundred dollars. Although many loved the book religious leaders condemned it. In modern times other forms of media would tell the books story. This includes opera, plays, music, television and film.

Nathaniel Hawthorne was born in Salem, Massachusetts in 1804. His surname was actually spelled "Hathorne" without the "w." It is suspected that he added the letter to disassociate himself with his great, great grandfather John Hathorne. John Hathorne was a judge who presided over the Salem Witch Trials in the late Seventeenth Century. The questionable actions of Judge Hathorne shamed Nathaniel as an adult and he would add the "w" and become Nathaniel Hawthorne for the rest of his life.

Hawthorne would graduate from Bowdoin College where he attended school not only with future President of the United States Franklin Pierce but renown poet Henry Wadsworth Longfellow as well. In his young adult years he would live next door to Ralph Waldo Emerson and become good friends with Herman Melville who was a great admirer of his work.

His college friendship with Franklin Pierce would send him to Europe when he was appointed United States Consul to Liverpool, England during Pierce's presidency. This also afforded him an opportunity to travel extensively throughout France and Italy.

Darryl Murphy

Hawthorne died in May, 1864. His other works completed in the 1850s include The House of the Seven Gables in 1851, the Blithedale Romance in 1852, and selected short stories. These include The Snow-Image and Other Twice-Told Tales and A Wonder-Book for Girls and Boys, both completed in 1852. In 1853 he wrote Tanglewood Tales.

"Call me Ishmael." This has become one of the most famous opening lines to a novel ever written. The sentence starts us all on the journey that became Moby Dick. It was completed by Herman Melville in 1851. As narrated by Ishamel he tells the story of the monomaniacal Captain Ahab. He is the Skipper of the whaling boat Pequod. Ahab is on a quest of revenge as he hunts the ferocious white whale known as Moby Dick.

Ultimately, Moby Dick ends up killing every fucking body. The story became known for its detail about the whaling industry. In addition, the work examines themes of cause and effect as motivated by misguided revenge. The book would live on as Melville's masterpiece. Ironically, it received a lukewarm response when it was first released to the public. It was originally published in England under the title "The Whale." The American edition was changed to "Moby Dick" because it was deemed a better selling title.

Adding to its lackluster reception was the subject matter in general. With the advent of the California Gold Rush and subsequent opportunities being sought in the western half of the United States, America's interest in seagoing adventures had waned considerably. Herman Melville was born in the City of New York, New York. His family had strong Revolutionary roots as both his paternal and maternal grandfathers left their marks on the annals of American history.

Three Blind Mice

His paternal grandfather was Thomas Melvill. A Major in the Continental Army Melvill became famous for boisterous participation in the Boston Tea party. He also served during the fighting for independence in Rhode Island during the years 1777 and 1779. He also would be a great contributor to the Commonwealth of Massachusetts after the American Revolutionary War. In Boston he was a longtime member of the Boston Fire Department. He also served in the Massachusetts State Legislature and was one of the founders of the Massachusetts General Hospital.

On his maternal side his grandfather was General Peter Gansevoort. Gansevoort served as a Colonel in the Continental Army during the American Revolutionary War. He became famous for his gallantry during the Siege of Fort Stanwix in 1777. Fort Stanwix was part of the strategically important Hudson River Valley. For the British control of the Hudson River meant control of the Northeastern half of the American colonies.

The British detachment was commanded by General Barry St. Leger. Among his troops were British regulars, American Loyalists, Hessians and a group of Native Americans. St. Leger offered to Gansevoort a chance to surrender and the Colonel told him to go fuck himself. Colonel Gansevoort and his men would hold off the British until reinforcements could arrive and provide relief. That relief would come from none other than Major General Benedict Arnold. St. Leger, thinking he was outnumbered decided to retreat and live to fight another day.

For the British, not taking Fort Stanwix would lead directly their surrender at the Battle of Saratoga in October of 1777. Colonel Peter

Gansevoort and his men would be widely praised for his standing his ground. Ironically, one hundred and sixty seven years later a similar scene would take place during World War Two at the Battle of the Bulge. General Anthony McAuliffe, commanding the 101st Airborne Division would have to hold off the German Army until he could be relieved by General George S. Patton. McAuliffe was also offered the chance to surrender and responded with now famous reply "Nuts."

So the exploits of his grandfathers were a great source of pride for Herman Melville. He would take from their lives in his 1852 novel Pierre. In his twenties the young Melville would take to sea. He would even name his second son "Stanwix." He sailed on such vessels as the merchant ship St. Lawrence, the American whaler Acushnet, the Australian whaler Lucy Ann and the United States Navy frigate USS United States. His time aboard the Acushnet would greatly influence his writing in Moby Dick.

He disembarked the Acushnet in the Marquesas Islands and spent time with a native tribe called the Typee. All of these adventures would direct his story telling. He was not able to live financially off of his writings. His other 1850 works included White-Jacket, Isle of the Cross, The Encatadas, Benito Cereno, Israel Potter: His Fifty Years of Exile and The Confidence-Man: His Masquarade. Melville died in New York City at the age of seventy two years.

Victor Hugo would scribe three pieces of note in the 1850s. They would be Napoleon Le Petit, Les Chatiments and La Legende des Sicecles. He would become most famous for Les Miserables and The Hunchback of Notre Dame. Napoleon Le Petit in particular caused quite a stir as the writing was quite critical of Napoleon III. Hugo accuses Napoleon III of abuse of power and basically calls him a fucking liar through and through.

Leo Tolstoy would become known as one of the greatest novelist the world has ever known. Along with Henry David Thoreau his writings regarding civil disobedience and non-violent protest would have a profound on such luminaries such as Mohandas Gandhi and Dr. Martin Luther King Jr. His 1850s work includes Childhood, Brotherhood and Youth and the relatable Sevastopol Sketches. These were two stories written about his experiences during the Crimean War. He is best remembered for War and Peace and Anna Karenina. Tolstoy was a friend and admirer of Victor Hugo.

When it came to historical non-fiction, in the Nineteenth Century the king of the genre was Washington Irving. He was the David McCullough of his day. He is best known for The Sketch Book of Geoffrey Crayon, Gent. This was the book from which we get the short stories The Legend of Sleepy Hollow and Rip Van Winkle. In the 1850s he penned the five volume biography The Life of George Washington which he finished in 1859. Also in the 1850s he would write Wolfert's Roost and Mahomet and His Successors. Additionally he would author biographies on Christopher Columbus, Muhammad and the Moors. He also served as the United States Ambassador to Spain (1842-1846) during the time when John Tyler was President of the United States.

Although he would become most famous for The Three Musketeers and The Count of Monte Cristo, Alexandre Dumas would show the world his writing range in the 1850s with a series of novels, plays and non-fiction accounts of his many travels. These would include the novels The Black Tulip, The New Troy and The Wolf-Leader. His main play of the 1850s was an unpublished five-act play called The Gold Thieves. One of his travel pieces included Voyage to the Caucasus.

Alexandre Dumas was born in France to Haitian parents. He would become one of the most well known Black writers in the world during the 1800s. His mother was enslaved Black woman. His father was Thomas Alexandre Dumas. Alexandre Dumas' father was a Black man of high nobility. He would become one of the highest ranking Generals in the France's history. Not an easy feat. General Dumas had a key military role in the French Revolution.

Although General Dumas would fall out of favor with Napoleon Bonaparte a young Alexandre would retain all of the good parts of his father's military rank, reputation and nobility. With the restoration of the French monarchy Alexandre would eventually find work at the Royal Palace. Unlike many writers Dumas starting making money (enough to live off of) with his pen at an early age (his twenties). And although he attained great wealth he had quite the appetite for high living and pussy.

He traveled extensively and despite his "regal" status because of his father's exploits he was still considered a nigger when it was all said and done. One of Dumas' responses to a racist still lives on to this day. He is reported to have said "My father was a mulatto, my grandfather was a Negro, and my great grandfather a monkey. You see sir my family starts where yours ends." Alexandre Dumas died in 1870 at the age of sixty eight.

Three Blind Mice

A major playwright of the 1850s was Henrik Johan Ibsen. Ibsen would become known as the most significant playwright since William Shakespeare. Born in Norway he wrote all of his work in Danish which was common in many parts of Scandinavia. He would write, produce or direct over one hundred forty five plays during his lifetime. His most famous play was A Doll's House. A Doll's House is the controversial story about women and marriage in the Nineteenth Century. It would go on to become the most performed play in the world. In the 1850s his noted works included Catalina, The Burial Ground, Norma, Saint John's Eve, Lady Inger of Oestraat, The Feast of Solhaug, Olaf Liljekrans and The Vikings at Helgelan.

Henry David Thoreau would become famous with his publishing of Walden in 1854. The book was a retrospective about the simple life. In 1854 he would also write Slavery in Massachusetts. He would canonize abolitionist John Brown in 1859 with A Plea for Captain John Brown and Remarks After the Hanging of John Brown. In 1860 he would write The Last Days of John Brown.

Thoreau himself was an unabashed abolitionist also advocated civil disobedience. His writings would also greatly influence Leo Tolstoy, Mohandas Ghandi and Dr. Martin Luther King Jr. Thoreau was a transcendentalist and early in life befriended Ralph Waldo Emerson and Nathaniel Hawthorne. Later in life he would write extensively on ecology and environmental issues. He would die in 1862 from the effects of tuberculosis at the young age of forty four.

Ralph Waldo Emerson was a profound lecturer of the 1850s. He left his mark on literature by publishing many of his speeches as essays.

His most significant 1850 work was Representative Men. Representative Men was a book of essays that extolled the virtues of great men. These included Plato, Napoleon Bonaparte and William Shakespeare.

On Good Friday, 1865 Abraham Lincoln was assassinated by the actor John Wilkes Booth. The events of the day are well known and have left an indelible mark on the history of the United States. The story has been recounted in books, television and film. Lincoln was shot at Ford's Theatre in Washington, D.C. After his assassination the theatre was closed and went into a state of disrepair. Many years later it would be rebuilt and today it is both a museum and, to a nod that the show must go on, is once again open to theatrical performances. Located at Five Eleven Tenth Street in Washington, D.C. it is a quiet gem of the District's historical heritage.

The play the Lincolns had gone to see that night was called Our American Cousin. Our American Cousin was written by an Englishman named Tom Taylor. If Taylor never writes Our American Cousin and it never plays at Ford's Theatre does President Lincoln's assassination ever happen? What happens to the course of world history? What was Our American Cousin about and who was Tom Taylor?

As far as Lincoln going to see the play he went for the same reason people go to the theatre today. He went because it got good reviews and heard it was worth seeing. Our American Cousin is a play about an American who goes back to England to claim an estate left to him by relatives. Ultimately the play is about the humorous clash of the two cultures. It was first performed in New York City in 1858 at Laura Keene's Theatre. Keene was the female lead in the play. She was not only an actress, but a keen (pun intended) businesswoman as well. Keene was an

English woman born Mary Frances Moss and got her acting bug from her aunt, Elizabeth Yates.

She married a man named John Taylor. Taylor was real fucking loser who ended up getting arrested and imprisoned in Australia. He left her with nothing but two kids so she decided to change her name and get into acting. To have complete control over her career she decided she would take control over the whole process. She acted, produced, directed and managed.

As the play had done very well in New York, she thought the timing was perfect to take the show to Washington, D.C. This would be the main impetus for booking Ford's Theatre for April 14th, 1865. Keene also knew that if Lincoln attended she could sell the shit out of the play. The great thing was that good seats could be had for seventy five cents.

In Our American Cousin the main character of Asa Trenchard was originally played by an actor named Joseph Jefferson. Jefferson was a noted actor in the 1850s and made his fame portraying the stage version of Washington Irving's Rip Van Winkle. It was this role he was doing in Australia that precluded him from doing Our American Cousin in Washington, D.C. in April, 1865. He was replaced by an actor named Harry Hawk. John Wilkes Booth shot Lincoln as Hawk was alone on the stage delivering dialogue. Booth knew the play well two things came along with Hawks timing.

One was that Hawk was about to say the funniest line in the play and Booth knew that the line would get the loudest laughter from the audience therefore drowning out the sound of the gunshot. The other was that leaping onto the stage Booth knew he would only have to deal with one Good Samaritan if it came down to it on his way out of Ford's Theatre.

Another notable role in the play was Lord Dundreary. It was most prominently played by the British actor E.A. Sothern. Sothern was initially reluctant to play the role citing the part as too small. In talking to actor Joseph Jefferson, Jefferson would remind him that "there are no small parts, only small actors." That surely lit a thespian fire under Sothern's ass. Not only would he make the character famous, but three other plays would be created as spinoffs based on the Lord Dundreary character. The first was Lord Dundreary Abroad, the second was Dundreary Married and Done For and the third was Brother Sam, a play about Dundreary's brother.

In addition to Our American Cousin Tom Taylor also wrote over one hundred plays in his lifetime. Among his 1850s work included Masks and Faces, Plot and Passion, Still Waters Run Deep, Victims and The Contested Election.

William Makepeace Thackeray had an almost backward artist journey. While he lived, as a novelist he was second only to Charles Dickens in fame. In death he is today known best only for writing Vanity Fair. His most famous work of the 1850s was The History of Henry Esmond. Other works included Men's Wives, The Newcomers, The Virginians and The Rose and the Ring.

Charles Dickens was the genius of the literary world in the Nineteenth Century. His writings continue to be widely read. From a Tale of Two

Three Blind Mice

Cities to A Christmas Carol to The Haunted House to The Adventures of Oliver Twist his impact was widely felt in the writing world. Dickens would bring us characters like Ebenezer Scrooge, Oliver Twist and The Artful Dodger. He traveled extensively as well and his work reflected his travels. He visited America twice during his lifetime and became good friends with Washington Irving. He would die from a stroke in 1870.

Epilogue

In posing the question of what if the Civil War didn't have to happen it's important to take a wide view of the many aspects of life in the 1850s. In national politics the Executive Branch of the United States Government was not especially powerful. After the death of President Zachary Taylor the nation didn't know what to expect from Millard Fillmore. He was a man with good intentions but woefully inept for the Presidency.

The western part of the United States was still finding its legs and the question of slavery and what was to become of it was just beginning to rip the country apart. Americans moving west took the opportunity to shape the newest parts of American into everything their wanted, but didn't have when they lived on back east. The California Gold Rush exploded on the scene and the dreams of finding riches would elude many. Others would get rich from supplying resources for the dream seekers. They provided pick axes, shovels, hotels, brothels and saloons. These were the real benefactors of the Gold Rush.

In the legislature, the 1850s was dominated by the question of slavery and many of those answers would be found under the guise of Southern manipulation both politically and emotionally. The South was overrepresented in Congress as a result of three specific events. The Three-Fifths

Compromise established in the United States Constitution let Southern states count slaves as part of the population for purposes of representation in the United States House of Representatives.

The Fugitive Slave Law of 1850 was disastrous. With its passage slave owners now had the assistance of the United States Federal Government to help them not only catch runaways, but also steal free Blacks off the streets and psychologically scare the shit out of an entire population. The invention of Eli Whitney's cotton gin, on its own, increased cotton production in the Southern United States ten-fold and this in turn increased the need for slave labor.

This led to the election of more representatives to the United States House of Representatives than Southern States had "legal" citizens in reality. The unequal distribution of national power and greed led directly to the American Civil War. Pro slavery Congressmen on both sides of the aisle led the charge to keep a balance of slave states versus "free" states as new territories joined the Union. Fillmore was replaced by President Franklin Pierce who, frankly, was too consumed by personal demons to ever be an effective President. The mix of his alcoholism, the deaths of his three boys and his general indifference to the duties of his office led to a Presidential term filled with political stagnation.

He would be replaced by James Buchanan who had spent much of his political career in diplomatic service to the United States. Ironically it was the fact that his overseas service kept him from scandal that made him such an attractive candidate in the first place. Since the United States was hardly a superpower in those days his foreign policy experience meant little to the Presidency. Another caretaker President he simply hoped the nation's problems would just go away. As Southern voices to break away from the Union grew louder he did nothing. Yes, he protested but took no definitive action as Commander-in-Chief leaving his military leaders to twist in the wind.

As a result of the non-action of the Three Blind Mice the new Republican Party would not only be founded but take hold as a national political force and sweep Abraham Lincoln into the Presidency. Buchanan would leave the mess of fighting the Civil War to him and spend the rest of his post Presidency trying to convince people it wasn't his fault and he did all he could.

At a minimum for not dealing with the Secessionists, James Buchanan was guilty of the impeachable offense of high crimes and misdemeanors. At a maximum he was guilty of the only crime specifically mentioned in the United States Constitution, treason. And somewhere in between he could be accused of negligent manslaughter after the fact. No matter how anyone looks at Mr. Buchanan his lack of effective Presidential leadership lead to the death of hundreds of thousands of Americans. Americans killed during the Civil War represent more dead than all of the wars the United States has fought COMBINED.

In addition to slavery, domestically the United States was dominated by western expansion, Native American displacement, women's suffrage and a subtle underbelly of religious intolerance. America was a nation of Protestants political parties like the Know Nothings were, among other things, quite anti-Catholic and anti-Semitic. Many Americans feared the "Poperization" of the United States.

Darryl Murphy

Although Poperaizaton is exactly what has happened to the United States Supreme Court in Twentieth Century as the Chief Justice and five other Associate Justices on the Court are Roman Catholic. And some do argue that the current Pope Francis is a de facto "Capo di Tutti" or "Boss of all" of the United States Supreme Court. The Pope of the 1850s was Pope Pius IX. Unlike some of the scoundrels of the Fifteenth and Sixteenth Centuries by all accounts he was a good man and revered among the faithful. The Know Nothing Party played on this thought that giving power to Catholics meant giving power to the Pope. Anti Semitism was fueled by European attitudes towards Jews in the Nineteenth Century. The Germans were spouting that Aryan bullshit about racial superiority and blaming the Jews for society's ills way before Hitler came along.

Newly acquired lands as a result of the Mexican American War were finally made and set the boundaries of the United States from "sea to shining sea." Women would participate, but only in the shadows of men. Although 1850s America was largely a country run on marginalization many people thrived anyway. From the Gold Rushers to performers to artists to writers creativity strived throughout the decade.

P. T. Barnum made a killing with Jenny Lind who turned around and made a killing herself. Harriet Beecher Stowe unintentionally ended up writing a book whose sales had no equal in the Nineteenth Century. In the 1850s wars with Native American tribes would prove to be fertile training ground for the future Generals that would conduct the American Civil War. The United States Military Academy would show its relevancy while the United States Naval Academy was in its infancy.

Three Blind Mice

The railroads were laying track like crazy and financiers would see themselves get rich on non-union labor. In Alabama three brothers would start a consignment business that would trade standard goods for cotton instead of cash. It became so profitable they damn near cornered the cotton market in the South. They would eventually move to New York and help found the New York Cotton Exchange. Those siblings and company was named Lehman Brothers.

Levi Strauss would move to San Francisco in 1853 and begin to sell supplies to Forty Niners including a pair of denim pants then called "waist overalls." Today we know them as blue jeans and their still going strong. Joel Houghton would be granted the first patent for the dishwasher in 1850. Other inventions in the decade would be Issac Singer's sewing machine, Jean Foucault's gyroscope, Georges Audemar would invent rayon and Louis Pasteur would invent Pasteurization.

On the organized crime side, like Prohibition of the 1920s the Fugitive Slave Law would create the Reverse Underground Railroad. Like the Underground Railroad the process would work backward. Free Blacks would be kidnapped off the streets and sent to plantations to the South and forced into slavery. Solomon Northup would become the most famous case. Additionally, slaves would be stolen from one plantation and resold to other unsuspecting slave owners. A good ass beating would suffice to make the stolen slave keep his fucking mouth shut.

One of the most notorious of these criminals was John Hart Crenshaw. He was a landowner and slave trader based out of the state of Illinois. Although Illinois was a free state Crenshaw benefited from the

Fugitive Slave Act and later the Dred Scott decision, which declared that all Blacks were property (by declaring no Blacks were citizens) no matter where they were on American soil.

American in the 1850s loved the idea that "all men are created equal," but lived the reality of "some men were created equal." This very truth would relegate the three Presidents before Lincoln to historical used cat litter whose relevance would be reduced to the fact that somebody had to be President.

History provides many lessons and the 1850s left us with plenty on which to draw from. Thanks for reading.

Bibliography

"Andrew Jackson: The Petticoat Affair, Scandal in Jackson's White House", History Net, accessed August 4, 2009.

Widmer, Edward L. 2005. *Martin Van Buren*: The American Presidents Series, The 8th President, 1837–1841. Time Books. ISBN 978-0-7862-7612-7

William Meigs, *The life of John Caldwell Calhoun* (1917) p. 221

John C. Calhoun, 7th Vice President 1825–1832, *Senate.gov*

Abraham, Henry J. (1992). *Justices and Presidents: A Political History of Appointments to the Supreme Court* (3rd ed.). New York: Oxford University Press. ISBN 0-19-506557-3.

Cushman, Clare (2001). *The Supreme Court Justices: Illustrated Biographies, 1789–1995* (2nd ed.). (Supreme Court Historical Society, Congressional Quarterly Books). ISBN 1-56802-126-7.

Flanders, Henry (1874). *The Lives and Times of the Chief Justices of the United States Supreme Court*. Philadelphia: J. B. Lippincott & Co. (at Google Books)

Frank, John P. (1995). Friedman, Leon; Israel, Fred L., eds. *The Justices of the United States Supreme Court: Their Lives and Major Opinions*. Chelsea House Publishers. ISBN 0-7910-1377-4.

Hall, Kermit L., ed. (1992). *The Oxford Companion to the Supreme Court of the United States*. New York: Oxford University Press. ISBN 0-19-505835-6.

Huebner, Timothy S. (2003). *The Taney Court, Justice Rulings and Legacy*. Santa Barbara, Calif.: ABC-Clio. ISBN 1-57607-368-8.

———— (2010). "Roger Taney and the Slavery Issue: Looking Beyond—and Before—*Dred Scott*". *Journal of American History* **97**: 39–62.

Lewis, Walker (1965). *Without Fear or Favor: A Biography of Chief Justice Roger Brooke Taney*. Boston: Houghton Mifflin.

Martin, Fenton S.; Goehlert, Robert U. (1990). *The U.S. Supreme Court: A Bibliography*. Washington, D.C.: Congressional Quarterly Books. ISBN 0-87187-554-3. Cite uses deprecated parameters (help)

Simon, James F. (2006). *Lincoln and Chief Justice Taney: Slavery, Secession, and the President's War Powers* (Paperback ed.). New York: Simon & Schuster. ISBN 0-7432-9846-2.

Urofsky, Melvin I. (1994). *The Supreme Court Justices: A Biographical Dictionary*. New York: Garland Publishing. p. 590. ISBN 0-8153-1176-1.

Roger B. Taney at the *Biographical Directory of Federal Judges*, a public domain publication of the Federal Judicial Center.

Holt, Michael F. (2004). "Millard Fillmore". In Brinkley Alan; Dyer, Davis. *The American Presidency*. pp. 145–151. ISBN 9780618382736.

Van Deusen, Glyndon G. "Fillmore, Millard". Encyclopedia Americana. Retrieved 2007-05-09.

Overdyke, W. Darrell (1950). *The Know-Nothing Party in the South*. Baton Rouge: Louisiana State University Press. OCLC 1377033.

Rayback, Robert J. (1959). *Millard Fillmore: Biography of a President*. Buffalo, New York: Buffalo Historical Society. OCLC 370863.

Grayson, Benson Lee (1981). *The Unknown President: The Administration of Millard Fillmore*. Washington, D.C.: University Press of America. ISBN 9780819114570.

Baxter, Maurice G. *Henry Clay and the American System* (1995)

Baxter, Maurice G. *Henry Clay the Lawyer* (2000).

Bordewich, Fergus M. *America's Great Debate: Henry Clay, Stephen A. Douglas, and the Compromise That Preserved the Union* (2012) excerpt and text search, on Compromise of 1850

Bowman, Shearer Davis. "Comparing Henry Clay and Abraham Lincoln," *Register of the Kentucky Historical Society*, 106 (Summer–Autumn 2008), 495–512

Brown, Thomas. *Politics and Statesmanship: Essays on the American Whig Party* (1985) ch 5

Eaton, Clement. *Henry Clay and the Art of American Politics* (1957)

Gammon, Samuel R. *The Presidential Campaign of 1832* (1922) online free

Heidler, David S., and Jeanne T. Heidler. *Henry Clay: The Essential American* (2010), major scholarly biography; 624pp

Holt, Michael F. *The Rise and Fall of the American Whig Party: Jacksonian Politics and the Onset of the Civil War* (1999)

Knupfer, Peter B. "Compromise and Statesmanship: Henry Clay's Union." in Knupfer, *The Union As It Is: Constitutional Unionism and Sectional Compromise, 1787–1861* (1991), pp. 119–57.

Mayo, Bernard. *Henry Clay, Spokesman of the West* (1937)

Peterson, Merrill D. *The Great Triumvirate: Webster, Clay, and Calhoun* (1987)

Poage, George Rawlings. *Henry Clay and the Whig Party* (1936)

Remini, Robert. *Henry Clay: Statesman for the Union* (1991), a standard scholarly biography

Remini, Robert. *At the Edge of the Precipice: Henry Clay and the Compromise That Saved the Union* (2010) 184 pages; the Compromise of 1850

Schurz, Carl. *Life of Henry Clay*, 2 vols., 1899. Outdated biography.

Schurz, Carl (1911). "Clay, Henry". In Chisholm, Hugh. *Encyclopædia Britannica* (11th ed.). Cambridge University Press

Strahan, Randall. *Leading Representatives: The Agency of Leaders in the Politics of the U.S. House.* Johns Hopkins University Press, 2007

Strahan, Randall; Moscardelli, Vincent G.; Haspel, Moshe; and Wike, Richard S. "The Clay Speakership Revisited" *Polity* 2000 32(4): 561–593. ISSN 0032-3497

Van Deusen, Glyndon G. *The Life of Henry Clay* (1937), scholarly biography

Watson, Harry L. ed. *Andrew Jackson vs. Henry Clay: Democracy and Development in Antebellum America* (1998)

Zarefsky, David. "Henry Clay and the Election of 1844: the Limits of a Rhetoric of Compromise" *Rhetoric & Public Affairs* 2003 6(1): 79–96. ISSN 1094-8392

Campbell, Stanley W (1970). *The Slave Catchers: Enforcement of the Fugitive Slave Law, 1850-1860.* Chapel Hill: University of North Carolina Press.

Fehrenbacher, Don E. (February 8, 2001/December 19, 2002). *The Slaveholding Republic: An Account of the United States Government's Relations to Slavery.* Oxford University Press/NetLibrary, Incorporated. ISBN 9780198032472. Retrieved February 11, 2013. Check date values in: |date= (help)

Franklin, John Hope; Schweninger, Loren (1999). *Runaway Slaves: Rebels on the Plantation*. Oxford University Press.

"Fugitive Slave Law" (2008)

Nevins, Allan (1947/August 1992). *Ordeal of the Union: Fruits of Manifest Destiny, 1847–1852* **1**. Collier Books. ISBN 002035441X. Check date values in: | date= (help) ISBN 978-0020354413

Giles, Ted. *Patty Cannon: Woman of Mystery*. Easton, MD: Easton Publishing Company, 1965.

Cannon House PDF transcript of the Season 1, Episode 4 segment on History Detectives, broadcast by PBS. Accessed online August 29, 2007.

Shields, J. "The infamous Patty Cannon in history and legend." Dover, DE: Bibliotheca Literaria Press, 1990.

Frank, William P. Interview with genealogist George Valentine Massey, published in the *Wilmington News* of Delaware, September 2, 1960, quoted in *Patty Cannon: Woman of Mystery*, by Ted Giles, 1965.

The Domestic Slave Trade of the United States Winfield Hazlitt Collins, 1904, pp. 90-92. Accessed August 29, 2007.

Abraham, Henry J. (1992). *Justices and Presidents: A Political History of Appointments to the Supreme Court* (3rd ed.). New York: Oxford University Press. ISBN 0-19-506557-3.

Cushman, Clare (2001). *The Supreme Court Justices: Illustrated Biographies, 1789–1995* (2nd ed.). (Supreme Court Historical Society, Congressional Quarterly Books). ISBN 1-56802-126-7.

- Flanders, Henry. *The Lives and Times of the Chief Justices of the United States Supreme Court.* Philadelphia: J. B. Lippincott & Co., 1874 at Google Books.

Frank, John P. (1995). Friedman, Leon; Israel, Fred L., eds. *The Justices of the United States Supreme Court: Their Lives and Major Opinions.* Chelsea House Publishers. ISBN 0-7910-1377-4.

Hall, Kermit L., ed. (1992). *The Oxford Companion to the Supreme Court of the United States.* New York: Oxford University Press. ISBN 0-19-505835-6.

Huebner, Timothy S.; Renstrom, Peter; coeditor. (2003) *The Taney Court, Justice Rulings and Legacy.* City: ABC-Clio Inc.ISBN 1-57607-368-8.

Leach, Richard H. *Benjamin Robins Curtis, Judicial Misfit.* The New England Quarterly, Vol. 25, No. 4 (Dec., 1952), pp. 507-523 (article consists of 17 pages) Published by: The New England Quarterly, Inc.

Leach, Richard H. *Benjamin R. Curtis: Case Study of a Supreme Court Justice* (Ph.D. diss., Princeton University, 1951).

Lewis, Walker (1965). *Without Fear or Favor: A Biography of Chief Justice Roger Brooke Taney.* Boston: Houghton Mifflin.

Martin, Fenton S.; Goehlert, Robert U. (1990). *The U.S. Supreme Court: A Bibliography*. Washington, D.C.: Congressional Quarterly Books. ISBN 0-87187-554-3. Cite uses deprecated parameters (help)

Simon, James F. (2006) *Lincoln and Chief Justice Taney: Slavery, Secession, and the President's War Powers* (Paperback) New York: Simon & Schuster, 336 pages. ISBN 0-7432-9846-2.

Urofsky, Melvin I. (1994). *The Supreme Court Justices: A Biographical Dictionary*. New York: Garland Publishing. p. 590. ISBN 0-8153-1176-1.

Allen, Felicity. *Jefferson Davis, Unconquerable Heart*. St. Louis, Missouri: University of Missouri Press. 1999. ISBN 0-8262-1219-0.

Bergen, Anthony. (2010) "Pierce and the Consequences of Ambition" [1]

Boulard, Garry, "The Expatriation of Franklin Pierce—The Story of a President and the Civil War". (iUniverse, 2006)

Brinkley, A. and Dyer, D. *The American Presidency*. 2004. Houghton Mifflin Company.

DiConsiglio, John. Franklin Pierce. Vol. 14. New York: Children's Press-Scholastic, 2004. ISBN 0-516-24235-0

Gara, Larry, *The Presidency of Franklin Pierce* (1991), standard history of his administration

Nichols; Roy Franklin. *Franklin Pierce, Young Hickory of the Granite Hills* (1931), standard biography

Nichols; Roy Franklin.*The Democratic Machine, 1850–1854*. Columbia University Press, 1923. online version

Potter, David M, *The Impending Crisis, 1848–1861*. New York, New York: Harper & Row, 1976. ISBN 0-06-013403-8.

Taylor; Michael J.C. "Governing the Devil in Hell: 'Bleeding Kansas' and the Destruction of the Franklin Pierce Presidency (1854–1856)" *White House Studies*, Vol. 1, 2001, pp 185–205

Wallner, Peter A. (2004). *Franklin Pierce: New Hampshire's Favorite Son*. Concord, New Hampshire: Plaidswede. ISBN 0-9755216-1-6.

Wallner, Peter A. (2007). *Franklin Pierce: Martyr for the Union*. Concord, New Hampshire: Plaidswede. ISBN 978-0-9790784-2-2.

Arndt, Jochen S., "The True Napoleon of the West: General Winfield Scott's Mexico City Campaign and the Origins of the U.S. Army's Combined-Arms Combat Division," *Journal of Military History*, 76 (July 2012), 649–71.

Bell, William Gardner (2005). "Winfield Scott". *Commanding Generals and Chiefs of Staff: Portraits and Biographical Sketchs*. United States Army Center of Military History. pp. 78–79.

Eisenhower, John S.D., *Agent of Destiny: The Life and Times of General Winfield Scott*, University of Oklahoma Press, 1999, ISBN 0-8061-3128-4.

Elliott, Charles Winslow, *Winfield Scott: The Soldier and the Man*, 1937.

Forney, John Wien (1880). *The Life and Military Career of Winfield Scott Hancock*. New York: United States Book Company. Retrieved July 6, 2009.

Johnson, Timothy D., *Winfield Scott: The Quest for Military Glory*, University Press of Kansas, 1998, ISBN 0-7006-0914-8, a standard scholarly biography

Mansfield, Edward Deering (1847). *Illustrated life of General Winfield Scott; illustrated by D.H. Strother*. New York: A.S. Barnes & Co.

Peskin, Allan, *Winfield Scott and the Profession of Arms*, 2003, a standard scholarly biography

William DeGregorio, *The Complete Book of U.S. Presidents*, Gramercy 1997

Biography of Franklin Pierce

Holt, Michael F. *The Rise and Fall of the American Whig Party: Jacksonian Politics and the Onset of the Civil War.* Oxford University Press, New York, New York: 1999.

"A Historical Analysis of the Electoral College". *The Green Papers.* Retrieved September 17, 2005.

Bemis, Samuel Flagg (1965). *A Diplomatic History of the United States.* New York: Henry Holt and Company. OCLC 1310959.

Brown, Charles Henry (1980). *Agents of Manifest Destiny: The Lives and Times of the Filibusters.* Chapel Hill: University of North Carolina Press. ISBN 0-8078-1361-3.

Hershey, Amos S (May 1896). "The Recognition of Cuban Belligerency". *Annals of the American Academy of Political and Social Science* **7**: 74–85.

Henderson, Gavin B. (August 1939). "Southern Designs on Cuba, 1854–1857 and Some European Opinions". *The Journal of Southern History* **5** (3): 371–385.

May, Robert E. (1973). *The Southern Dream of a Caribbean Empire, 1854-1861.* Baton Rouge: Louisiana State University Press. ISBN 0-8071-0051-X.

Moore, J. Preston (May 1955). "Pierre Soule: Southern Expansionist and Promoter". *The Journal of Southern History* **21** (2): 203–223.

Potter, David M. (1996). *The Impending Crisis 1848–1861.* New York: Harper & Row. ISBN 0-06-131929-5.

Rhodes, James Ford (1893). *History of the United States from the Compromise of 1850, Vol. II: 1854–1860.* New York: Harper & Bros. OCLC 272963.

Schoultz, Lars (1998). *Beneath the United States: A History of U.S. Policy Toward Latin America.* Cambridge, MA: Harvard University Press. pp. 39–58. ISBN 978-0-674-04328-2. Retrieved 5 December 2013.

Smith, Peter H. (April 1996). *Talons of the Eagle: Dynamics of U.S. - Latin American Relations* (2nd ed.). Oxford University Press, USA. p. 392. ISBN 0-19-508303-2

Connell, Thomas. (2002). America's Japanese Hostages: The US Plan For A Japanese Free Hemisphere. [9] Westport: Praeger-Greenwood. ISBN 9780275975357; OCLC 606835431

Conn, Stetson (2000 (reissue from 1960)). "5. The Decision to Evacuate the Japanese from the Pacific Coast". In Kent Roberts Greenfield. *Command Decisions.* United States Army Center of Military History. CMH Pub 70-7. Check date values in: | date= (help)

De Nevers, Klancy Clark. *The Colonel and the Pacifist: Karl Bendetsen, Perry Saito, and the Incarceration of Japanese Americans during World War II.* Salt Lake City: University of Utah Press, 2004. ISBN 978-0-87480-789-9

Drinnon, Richard. *Keeper of Concentration Camps: Dillon S. Meyer and American Racism.* Berkeley: University of California Press, 1989.

Gardiner, Clinton Harvey. (1981). *Pawns in a Triangle of Hate: The Peruvian Japanese and the United States.* Seattle: University of Washington Press. 10-ISBN 0-295-95855-3; ISBN 978-0-295-95855-2

Harth, Erica. (2001). *Last Witnesses: Reflections on the Wartime Internment of Japanese Americans.* Palgrave, New York. ISBN 0-312-22199-1.

Higashide, Seiichi. (2000). *Adios to Tears: The Memoirs of a Japanese-Peruvian Internee in U.S. Concentration Camps.* Seattle: University of Washington Press. 10-ISBN 0-295-97914-3; 13-ISBN 978-0-295-97914-4

Hirabayashi, Lane Ryo. *The Politics of Fieldwork: Research in an American Concentration Camp.* Tucson: The University of Arizona Press, 1999.

Gordon, Linda and Gary Y. Okihiro (eds.), *Impounded: Dorothea Lange and the Censored Images of Japanese American Internment.* New York: W.W. Norton, 2006.

Lyon, Cherstin M. *Prisons and Patriots: Japanese American Wartime Citizenship, Civil Disobedience, and Historical Memory.* Philadelphia: Temple University Press, 2012.

Mackey, Mackey, ed. *Remembering Heart Mountain: Essays on Japanese American Internment in Wyoming.* Wyoming: Western History Publications, 1998.

Miyakawa, Edward T. *Tule Lake.* Trafford Publishing, 2006. ISBN 1-55369-844-4

Robinson, Greg. *By Order of the President: FDR and the Internment of Japanese Americans*. Cambridge and others: Harvard University Press, 2001.

Robinson, Greg (2009). *A Tragedy of Democracy: Japanese Confinement in North America*. Columbia University Press. ISBN 978-0-231-12922-0.

Weglyn, Michi. (1976, 1996). *Years Of Infamy: The Untold Story Of America's Concentration Camps*. University of Washington Press. ISBN 0-295-97484-2. Check date values in: | date= (help)

Civil Liberties Public Education Fund. (1997). *Personal Justice Denied: Report of the Commission on Wartime Relocation and Internment of Civilians*. Civil Liberties Public Education Fund and University of Washington Press. ISBN 0-295-97558-X.

Elleman, Bruce (2006). *Japanese-American civilian prisoner exchanges and detention camps, 1941–45*. Routledge. p. 179. ISBN 978-0-415-33188-3. Retrieved 14 September 2009.

Caldwell, J. G; E. V. Price, et al. (1973). "Aortic regurgitation in the Tuskegee study of untreated syphilis". *J Chronic Dis* **26** (3): 187–94. doi:10.1016/0021-9681(73)90089-1. PMID 4695031. Cite uses deprecated parameters (help)

Hiltner, S. (1973). "The Tuskegee Syphilis Study under review". *Christ Century* **90** (43): 1174–6. PMID 11662609.

Kampmeier, R. H. (1972). "The Tuskegee study of untreated syphilis". *South Med J* **65** (10): 1247–51. PMID 5074095.

Kampmeier, R. H. (1974). "Final report on the "Tuskegee syphilis study". *South Med J* **67** (11): 1349–53. PMID 4610772.

Olansky, S.; L. Simpson, et al. (1954). "Environmental factors in the Tuskegee study of untreated syphilis". *Public Health Rep* **69** (7): 691–8. PMC 2024316. PMID 13177831. Cite uses deprecated parameters (help)

Rockwell, D. H.; A. R. Yobs, et al. (1964). "The Tuskegee Study of Untreated Syphilis; the 30th Year of Observation". *Arch Intern Med* **114**: 792–8. PMID 14211593. Cite uses deprecated parameters (help)

Schuman, S. H.; S. Olansky, et al. (1955). "Untreated syphilis in the male negro; background and current status of patients in the Tuskegee study.". *J Chronic Dis* **2** (5): 543–58. doi:10.1016/0021-9681(55)90153-3. PMID 13263393

Gjestland T (1955). "The Oslo study of untreated syphilis: an epidemiologic investigation of the natural course of the syphilitic infection based upon a re-study of the Boeck-Bruusgaard material". *Acta Derm Venereol* **35** (Suppl 34): 3–368.

Gray, Fred D. (1998). *The Tuskegee Syphilis Study: The Real Story and Beyond*. Montgomery, Alabama: NewSouth Books.

Jones, James H. (1981). *Bad Blood: The Tuskegee Syphilis Experiment*. New York: Free Press.

The Deadly Deception, by Denisce DiAnni, PBS/WGBH NOVA documentary video, 1993.

Reverby, Susan M. (1998). "History of an Apology: From Tuskegee to the White House". *Research Nurse*.

Reverby, Susan M. (2000). *Tuskegee's Truths: Rethinking the Tuskegee Syphilis Study*. University of North Carolina Press.

Reverby, Susan M. (2009). *Examining Tuskegee: The Infamous Syphilis Study and its Legacy*. University of North Carolina Press.

Jean Heller (Associated Press), "Syphilis Victims in the U.S. Study Went Untreated for 40 Years" *New York Times*, July 26, 1972: 1, 8.

Thomas, Stephen B; Sandra Crouse Quinn (1991). "The Tuskegee Syphilis Study, 1932–1972: Implications for HIV Education and AIDS Risk Programs in the Black Community". *American Journal of Public Health* **81** (1503). doi:10.2105/AJPH.81.11.1498. PMC 1405662. PMID 1951814. Cite uses deprecated parameters (help)

Carlson, Elof Axel (2006). *Times of triumph, times of doubt: science and the battle for the public trust*. Cold Spring Harbor Press. ISBN 0-87969-805-5.

Washington, Harriet A. (2007). *Medical Apartheid: The Dark History of Medical Experimentation on Black Americans From Colonial Times to the Present*.

Baker, Jean H. (2004). *James Buchanan*. New York: Times Books. ISBN 0-8050-6946-1. excerpt and text search

Curtis, George Ticknor (1883). *Life of James Buchanan*. Harper & Brothers. Retrieved 2009-04-15.

Klein, Philip S. (1962). *President James Buchanan: A Biography* (1995 ed.). Newtown, Connecticut: American Political Biography Press. ISBN 0-945707-11-8.

Nevins, Allan (1950). *The Emergence of Lincoln: Douglas, Buchanan, and Party Chaos, 1857–1859*. New York: Scribner. ISBN 9780684104157.

Potter, David M. (1976). *The Impending Crisis, 1848–1861*. New York: Harper & Row. ISBN 9780060905248.

Rhodes, James Ford (1906). *History of the United States from the Compromise of 1850 to the End of the Roosevelt Administration* **2**. Macmillan.

Stampp, Kenneth M. (1990). *America in 1857: A Nation on the Brink*. New York: Oxford University Press. ISBN 9780195074819.

Binder, Frederick Moore. "James Buchanan: Jacksonian Expansionist" *Historian* 1992 55(1): 69–84. ISSN 0018-2370 Full text: in Ebsco

Binder, Frederick Moore. *James Buchanan and the American Empire.* Susquehanna U. Press, 1994. 318 pp.

Birkner, Michael J., ed. *James Buchanan and the Political Crisis of the 1850s.* Susquehanna U. Press, 1996. 215 pp.

George Ticknor Curtis (1883). *Life of James Buchanan: Fifteenth President of the United States.* Harper & Brothers. vol 2 online

Meerse, David. "Buchanan, the Patronage, and the Lecompton Constitution: a Case Study" *Civil War History* 1995 41(4): 291–312. ISSN 0009-8078

Nevins, Allan. *The Emergence of Lincoln* 2 vols. (1960) highly detailed narrative of his presidency

Nichols, Roy Franklin; *The Democratic Machine, 1850–1854* (1923), detailed narrative; online

Potter, David Morris. *The Impending Crisis, 1848–1861* (1976). ISBN 0-06-013403-8 Pulitzer prize.

Rhodes, James Ford *History of the United States from the Compromise of 1850 to the McKinley-Bryan Campaign of 1896* vol 2. (1892)

Smith, Elbert B. *The Presidency of James Buchanan* (1975). ISBN 0-7006-0132-5, standard history of his administration

Updike, John *Buchanan Dying: A Play* (1974). ISBN 0-394-49042-8, ISBN 0-8117-0238-3, containing an 80-page historical "Afterword" that discusses sources, etc.

Robert Watson, *Affairs of State: The untold story of presidential love sex and scandal, 1789-1900*, Plymouth, 2012

Barney, William L. "Brown, John." *The Civil War and Reconstruction: A Student Companion*. New York: Oxford University Press, Inc., 2001.

Chowder, Ken "The Father of American Terrorism." *American Heritage* (2000) 51(1): pp. 81+; online version

DeCaro, Louis A. Jr. *"Fire from the Midst of You": A Religious Life of John Brown* (2002)

Du Bois, W. E. B. *John Brown* (ISBN 0-679-78353-9) (1909).

Finkelman, Paul, ed. *His Soul Goes Marching On: Responses to John Brown and the Harpers Ferry Raid* (1995)

Furnas, J. C. *The Road to Harpers Ferry*. New York, William Sloane Associates, 1959

Goodrich, Thomas *War to the Knife: Bleeding Kansas, 1854–1861* (1998).

Horwitz, Tony. *Midnight Rising: John Brown and the Raid That Sparked the Civil War*. New York: Henry Holt & Co., 2011.

Hotchkiss, Jed. "John Brown's Raid." The Confederate Military History. Oct. 27, 2009. John Brown's Raid

Long, Roderick (2008). "Brown, John (1800–1859)". In Hamowy, Ronald. *The Encyclopedia of Libertarianism*. Thousand Oaks, CA: SAGE; Cato Institute. pp. 39–40. ISBN 978-1-4129-6580-4. LCCN 2008009151. OCLC 750831024.

Malin, James. *John Brown & the Legend of Fifty-Six* (1942), the most influential scholarly attack on Brown (ISBN 0-8383-1021-4)

McGlone, Robert E. *John Brown's War against Slavery*. Cambridge, CUP, 2009.

Nevins, Allan. *Ordeal of the Union*. 2 vols. (1947), in depth scholarly history.

Nichols, Roy F. "The Kansas-Nebraska Act: A Century of Historiography." *Mississippi Valley Historical Review* 43 (September 1956): 187–212. in JSTOR

Nudelman, Franny, *John Brown's Body: Slavery, Violence, and the Culture of War* (2004).

Oates, Stephen B. *To Purge This Land With Blood: A Biography of John Brown* (1970).

Oates, Stephen B. *Our Fiery Trial: Abraham Lincoln, John Brown, and the Civil War Era (1979)*

Peterson, Merrill D. (2002): *John Brown: The Legend Revisited* (ISBN 0-8139-2132-5), how history has treated Brown

Potter, David M. *The Impending Crisis, 1848–1861* (1976), Pulitzer prize; scholarly national history

Renehan, Edward J. *The Secret Six: The True Tale of the Men Who Conspired with John Brown.* 1995.

Reynolds, David S. (2005): *John Brown, Abolitionist: The Man Who Killed Slavery, Sparked the Civil War, and Seeded Civil Rights* (2005)[secondary sources 1]

Rodriguez, Junius P., ed. *Encyclopedia of Slave Resistance and Rebellion.* Westport, CT: Greenwood, 2006.

Scott, Otto, *The Secret Six: John Brown and The Abolitionist Movement* (1979).

SenGupta, Gunja. "Bleeding Kansas: A Review Essay." *Kansas History* 24 (Winter 2001/2002): 318–341.

Villard, Oswald Garrison, *John Brown 1800–1859: A Biography Fifty Years After* (1910). full text online

Martis, Kenneth C. (1989). *The Historical Atlas of Political Parties in the United States Congress.* New York: Macmillan Publishing Company.

Martis, Kenneth C. (1982). *The Historical Atlas of United States Congressional Districts.* New York: Macmillan Publishing Company.

Garber, Paul Neff. *The Gadsden Treaty* (1923) 222 pp; the standard diplomatic history

Kluger, Richard. *Seizing Destiny: How America Grew From Sea to Shining Sea.* (2007) ISBN 978-0-375-41341-4.

Nevins, Allan. *Ordeal of the Union: A House Dividing 1852-1857.* (1947) SBN 684-10424-5.

Nichols, Roy Franklin. *Franklin Pierce: Young Hickory of the Granite Hills.* (1969 2nd. Edition) 8122-7044-4.

Richards, *The California Gold Rush and the Coming of the Civil War.* (2007) ISBN 0-307-26520-X.

Roberson, Jere W. "The South and the Pacific Railroad, 1845-1855". *The Western Historical Quarterly*, Vol. 5, No. 2, (Apr. 1974), pp. 163–186. JSTOR.

Terrazas, Marcela. "The Regional Conflict, the Contractors, and the Construction Projects of a Road to the Pacific at the End of the War Between Mexico and the United States". *Journal of Popular Culture* 2001 35(2): 161-169. Issn: 0022-3840 Fulltext: Ebsco, stresses railroad speculation and corruption themes

Truett, Samuel. "The Ghosts of Frontiers Past: Making and Unmaking Space in the Borderlands". *Journal of the Southwest*. Volume: 46. Issue: 2. 2004. pp: 309+.

Chambers, William Nisbet. *Old Bullion Benton: Senator From the New West* (1956)

Childers, Christopher. "Interpreting Popular Sovereignty: A Historiographical Essay", *Civil War History* Volume 57, Number 1, March 2011 pp. 48–70 in Project MUSE

Etcheson, Nicole. *Bleeding Kansas: Contested Liberty in the Civil War Era* (2006)

Foner, Eric. *Free Soil, Free Labor, Free Men: The Ideology of the Republican Party Before the Civil War.* (1970) ISBN 0-19-509497-2

Freehling, William W. *The Road to Disunion: Secessionists at Bay 1776–1854.* (1990) ISBN 0-19-505814-3

Holt, Michael. *The Political Crisis of the 1850s* (1978)

Huston, James L. *Stephen A. Douglas and the dilemmas of democratic equality* (2007)

Johannsen. Robert W. *Stephen A. Douglas* (1973) ISBN 0-19-501620-3

Morrison, Michael. *Slavery and the American West: The Eclipse of Manifest Destiny and the Coming of the Civil War* (1997) online edition

Nevins, Allan. *Ordeal of the Union: A House Dividing 1852–1857.* (1947) SBN 684-10424-5

Nichols, Roy F. "The Kansas-Nebraska Act: A Century of Historiography." *Mississippi Valley Historical Review* 43 (September 1956): 187–212. Online at JSTOR

Potter, David M. *The Impending Crisis, 1848–1861* (1976), Pulitzer prize winning scholarly history.

SenGupta, Gunja. "Bleeding Kansas: A Review Essay." *Kansas History* 24 (Winter 2001/2002): 318–341. online

Wolff, Gerald W., *The Kansas-Nebraska Bill: Party, Section, and the Coming of the Civil War,* (Revisionist Press, 1977), 385 pp.

Bartlett, Irving H. *Daniel Webster* (1978) online edition

Baxter, Maurice G. "Webster, Daniel"; *American National Biography Online* Feb. 2000. online edition at academic libraries

Baxter, Maurice G. *One and Inseparable: Daniel Webster and the Union.* (1984).

Current, Richard Nelson. *Daniel Webster and the Rise of National Conservatism* (1955), short biography

Curtis, George Ticknor. *Life of Daniel Webster* (1870), useful for quotations online edition vol 1; online edition vol 2

Fuess, Claude M. *Daniel Webster.* (2 vols. 1930). scholarly biography

Ogg, Frederic Austin. *Daniel Webster* (1914) online edition, old scholarly biography

Peterson, Merrill D. *The Great Triumvirate: Webster, Clay, and Calhoun* (1983)

Remini, Robert V. *Daniel Webster* (1997), 796pp; the standard scholarly biography and the most important place to start excerpt and text search

Allen, William B. (1872). *A History of Kentucky: Embracing Gleanings, Reminiscences, Antiquities, Natural Curiosities, Statistics, and Biographical Sketches of Pioneers, Soldiers, Jurists, Lawyers, Statesmen, Divines, Mechanics, Farmers, Merchants, and Other Leading Men, of All Occupations and Pursuits*. Louisville, Kentucky: Bradley & Gilbert.

Bradley, George C.; Richard L. Dahlen (2006). *From Conciliation to Conquest: The Sack of Athens and the Court-Martial of Colonel John B. Turchin*. Tuscaloosa, Alabama: University of Alabama Press. ISBN 0-8173-1526-8. Cite uses deprecated parameters (help)

Coleman, Mrs. Chapman (1873). *The Life of John J. Crittenden: With Selections from His Correspondence and Speeches* **I**. Philadelphia, Pennsylvania: J. B. Lippincott & Co.

"Crittenden, John Jordan". *Biographical Directory of the United States Congress*. United States Congress. Retrieved 2010-01-14.

Coulter, Ellis Merton (1937). "John Jordan Crittenden". *Dictionary of American Biography*. New York City, New York: Charles Scribner's Sons.

Finkelman, Paul (2000). "Crittenden, John J. (1787–1863)". In Leonard W. Levy and Kenneth L. Karst. *Encyclopedia of the American Constitution*. New York City, New York: Macmillan Reference USA.

Harrison, Lowell H.; Frank F. Mathias (1992). "Crittenden, John Jordan". In Kleber, John E. *The Kentucky Encyclopedia*. Associate editors: Thomas D. Clark, Lowell H. Harrison, and James C. Klotter. Lexington, Kentucky: The University Press of Kentucky. ISBN 0-8131-1772-0. Cite uses deprecated parameters (help)

Hatter, Russell; Gene Burch (2003). *A Walking Tour of Historic Frankfort*. Frankfort, Kentucky: Gene Burch. ISBN 0-9637008-3-9. Cite uses deprecated parameters (help)

Howard, Victor B. (2004). "John Jordan Crittenden". In Lowell Hayes Harrison. *Kentucky's Governors*. Lexington, Kentucky: The University Press of Kentucky. ISBN 0-8131-2326-7.

"John Jordan Crittenden". *American Law Encyclopedia* **3**. Net Industries. Retrieved 2011-01-13.

Jones, Terry L. (2002). *Historical Dictionary of the Civil War: A-L*. Lanham, Maryland: Scarecrow Press. ISBN 0-8108-4112-6.

"Kentucky Governor John Jordan Crittenden". National Governors Association. Retrieved 2012-03-30.

Kirwan, Albert Dennis (1974). *John J. Crittenden: The Struggle for the Union*. Lexington, Kentucky: University Press of Kentucky. ISBN 0-8371-6922-4.

Levin, H. (1897). *Lawyers and Lawmakers of Kentucky*. Chicago, Illinois: Lewis Publishing Company.

Ragan, Allen E. (January 1944). "John J. Crittenden, 1787–1863". *Filson Club Historical Quarterly* **18** (1): 3–28. Retrieved 2011-12-06.

Rennick, Robert M. (1988). *Kentucky Place Names*. Lexington, Kentucky: University Press of Kentucky. ISBN 0-8131-0179-4.

Taylor, Jeremiah R. (Summer 2000). "A Leaf Upon a Torrent: John Jordan Crittenden's 1828 Nomination to the Supreme Court as a Study in Political Determinism". *The Upsilonian* **12**. Archived from the original on 2010-12-27. Retrieved 2011-01-13.

Allen, Felicity (1999). *Jefferson Davis: Unconquerable Heart*. Columbia: The University of Missouri Press. ISBN 9780826212191.

Ballard, Michael B. (1986). *A Long Shadow: Jefferson Davis and the Final Days of the Confederacy*. Jackson: University Press of Mississippi. ISBN 9780820319414.

Collins, Donald E. (2005). *The Death and Resurrection of Jefferson Davis*. Lanham, MD: Rowman & Littlefield Publishers. ISBN 9780742543041.

Cooper, William J. (2000). *Jefferson Davis, American*. New York: Alfred A. Knopf. ISBN 9780307772640.

Cooper, William J. (2008). *Jefferson Davis and the Civil War Era*. Baton Rouge: Louisiana State University Press. ISBN 9780807153116.

Current, Richard, *et al.* (1993). *Encyclopedia of the Confederacy*. New York: Simon & Schuster.

Coulter, Ellis Merton (1950). *The Confederate States of America, 1861–1865, Volume 7*. Baton Rouge: Louisiana State University Press. ISBN 9780807100073.

Davis, William C. (1996). *Jefferson Davis: The Man and His Hour*. Louisiana State University Press. ISBN 9780807120798.

Dodd, William E. (1907). *Jefferson Davis*. Philadelphia: George W. Jacobs and Company.

Eaton, Clement (1977). *Jefferson Davis*. New York: The Free Press.

Escott, Paul (1978). *After Secession: Jefferson Davis and the Failure of Confederate Nationalism*. Baton Rouge: Louisiana State University Press. ISBN 9780807118078.

Hattaway, Herman and Beringer, Richard E. (2002). *Jefferson Davis, Confederate President*. Lawrence: University Press of Kansas. ISBN 9780700611706.

McPherson, James M. (1989). *Battle Cry of Freedom: The Civil War Era*. New York: Bantam Books. ISBN 9780195038637.

Neely Jr., Mark E. (1993). *Confederate Bastille: Jefferson Davis and Civil Liberties*. Milwaukee: Marquette University Press. ISBN 9780874623253.

Patrick, Rembert W. (1944). *Jefferson Davis and His Cabinet*. Baton Rouge: Louisiana State University Press.

Rable, George C. (1994). *The Confederate Republic: A Revolution against Politics*. Chapel Hill: University of North Carolina Press. ISBN 9780807863961.

Stoker, Donald, "There Was No Offensive-Defensive Confederate Strategy," *Journal of Military History*, 73 (April 2009), 571–90.

Strode, Hudson (1955). *Jefferson Davis, Volume I: American Patriot*. New York: Harcourt, Brace & Company.

Strode, Hudson (1959). *Jefferson Davis, Volume II: Confederate President*. New York: Harcourt, Brace & Company.

Strode, Hudson (1964). *Jefferson Davis, Volume III: Tragic Hero*. New York: Harcourt, Brace & Company.

Swanson, James L. (2010). *Bloody Crimes: The Chase for Jefferson Davis and the Death Pageant for Lincoln's Corpse*. New York: HarperCollins. ISBN 9780061233791.

Thomas, Emory M. (1979). *The Confederate Nation, 1861–1865*. New York: Harper & Row. ISBN 9780062069467.

Woodworth, Steven E. (1990). *Jefferson Davis and His Generals: The Failure of Confederate Command in the West*. Lawrence: University Press of Kansas. ISBN 9780700604616.

Cashin, Joan (2006). *First Lady of the Confederacy: Varina Davis's Civil War*, Cambridge, MA: Belknap Press of Harvard University Press.

Strode, Hudson (1955). *Jefferson Davis, Volume I: American Patriot*. New York: Harcourt, Brace & Company.

Strode, Hudson (1964). *Jefferson Davis, Volume III: Tragic Hero*. New York: Harcourt, Brace & Company.

Wyatt-Brown, Bertram (1994). *The House of Percy: Honor, Melancholy and Imagination in a Southern Family*, New York: Oxford University Press.

Eicher, John H., and Eicher, David J., *Civil War High Commands*, Stanford University Press, 2001, ISBN 0-8047-3641-3.

Union Pacific Railroad, *UP - History of the UP logo*. Retrieved June 8, 2005. Timeline that also includes UP presidency successions.

Warner, Ezra J., *Generals in Blue: Lives of the Union Commanders*, Louisiana State University Press, 1964, ISBN 0-8071-0822-7.

Lewis Cass at the *Biographical Directory of the United States Congress*

Klunder, Willard Carl. "Lewis Cass, Stephen Douglas, and Popular Sovereignty: The Demise of Democratic Party Unity," in *Politics and Culture of the Civil War Era* ed by Daniel J. McDonough and Kenneth W. Noe, (2006) pp. 129–53

Silbey, Joel H. *Party Over Section: The Rough and Ready Presidential Election of 1848* (2009), 205 pp.

Bell, William Gardner (1992). "Lewis Cass". *Secretaries of War and Secretaries of the Army*. United States Army Center of Military History. CMH pub 70-12.

Baker, Jean H. *Sisters: The Lives of America's Suffragists*. Hill and Wang, New York, 2005. ISBN 0-8090-9528-9.

Dubois, Ellen Carol. *Feminism and Suffrage: The Emergence of an Independent Women's Movement in America, 1848–1869* (1999)

Hemming, Heidi, and Julie Hemming Savage, *Women Making America*. Clotho Press, 2009. ISBN 978-0-9821271-7-7

Kraditor, Aileen S. *The Ideas of the Woman Suffrage Movement: 1890–1920* (1965) excerpt and text search

Mead, Rebecca J. *How the Vote Was Won: Woman Suffrage in the Western United States, 1868–1914* (NYU Press, 2006)

Ward, Geoffrey C. *Not Ourselves Alone: the story of Elizabeth Cady Stanton and Susan B. Anthony* (1999),

Wellman, Judith. *The Road to Seneca Falls*, University of Illinois Press, 2004. ISBN 0-252-02904-6

Blackwell, Alice Stone. *Lucy Stone: Pioneer of Woman's Rights*. Charlottesville and London: University Press of Virginia, 2001. ISBN 0-8139-1990-8

Hays, Elinor Rice. *Morning Star: A Biography of Lucy Stone 1818–1893*. Harcourt, Brace & World, 1961. ISBN 0-347-93756-7

Kerr, Andrea Moore. *Lucy Stone: Speaking Out for Equality*. New Jersey: Rutgers University Press, 1992. ISBN 0-8135-1860-1

Burns, Ken and Geoffrey C. Ward; *Not for Ourselves Alone: The Story of Elizabeth Cady Stanton and Susan B. Anthony;* Alfred A. Knoph; New York, NY, 1999. ISBN 0-375-40560-7.

Dubois, Ellen Carol. *Feminism & Suffrage: The Emergence of an Independent Women's Movement in America, 1848–1869*. Cornell University Press; Ithaca, NY, 1999. ISBN 0-8014-8641-6.

Dubois, Ellen Carol and Candida-Smith, Richard editors. "Elizabeth Cady Stanton, Feminist as Thinker. *New York University Press; New York, NY, 2007. ISBN*

Griffith, Elisabeth. *In Her Own Right: The Life of Elizabeth Cady Stanton*. Oxford University Press; New York, NY, 1985. ISBN 0-19-503729-4.

Three Blind Mice

"Stampede of Slaves: A Tale of Horror" *The Cincinnati Enquirer*, January 29, 1856.

Weisenburger, Steven. *Modern Medea: A Family Story of Slavery and Child Murder from the Old South* (New York: Hill and Wang), 1998. ISBN 0-8090-6953-9

Harper, Ida Husted (1898–1908). *The Life and Work of Susan B. Anthony* in three volumes. Indianapolis: Hollenbeck Press. Harper's biography was commissioned by and written with the assistance of Susan B. Anthony. The complete text is available on the web:

Volume I: Internet Archive and Project Gutenberg

Volume 2: Internet Archive, Google Books and Project Gutenberg

Volume 3: Internet Archive and Google Books

Gordon, Ann D.(1997). *The Selected Papers of Elizabeth Cady Stanton and Susan B. Anthony: In the School of Anti-Slavery, 1840 to 1866*. Vol. 1 of 6. New Brunswick, NJ: Rutgers University Press. ISBN 0-8135-2317-6.

Gordon, Ann D.(2000). *The Selected Papers of Elizabeth Cady Stanton and Susan B. Anthony: Against an aristocracy of sex, 1866 to 1873*. Vol. 2 of 6. New Brunswick, NJ: Rutgers University Press. ISBN 0-8135-2318-4.

Gordon, Ann D.(2003). *The Selected Papers of Elizabeth Cady Stanton and Susan B. Anthony: National protection for national citizens, 1873 to 1880*.

Vol. 3 of 6. New Brunswick, NJ: Rutgers University Press. ISBN 0-8135-2319-2.

Gordon, Ann D.(2006). *The Selected Papers of Elizabeth Cady Stanton and Susan B. Anthony: When clowns make laws for queens, 1880-1887*. Vol. 4 of 6. New Brunswick, NJ: Rutgers University Press. ISBN 0-8135-2320-6.

Gordon, Ann D.(2009). *The Selected Papers of Elizabeth Cady Stanton and Susan B. Anthony: Place Inside the Body-Politic, 1887 to 1895*. Vol. 5 of 6. New Brunswick, NJ: Rutgers University Press. ISBN 0-8135-2321-7.

Gordon, Ann D.(2013). *The Selected Papers of Elizabeth Cady Stanton and Susan B. Anthony: An Awful Hush, 1895 to 1906*. Vol. 6 of 6. New Brunswick, NJ: Rutgers University Press. ISBN 0-8135-2320-6.

Anderson, E. M. (2005). *Home, Miss Moses: A novel in the time of Harriet Tubman*. Higganum, Connecticut: Higganum Hill Books. ISBN 0-9776556-0-1.

Bradford, Sarah Hopkins (orig. pub. 1886), (1961). *Harriet Tubman: The Moses of Her People*. New York: Corinth Books, lccn = 61008152.

Bradford, Sarah Hopkins (orig. pub. 1869), (1971). *Scenes in the Life of Harriet Tubman*. Freeport: Books for Libraries Press. ISBN 0-8369-8782-9.

Clinton, Catherine (2004). *Harriet Tubman: The Road to Freedom*. New York: Little, Brown and Company. ISBN 0-316-14492-4.

Conrad, Earl (1942). *Harriet Tubman: Negro Soldier and Abolitionist*. New York: International Publishers. OCLC 08991147.

Douglass, Frederick (1969). *Life and times of Frederick Douglass: his early life as a slave, his escape from bondage, and his complete history, written by himself*. London: Collier-Macmillan. OCLC 39258166.

Humez, Jean (2003). *Harriet Tubman: The Life and Life Stories*. Madison: University of Wisconsin Press. ISBN 0-299-19120-6.

Larson, Kate Clifford (2004). *Bound For the Promised Land: Harriet Tubman, Portrait of an American Hero*. New York: Ballantine Books. ISBN 0-345-45627-0.

Lowry, Beverly (2008). *Harriet Tubman: Imagining a Life*. Random House. ISBN 978-0-385-72177-6.

Sterling, Dorothy (1970). *Freedom Train: The Story of Harriet Tubman*. New York: Scholastic, Inc. ISBN 0-590-43628-7.

Narrative of Sojourner Truth: A Northern Slave (1850).

- Dover Publications 1997 edition: ISBN 0-486-29899-X
- Penguin Classics 1998 edition: ISBN 0-14-043678-2. Introduction & notes by Nell Irvin Painter.
- University of Pennsylvania online edition (html format, one chapter per page)

- University of Virginia online edition (HTML format, 207 kB, entire book on one page)

Alison Piepmeier, *Out in Public: Configurations of Women's Bodies in Nineteenth-Century America* (The University of North Carolina Press, 2004) ISBN 0-8078-5569-3

Paul E. Johnson and Sean Wilentz, *The Kingdom of Matthias: A Story of Sex and Salvation in 19th-Century America* (New York and Oxford: Oxford University Press, 1994) ISBN 0-19-509835-8

Carleton Mabee with Susan Mabee Newhouse, *Sojourner Truth: Slave, Prophet, Legend* (New York and London: New York University Press, 1993) ISBN 0-8147-5525-9

Nell Irvin Painter, *Sojourner Truth: A Life, A Symbol* (New York and London: W. W. Norton & Co., 1996) ISBN 0-393-31708-0

Jacqueline Sheehan, *Truth: A Novel* (New York: Free Press, 2003) ISBN 0-7432-4444-3

Erlene Stetson and Linda David, *Glorying in Tribulation: The Lifework of Sojourner Truth* (East Lansing: Michigan State University Press, 1994) ISBN 0-87013-337-3

Michael Warren Williams, *The African American encyclopedia, Volume 6*, Marshall Cavendish Corp., 1993, ISBN 1-85435-551-1

Three Blind Mice

William Leete Stone, *Matthias and his Impostures- or, The Progress of Fanaticism* (New York, 1835) Internet Archive online edition (pdf format, 16.9 MB, entire book on one pdf)

Gilbert Vale, *Fanaticism – Its Source and Influence Illustrated by the Simple Narrative of Isabella, in the Case of Matthias, Mr. and Mrs. B. Folger, Mr. Pierson, Mr. Mills, Catherine, Isabella, &c. &c.* (New York, 1835) Google Books online edition (pdf format, 9.9 MB, entire book on one pdf or one page per page)[14]

Janus Adams (11 January 2000). *Sister days: 365 inspired moments in African-American women's history*. John Wiley and Sons. p. 8. ISBN 978-0-471-28361-4. Retrieved 28 February 2011.

Julius Eric Thompson; James L. Conyers (2010). *The Frederick Douglass encyclopedia*. ABC-CLIO. pp. 124–125. ISBN 978-0-313-31988-4. Retrieved 27 February 2011.

"Discovering Anna Murray Douglass". *South Coast Today*. 17 February 2008. Retrieved 27 February 2011.

"Anna Murray Douglass". *BlackPast.org*.

My Mother as I Recall Her, by Rosetta Douglass Sprague (1900), The Frederick Douglass Papers at the Library of Congress

Brough, James. *The Vixens*. Simon & Schuster, 1980. ISBN 0-671-22688-6

Caplan, Sheri J. *Petticoats and Pinstripes: Portraits of Women in Wall Street's History*. Praeger, 2013. ISBN 978-1-4408-0265-2

Carpenter, Cari M. *Selected Writings of Victoria Woodhull: Suffrage, Free Love, and Eugenics*, Lincoln: University of Nebraska Press, 2010

Frisken, Amanda. *Victoria Woodhull's Sexual Revolution*, University of Pennsylvania Press, 2004. ISBN 0-8122-3798-6

Gabriel, Mary. *Notorious Victoria: The Life of Victoria Woodhull Uncensored*, Algonquin Books of Chapel Hill, 1998, 372 pages. ISBN 1-56512-132-5

Goldsmith, Barbara. *Other Powers: The Age of Suffrage, Spiritualism, and the Scandalous Victoria Woodhull*, New York: Harper Perennial, 1998, 531 pages. ISBN 0-06-095332-2

Johnson, Gerald W. 1956. "Dynamic Victoria Woodhull". American Heritage Volume 7, No. 4, June 1956

Marberry, M.M. *Vicky*. Funk & Wagnalls, New York. 1967

Meade, Marion. *Free Woman*, Alfred A. Knopf, Harper & Brothers, 1976

Sachs, Emanie. *The Terrible Siren*, Harper & Brothers, 1928

The Staff of the Historian's Office and National Portrait Gallery. '*If Elected...*' *Unsuccessful candidates for the presidency 1796-1968*. Washington, DC: United States Government Printing Offices, 1972

Stern, Madeleine B., ed., *The Victoria Woodhull Reader*, Weston, Mass.: M&S Press, 1974

Underhill, Lois Beachy, *The Woman Who Ran for President: The Many Lives of Victoria Woodhull* (Bridgehampton, N.Y.: Bridge Works, 1st ed. 1995 (ISBN 1-882593-10-3))

Cook, Frances A. "Belva Ann Lockwood: for Peace, Justice, and President" (1997) *Women's Legal History Biography Project*, Robert Crown Law Library, Stanford Law School.

Kerr, Laura. *The Girl Who Ran for President*. Thomas Nelson, 1947.

Norgren, Jill. "Belva Lockwood, Blazing the Trail for Women in Law". *Prologue Magazine*. Spring 2005, Vol. 37, No. 1.

Norgren, Jill. "Belva Lockwood, Blazing the Trail for Women in Law, Part 2". *Prologue Magazine*. Spring 2005, Vol. 37, No. 1.

Norgren, Jill. *Belva Lockwood: The Woman Who Would Be President*. New York: New York University Press, 2007.

Aiken, George L. *Uncle Tom's Cabin*. New York: Garland, 1993.

Gates, Henry Louis; and Appiah, Kwame Anthony. *Africana: Arts and Letters: an A-to-Z reference of writers, musicians, and artists of the African American Experience*, Running Press, 2005.

Gates, Henry Louis; and Hollis Robbins. *The Annotated Uncle Tom's Cabin*, W. W. Norton. ISBN 0-393-05946-4

Gerould, Daniel C., ed. *American Melodrama*. New York: Performing Arts Journal Publications, 1983.

Jordan-Lake, Joy. *Whitewashing Uncle Tom's Cabin: Nineteenth-Century Women Novelists Respond to Stowe,* Vanderbilt University Press, 2005.

Lott, Eric. *Love and Theft: Blackface Minstrelsy and the American Working Class*. New York: Oxford University Press, 1993.

Lowance, Mason I. (Jr.); Westbrook, Ellen E.; De Prospo, R., *The Stowe Debate: Rhetorical Strategies in Uncle Tom's Cabin,* University of Massachusetts Press, 1994.

Parfait, Claire. *The Publishing History of Uncle's Tom's Cabin, 1852–2002*, Aldershot: Ashgate, 2007.

Reynolds, David S. *Mightier Than the Sword: Uncle Tom's Cabin and the Battle for America*, Norton, 2011. 351 pp.

Rosenthal, Debra J. *Routledge Literary Sourcebook on Harriet Beecher Stowe's Uncle Tom's Cabin*, Routledge, 2003.

Sundquist, Eric J., ed. *New Essays on Uncle Tom's Cabin,* Cambridge University Press, 1986.

Three Blind Mice

Tompkins, Jane. *In Sensational Designs: The Cultural Work of American Fiction, 1790–1860.* New York: Oxford University Press, 1985.

Weinstein, Cindy. *The Cambridge Companion to Harriet Beecher Stowe,* Cambridge University Press, 2004.

Williams, Linda. *Playing the Race Card: Melodramas of Black and White from Uncle Tom to O. J. Simpson,* Princeton University Press, 2001.

Addams, Jane, in *Crisis: A Record of Darker Races,* X (May 1915), 19, 41, and (June 1915), 88.

Bogle, Donald. *Toms, Coons, Mulattoes, Mammies and Bucks: An Interpretive History of Blacks in American Films* (1973).

Brodie, Fawn M. *Thaddeus Stevens, Scourge of the South* (New York, 1959), p. 86–93. Corrects the historical record as to Dixon's false representation of Stevens in this film with regard to his racial views and relations with his housekeeper.

Chalmers, David M. *Hooded Americanism: The History of the Ku Klux Klan* (New York: 1965), p. 30 *Cook, Raymond Allen. *Fire from the Flint: The Amazing Careers of Thomas Dixon* (Winston-Salem, N.C., 1968).

Franklin, John Hope. "Silent Cinema as Historical Mythmaker". **In** *Myth America: A Historical Anthology, Volume II.* 1997. Gerster, Patrick, and Cords, Nicholas. (editors.) Brandywine Press, St. James, NY. ISBN 978-1-881089-97-1

Franklin, John Hope, "Propaganda as History" pp. 10–23 in *Race and History: Selected Essays 1938–1988* (Louisiana State University Press, 1989); first published in *The Massachusetts Review*, 1979. Describes the history of the novel *The Clan* and this film.

Franklin, John Hope, *Reconstruction After the Civil War* (Chicago, 1961), p. 5–7.

Hickman, Roger. *Reel Music: Exploring 100 Years of Film Music* (New York: W. W. Norton & Company, 2006).

Hodapp, Christopher L., VonKannon, Alice, *Conspiracy Theories & Secret Societies For Dummies* (Hoboken: Wiley, 2008) p. 235–6.

Korngold, Ralph, *Thaddeus Stevens. A Being Darkly Wise and Rudely Great* (New York: 1955) pp. 72–76. corrects Dixon's false characterization of Stevens' racial views and of his dealings with his housekeeper.

Leab, Daniel J., *From Sambo to Superspade* (Boston, 1975), p. 23–39.

New York Times, roundup of reviews of this film, March 7, 1915.

The New Republica, II (March 20, 1915), 185

Poole, W. Scott, *Monsters in America: Our Historical Obsession with the Hideous and the Haunting* (Waco, Texas: Baylor, 2011), 30. ISBN 978-1-60258-314-6

Simkins, Francis B., "New Viewpoints of Southern Reconstruction", *Journal of Southern History*, V (February, 1939), pp. 49–61.

Stokes, Melvyn, *D. W. Griffith's The Birth of a Nation: A History of "The Most Controversial Motion Picture of All Time"* (New York: Oxford University Press, 2007). The latest study of the film's making and subsequent career.

Williamson, Joel, *After Slavery: The Negro in South Carolina During Reconstruction* (Chapel Hill, 1965). This book corrects Dixon's false reporting of Reconstruction, as shown in his novel, his play and this film.

Gooch, Brison D. "A Century of Historiography on the Origins of the Crimean War", *American Historical Review* Vol. 62, No. 1 (Oct. 1956), pp. 33–58 in JSTOR

Kozelsky, Mara. "The Crimean War, 1853–56," *Kritika* (2012) 13#4 online

Markovits, Stefanie. *The Crimean War in the British Imagination* (Cambridge University Press: 2009) 287 pp. ISBN 0-521-11237-0

Russell, William Howard, "The Crimean War: As Seen by Those Who Reported It". (Louisiana State University Press, 2009) ISBN 978-0-8071-3445-0

Girard, Louis (1986), *Napoléon III*, Paris: Fayard, ISBN 2-01-27-9098-4

Milza, Pierre (2006), *Napoléon III*, Paris: Tempus, ISBN 978-2-262-02607-3

Milza, Pierre (2009), *L'Année Terrible- La guerre franco-prussienne (september 1870-march 1871)*, Perrin, ISBN 978-2-262-02498-7

Cobban, Alfred (1965), *A History of Modern France: Volume 2: 1799-1871*, London: Penguin

Séguin, Philippe (1990), *Louis Napoléon Le Grand*, Paris: Bernard Grasset, ISBN 2-246-42951-X

McMillan, J. *Napoleon III* (Longman, 1991)

Thompson, J.M. *Louis Napoleon and the Second Empire*. Oxford: Basil Blackwell, 1965. online edition

Plessis, Alain (1989), *The Rise & Fall of the Second Empire 1852–1871*, Paris: Cambridge University Press

Randell, Keith (1991), *Monarchy, Republic & Empire*, Access to History, Hodder & Stoughton, ISBN 0-340-51805-7

Markham, Felix (1975), *The Bonapartes*, London: Weidenfeld & Nicolson, ISBN 0-297-76928-6

Bresler, Fenton (1999), *Napoleon III: A Life*, London: Harper Collins, ISBN 0-00-255787-8

Baguley, David. *Napoleon III and His Regime: An Extravaganza* (2000)

Bury J. P.T. *Napoleon III and the Second Empire* (1964).

Case Lynn M. *French Opinion on War and Diplomacy during the Second Empire* (1954)

Corley, T. A. B. *Democratic Despot: A Life of Napoleon III* (1961) online edition

Cunningham; Michele. *Mexico and the Foreign Policy of Napoleon III* (Palgrave, 2001) online edition

Duff, David. *Eugenie and Napoleon III* (Collins, 1978)

Gooch, Brison D., ed. *Napoleon III – Man of Destiny: Enlightened Statesman or Proto-Fascist?*, (1966) excerpt

Gooch, Brison D., ed. *The Reign of Napoleon III,* (1969)

Pinkney, David H. "Napoleon III's Transformation of Paris: The Origins and Development of the Idea," *Journal of Modern History* (1955) 27#2 pp. 125–134 in JSTOR

Pinkney, David H. *Napoleon III and the Rebuilding of Paris* (Princeton University Press, 1958) ISBN 0-691-00768-3.

Price, Roger. "Napoleon III: 'hero' or 'grotesque mediocrity'?" *History Review* (2003) pp 14+

Price, Roger. *Napoleon III and the Second Empire* (Routledge, 1997)

Price, Roger. *The French Second Empire: an anatomy of political power* (Cambridge University Press, 2001) online edition

Wawro, Geoffrey. *The Franco-Prussian War: The German Conquest of France in 1870–1871*(2005)

Wetzel, David *A Duel of Giants: Bismarck, Napoleon III, and the Origins of the Franco-Prussian War* (University of Wisconsin Press, 2001)

Wetzel, David. *A Duel of Nations: Germany, France, and the Diplomacy of the War of 1870–1871* (University of Wisconsin Press; 2012) 310 pages

Wittmann, Heiner. *Napoleon III. Macht und Kunst*(Reihe Dialoghi/ dialogues. Literatur und Kultur Italiens und Frankreichs. Hrsg. v. Dirk Hoeges, Band 17, Verlag Peter Lang, Frankfurt, Berlin, Bern u.a., 2013).

Zeldin, Theodore. *The Political System of Napoleon III* (Oxford University Press, 1958).

Fanning, Charles (1990/2000). *The Irish Voice in America: 250 Years of Irish-American Fiction.* Lexington: The University of Kentucky Press. ISBN 0-8131-0970-1

Glazier, Michael, ed. (1999). *The Encyclopedia of the Irish in America.* Notre Dame, IN: University of Notre Dame Press. ISBN 0-268-02755-2

Glynn, Irial: <u>Emigration Across the Atlantic: Irish, Italians and Swedes compared, 1800-1950, European History Online</u>, Mainz: Institute of European History, 2011, retrieved: June 16, 2011.

McGee, Thomas D'Arcy (1852). *<u>A History of the Irish Settlers in North America from the Earliest Period to the Census of 1850</u>*

Meagher, Timothy J. (2005). *The Columbia Guide to Irish American History*. New York: Columbia University Press. <u>ISBN 978-0-231-12070-8</u>

Merryweather (née Green), Kath (2009). *The Irish Rossiter: Ancestors and Their World Wide Descendents and Connections*. Bristol, UK: Irishancestors4u. <u>ISBN 978-0-9562976-0-0</u>

Miller, Kerby M. (1985). *Emigrants and Exiles: Ireland and the Irish Exodus to North America*. New York: Oxford University Press. <u>ISBN 0-19-505187-4</u>

Negra, Diane (ed.) (2006). *The Irish in Us*. Durham, NC: Duke University Press. <u>ISBN 0-8223-3740-1</u>

Quinlan, Kieran (2005). *Strange Kin: Ireland and the American South*. Baton Rouge: Louisiana State University Press. <u>ISBN 978-0-8071-2983-8</u>

Quinlin, Michael P. (2004). *Irish Boston: A Lively Look at Boston's Colorful Irish Past*. Gilford: Globe Pequot Press. <u>ISBN 978-0-7627-2901-2</u>

Blaustein, Richard. *The Thistle and the Brier: Historical Links and Cultural Parallels Between Scotland and Appalachia* (2003).

Blethen, Tyler; Wood, Curtis W. Jr.; Blethen, H. Tyler (Eds.) (1997). *Ulster and North America: Transatlantic Perspectives on the Scotch-Irish.* Tuscaloosa, AL: University of Alabama Press. ISBN 0-8173-0823-7

Cunningham, Roger (1991). *Apples on the Flood: Minority Discourse and Appalachia.* Knoxville, TN: University of Tennessee Press. ISBN 0-87049-629-8

Fischer, David Hackett (1991). *Albion's Seed: Four British Folkways in America.* New York: Oxford University Press USA. ISBN 0-19-506905-6

Ford, Henry Jones (1915). *The Scotch-Irish in America.* Full text online.

Griffin, Patrick (2001). *The People with No Name: Ireland's Ulster Scots, America's Scots Irish, and the Creation of a British Atlantic World, 1689–1764.* Princeton, NJ: Princeton University Press. ISBN 0-691-07462-3

Leyburn, James G. (1989). *The Scotch-Irish: A Social History.* Chapel Hill: University of North Carolina Press. ISBN 0-8078-4259-1

Lorle, Porter (1999). *A People Set Apart: The Scotch-Irish in Eastern Ohio.* Zanesville, OH: Equine Graphics Publishing. ISBN 1-887932-75-5

McWhiney, Grady (1988). *Cracker Culture: Celtic Ways in the Old South.* Tuscaloosa: University of Alabama Press. ISBN 0-8173-0328-6

Ray, Celeste. *Highland Heritage: Scottish Americans in the American South* (2001).

Webb, James H. (2004). *Born Fighting: How the Scots-Irish Shaped America*. New York: Broadway. ISBN 0-7679-1688-3.

Akiner, Shirin; Aldis, Anne, ed. (2004). *The Caspian: Politics, Energy and Security*. New York: Routledge. ISBN 978-0-7007-0501-6.

Bauer Georg, Bandy Mark Chance (tr.), Bandy Jean A.(tr.) (1546). "De Natura Fossilium". *vi* (in **Latin**)). translated 1955

Hyne, Norman J. (2001). *Nontechnical Guide to Petroleum Geology, Exploration, Drilling, and Production*. PennWell Corporation. ISBN 0-87814-823-X.

Mabro, Robert; Organization of Petroleum Exporting Countries (2006). *Oil in the 21st century: issues, challenges and opportunities*. Oxford Press. ISBN 0-19-920738-0, 9780199207381 Check |isbn= value (help). Cite uses deprecated parameters (help)

Maugeri, Leonardo (2005). *The Age of Oil: What They Don't Want You to Know About the World's Most Controversial Resource*. Guilford, CT: Globe Pequot. p. 15. ISBN 978-1-59921-118-3.

Speight, James G. (1999). *The Chemistry and Technology of Petroleum*. Marcel Dekker. ISBN 0-8247-0217-4.

Speight, James G; Ancheyta, Jorge, ed. (2007). *Hydroprocessing of Heavy Oils and Residua*. CRC Press. ISBN 0-8493-7419-7.

Vassiliou, Marius (2009). *Historical Dictionary of the Petroleum Industry*. Scarecrow Press (Rowman & Littlefield). ISBN 0-8108-5993-9.

Ambrose, Stephen (1966). *Duty, Honor, Country. A History of West Point*. Baltimore: Johns Hopkins University Press. ISBN 0-8018-6293-0.

Atkinson, Rick (1989). *The Long Gray Line*. Boston: Houghton Mifflin Company. ISBN 0-395-48008-6.

Barkalow, Carol (1990). *In the Men's House*. New York: Poseidon Press. ISBN 0-671-67312-2. , on integrating women

Betros, Lance. *Carved from Granite: West Point since 1902* (Texas A&M University Press, 2012), 458 pp.

Crackel, Theodore (1991). *The Illustrated History of West Point*. Boston: Harry N. Abrams, Inc. ISBN 0-8109-3458-2.

Crackel, Theodore (2002). *West Point: A Bicentennial History*. Lawrence, KS: University Press of Kansas. ISBN 0-7006-1160-6.

Crowley, Robert; Guinzburg, Thomas (2002). *West Point: Two Centuries of Honor and Tradition*. New York: Warner Books. ISBN 0-446-53018-2.

Endler, James (1998). *Other Leaders, Other Heroes*. Westport, CT: Praeger Publishers. ISBN 0-275-96369-1.

Lea, Russell (2003). *The Long Green Line*. Haverford, PA: Infinity Publishing. ISBN 0-7414-1459-7.

Lipsky, David (2003). *Absolutely American: Four Years at West Point*. Boston: Houghton Mifflin Company. ISBN 0-618-09542-X.

Hulse, Glenn (1994). *Bugle Notes, 86th Volume*. West Point, NY: Directorate of Cadet Activities.

McMaster, R.K. (1951). *West Point's Contribution to Education*. El Paso, TX: McMath Printing Co.

Miller, Rod (2002). *The Campus Guide: West Point US Military Academy*. New York: Princeton Architectural Press. ISBN 1-56898-294-1.

Murphy, Jr., Bill (2008). *In a Time of War: The Proud and Perilous Journey of West Point's Class of 2002*. New York: Henry Holt and Co. ISBN 0-8050-8679-X.

Neff, Casey (2007). *Bugle Notes: 99th Volume*. West Point, NY: Directorate of Cadet Activities.

Palka, Eugene; Malinowski, Jon C. (2008). *Historic Photos of West Point*. Nashville, TN: Turner Publishing Company. ISBN 978-1-59652-416-3. Cite uses deprecated parameters (help)

Poughkeepsie Journal (2003). *West Point: Legend on the Hudson*. Montgomery, NY: Walden Printing. ISBN 0-9674209-1-1.

Simpson, Jeffrey (1982). *Officers And Gentlemen: Historic West Point in Photographs*. Tarrytown, NY: Sleepy Hollow Press. ISBN 0-912882-53-0.

Garland, Hamlin (1898). *Ulysses S. Grant: His Life and Character*. New York: Doubleday & McClure Co

McFeely, William S. (1981). *Grant: A Biography*. Norton. ISBN 0-393-01372-3.; Pulitzer Prize

Sears, Stephen W. *George B. McClellan: The Young Napoleon*. New York: Da Capo Press, 1988. ISBN 0-306-80913-3.

Farwell, Byron. *Stonewall: A Biography of General Thomas J. Jackson*. New York: W. W. Norton and Co., 1993. ISBN 978-0-393-31086-3.

Blount, Roy, Jr. *Robert E. Lee*, Penguin Putnam, 2003. 210 pp., short popular biography, ISBN 0-670-03220-4.

Carmichael, Peter S., ed. *Audacity Personified: The Generalship of Robert E. Lee* Louisiana State University Press, 2004, ISBN 0-8071-2929-1.

Connelly, Thomas L. "Robert E. Lee and the Western Confederacy: A Criticism of Lee's Strategic Ability." *Civil War History* 15 (June 1969): 116–32.

Cooke, John E., *A Life of General Robert E. Lee*, Kessinger Publishing, 2004.

Dowdey, Clifford. *Lee* 1965.

Fellman, Michael (2000). *The Making of Robert E. Lee*. New York: Random House (ISBN 0-679-45650-3).

Fishwick, Marshall W. *Lee after the War* 1963.

Flood, Charles Bracelen. *Lee — The Last Years* 1981.

Freeman, Douglas Southall. *Lee* (4 vols, 1935); abridged one-volume edition, edited by Richard Harwell (1961); the standard biography

Gallagher, Gary W. *Lee the Soldier* (University of Nebraska Press, 1996)

Nolan, Alan T. *Lee Considered*, University of North Carolina Press, Chapel Hill, NC (1991)

Pryor, Elizabeth Brown. *Reading the Man: A Portrait of Robert E. Lee Through His Private Letters*. New York: Viking, 2007.

Smith, Eugene O. *Lee and Grant: a Dual Biography*, McGraw-Hill, New York (1991)

Thomas, Emory. *Robert E. Lee*, W.W. Norton & Co., 1995 (ISBN 0-393-03730-4) full-scale scholarly biography

Symonds, Craig L. *Joseph E. Johnston: A Civil War Biography*. New York: W. W. Norton, 1992. ISBN 978-0-393-31130-3.

Vandiver, Frank Everson. "Joseph Eggleston Johnston." In *Leaders of the American Civil War: A Biographical and Historiographical Dictionary*, edited by Charles F. Ritter and Jon L. Wakelyn. Westport, CT: Greenwood Press, 1998. ISBN 0-313-29560-3.

Lamers, William M. *The Edge of Glory: A Biography of General William S. Rosecrans, U.S.A.* Baton Rouge: Louisiana State University Press, 1961. ISBN 0-8071-2396-X.

Denison, Charles Wheeler, and George B. Herbert. *Hancock "The Superb": The Early life and Public Career of Winfield S. Hancock, Major-General U.S.A..* Philadelphia: The National Publishing Co., 1880. OCLC 81289926.

Goodrich, Frederick E., and Frederick O. Prince. *The Life and Public Services of Winfield Scott Hancock, Major-General, U.S.A.* Boston: Lee & Shepard, 1880. OCLC 6782477.

Marvel, William. *Burnside.* Chapel Hill: University of North Carolina Press, 1991. ISBN 0-8078-1983-2.

Wheelan, Joseph. *Terrible Swift Sword: The Life of General Philip H. Sheridan.* New York: Da Capo Press, 2012. ISBN 978-0-306-82027-4.

Hassler, William W. *A.P. Hill: Lee's Forgotten General.* Chapel Hill: University of North Carolina Press, 1962. ISBN 978-0-8078-0973-0.

Robertson, James I., Jr. *General A.P. Hill: The Story of a Confederate Warrior.* New York: Vintage Publishing, 1992. ISBN 0-679-73888-6.

Longacre, Edward G. *Pickett, Leader of the Charge: A Biography of General George E. Pickett, C.S.A.* Shippensburg, PA: White Mane Publishing, 1995. ISBN 978-1-57249-006-2.

Thomas, Emory M. *Bold Dragoon: The Life of J.E.B. Stuart*. Norman: University of Oklahoma Press, 1986. ISBN 0-8061-3193-4.

Wert, Jeffry D. *Cavalryman of the Lost Cause: A Biography of J.E.B. Stuart*. New York: Simon & Schuster, 2008. ISBN 978-0-7432-7819-5.

Ambrose, Stephen E. (1996 [1975]). *Crazy Horse and Custer: The Parallel Lives of Two American Warriors*. New York: Anchor Books. ISBN 0-385-47966-2.

Barnett, Louise *Touched by Fire: The Life, Death, and Mythic Afterlife of George Armstrong Custer* (1996) New York, Henry Holt and Company, Inc.

Sauers, Richard Allen. *Meade: Victor of Gettysburg*. Military Profiles. London: Brassey's, 2003. ISBN 978-1-57488-418-0.

Ward, James A. *That Man Haupt: A Biography of Herman Haupt*. Baton Rouge: Louisiana State University Press, 1973. ISBN 978-0-8071-0225-1.

Williams, T. Harry. *P.G.T. Beauregard: Napoleon in Gray*. Baton Rouge: Louisiana State University Press, 1955. ISBN 0-8071-1974-1.

Basso, Hamilton. *Beauregard: The Great Creole*. New York: Charles Scribner's Sons, 1933. OCLC 693265.

Marszalek, John F. *Commander of All Lincoln's Armies: A Life of General Henry W. Halleck*. Boston: Belknap Press of Harvard University Press, 2004. ISBN 0-674-01493-6.

Anders, Curt *Henry Halleck's War: A Fresh Look at Lincoln's Controversial General-in-Chief.* Guild Press of Indiana, 1999. ISBN 1-57860-029-4.

Ambrose, Stephen. *Halleck: Lincoln's Chief of Staff.* Baton Rouge: Louisiana State University Press, 1999. ISBN 0-8071-2071-5.

Hirshson, Stanley P., *The White Tecumseh: A Biography of General William T. Sherman,* John Wiley & Sons, 1997, ISBN 0-471-28329-0.

Clarke, Dwight L., *William Tecumseh Sherman: Gold Rush Banker,* California Historical Society, 1969.

McWhiney, Grady. *Braxton Bragg and Confederate Defeat.* Vol. 1. New York: Columbia University Press, 1969 (additional material, Tuscaloosa: University of Alabama Press, 1991). ISBN 0-8173-0545-9.

Gallagher, Gary W. *Jubal A. Early, the Lost Cause, and Civil War History: A Persistent Legacy (Frank L. Klement Lectures, No. 4).* Milwaukee, WI: Marquette University Press, 1995. ISBN 0-87462-328-6.

Morison, Samuel Eliot. (1967). "Old Bruin" Commodore Matthew Calbraith Perry Little, Brown and Company, Boston [1967]

Griffis, William Elliot (1887). *Matthew Calbraith Perry: a typical American naval officer.* Cupples and Hurd, Boston. p. 459. ISBN 1-163-63493-X. , Book

Hawks, Francis. (1856). *Narrative of the Expedition of an American Squadron to the China Seas and Japan Performed in the Years 1852, 1853 and 1854* under the Command of Commodore M.C. Perry, United States Navy. Washington: A.O.P. Nicholson by order of Congress, 1856; originally published in *Senate Executive Documents*, No. 34 of 33rd Congress, 2nd Session. [reprinted by London: Trafalgar Square, 2005. ISBN 1-84588-026-9 (paper)]

Askew, David. "The International Committee for the Nanking Safety Zone: An Introduction" *Sino-Japanese Studies* Vol. 14, April 2002 (Article outlining membership and their reports of the events that transpired during the massacre)

Askew, David, "The Nanjing Incident: An Examination of the Civilian Population" *Sino-Japanese Studies* Vol. 13, March 2001 (Article analyzes a wide variety of figures on the population of Nanking before, during, and after the massacre)

Bergamini, David, "Japan's Imperial Conspiracy," William Morrow, New York; 1971.

Brook, Timothy, ed. *Documents on the Rape of Nanjing*, Ann Arbor: The University of Michigan Press, 1999. ISBN 0-472-11134-5 (Does not include the Rabe diaries but does include reprints of "Hsu Shuhsi, *Documents of the Nanking Safety Zone*, Kelly & Walsh, 1939".)

Hua-ling Hu, *American Goddess at the Rape of Nanking: The Courage of Minnie Vautrin*, Foreword by Paul Simon; March 2000, ISBN 0-8093-2303-6

Fujiwara, Akira "The Nanking Atrocity: An Interpretive Overview" Japan Focus October 23, 2007.

Galbraith, Douglas, *A Winter in China*, London, 2006. ISBN 0-09-946597-3. A novel focussing on the western residents of Nanking during the massacre.

Higashinakano, Shudo, *The Nanking Massacre: Fact Versus Fiction: A Historian's Quest for the Truth*, Tokyo: Sekai Shuppan, 2005. ISBN 4-916079-12-4

Higashinakano, Kobayashi and Fukunaga, *Analyzing The Photographic Evidence' of The Nanking Massacre*, Tokyo: Soshisha, 2005. ISBN 4-7942-1381-6

Honda, Katsuichi, Sandness, Karen trans. *The Nanjing Massacre: A Japanese Journalist Confronts Japan's National Shame*, London: M.E. Sharpe, 1999. ISBN 0-7656-0335-7

Hsū Shuhsi, ed. (1939), Documents of the Nanking Safety Zone (reprinted in *Documents on the Rape of Nanjing* Brook ed. 1999)

Kajimoto, Masato "Mistranslations in Honda Katsuichi's the Nanjing Massacre" *Sino-Japanese Studies*, 13. 2 (March 2001) pp. 32–44

Lu, Suping, *They Were in Nanjing: The Nanjing Massacre Witnessed by American and British Nationals*, Hong Kong University Press, 2004.

Murase, Moriyasu, *Watashino Jyugun Cyugoku-sensen*(My China Front), Nippon Kikanshi Syuppan Center, 1987 (revised in 2005).(includes disturbing photos, 149 page photogravure) ISBN 4-88900-836-5 (村瀬守保,私の従軍中国戦線)

Qi, Shouhua. "When the Purple Mountain Burns: A Novel" San Francisco: Long River Press, 2005. ISBN 1-59265-041-4

Qi, Shouhua. *Purple Mountain: A Story of the Rape of Nanking* (A Novel) English Chinese Bilingual Edition (Paperback, 2009) ISBN 1-4486-5965-5

Rabe, John, *The Good Man of Nanking: The Diaries of John Rabe*, Vintage (Paper), 2000. ISBN 0-375-70197-4

Robert Sabella, Fei Fei Li and David Liu, eds. Nanking 1937: Memory and Healing (Armonk, NY: M.E. Sharpe, 2002). ISBN 0-7656-0817-0.

Takemoto, Tadao and Ohara, Yasuo *The Alleged "Nanking Massacre": Japan's rebuttal to China's forged claims*, Meisei-sha, Inc., 2000, (Tokyo Trial revisited) ISBN 4-944219-05-9

Tanaka, Masaaki, *What Really Happened in Nanking: The Refutation of a Common Myth*, Tokyo: Sekai Shuppan, 2000. ISBN 4-916079-07-8

Wakabayashi, Bob Tadashi "The Nanking 100-Man Killing Contest Debate: War Guilt Amid Fabricated Illusions, 1971–75", *The Journal of Japanese Studies*, Vol.26 No.2 Summer 2000.

Wakabayashi, Bob Tadashi *The Nanking Atrocity, 1937–1938: Complicating the Picture*, Berghahn Books, 2007, ISBN 1-84545-180-5

Yamamoto, Masahiro *Nanking: Anatomy of an Atrocity*, Praeger Publishers, 2000, ISBN 0-275-96904-5

Yang, Daqing. "Convergence or Divergence? Recent Historical Writings on the Rape of Nanjing" *American Historical Review* 104, 3 (June 1999)., 842–865.

Young, Shi; Yin, James. "Rape of Nanking: Undeniable history in photographs" Chicago: Innovative Publishing Group, 1997.

Zhang, Kaiyuan, ed. *Eyewitnesses to Massacre*, An East Gate Book, 2001 (includes documentation of American missionaries M.S. Bates, G.A. Fitch, E.H. Foster, J.G. Magee, J.H. MaCallum, W.P. Mills, L.S.C. Smyth, A.N. Steward, Minnie Vautrin and R.O. Wilson.) ISBN 0-7656-0684-4

Caldwell, Robert G. *The Lopez Expeditions to Cuba 1848–1851*. Princeton: Princeton University Press, 1915.

Lazo, Rodrigo *"Writing to Cuba: Filibustering and Cuban Exiles in the United States*. University of North Carolina Press, 2005 ISBN 0-8078-5594-4

May, Robert E. *Manifest Destiny's Underworld: Filibustering in Antebellum America*. Chapel Hill: University of North Carolina Press, 2002.

May, Robert E. *The Southern Dream of a Caribbean Empire*. Gainesville: University Press of Florida, 2002.

Quisenberry, Anderson G. *Lopez's Expeditions to Cuba, 1850 and 1851*. Louisville: Louisville University Press, 1906.

Villaverde, Cirilo 1882 (New translation by Sibylle Fischer and Helen Lane) *Cecilia Valdes or El Angel Hill.* Oxford University Press, USA 2005 ISBN 0-19-514395-7

Carr, Albert Z. *The World and William Walker*, 1963.

Dando-Collins, Stephen. *Tycoon's War: How Cornelius Vanderbilt Invaded a Country to Overthrow America's Most Famous Military Adventurer* (2008) excerpt and text search

Richard Harding Davis (1906), Real Soldiers of Fortune, "General William Walker, the King of the Filibusters" (Chapter 5).

Juda, Fanny. *California Filibusters: A History of their Expeditions into Hispanic America*

McPherson, James M. (1988). Battle Cry of Freedom: The Civil War Era. New York: Oxford University Press. p. 909. ISBN 0-19-503863-0.

May, Robert E. *Manifest Destiny's Underworld: Filibustering in Antebellum America*, 2002.

May, Robert E. *The Southern Dream of a Caribbean Empire*. Gainesville: University Press of Florida, 2002.

Moore, J. Preston. "Pierre Soule: Southern Expansionist and Promoter," *Journal of Southern History* 21:2 (May, 1955), 208 & 214.

Norvell, John Edward, "How Tennessee Adventurer William Walker became Dictator of Nicaragua in 1857: The Norvell Family origins of the Grey Eyed Man of Destiny," *The Middle Tennessee Journal of Genealogy and History*, Vol XXV, No.4, Spring 2012

"1855: American Conquistador," *American Heritage*, October 2005.

Recko, Corey. "Murder on the White Sands." University of North Texas Press. 2007

Scroggs, William O. (1916). *Filibusters and Financiers; the story of William Walker and his associates*. New York: The Macmillan Company.

"William Walker." Encyclopædia Britannica. 2008. Encyclopædia Britannica Online. 28 Oct. 2008 <http://www.britannica.com/EBchecked/topic/634642/William-Walker>.

Doubleday, C.W. *Reminiscences of the Filibuster War in Nicaragua*. New York: G.P. Putnam's Sons, 1886.

Jamison, James Carson. *With Walker in Nicaragua: Reminiscences of an Officer of the American Phalanx*. Columbia, MO: E.W. Stephens, 1909.

Wight, Samuel F. *Adventures in California and Nicaragua: a Truthful Epic*. Boston: Alfred Mudge & Son, 1860.

Fayssoux Collection. Tulane University. Latin American Library.

United States Magazine. Sept., 1856. Vol III No. 3. pp. 266–72

"Filibustering", *Putnam's Monthly Magazine* (New York), April 1857, 425–35.

"Walker's Reverses in Nicaragua," *Anti-Slavery Bugle*, November 17, 1856.

"The Lesson" *National Era*, June 4, 1857, 90.

"The Administration and Commodore Paulding," *National Era*, January 7, 1858.

"Wanted – A Few Filibusters," *Harper's Weekly*, January 10, 1857.

"Reception of Gen. Walker," *New Orleans Picayune*, May 28, 1857.

"Arrival of Walker," *New Orleans Picayune*, May 28, 1857.

"Our Influence in the Isthmus," *New Orleans Picayune*, February 17, 1856.

New Orleans Sunday Delta, June 27, 1856.

"Nicaragua and President Walker," *Louisville Times*, December 13, 1856.

"Le Nicaragua et les Filibustiers," *Opelousas Courier*, May 10, 1856.

"What is to Become of Nicaragua?," *Harper's Weekly*, June 6, 1857.

"The Late General Walker," *Harper's Weekly*, October 13, 1860.

"What General Walker is Like," *Harper's Weekly*, September, 1856.

"Message of the President to the Senate in Reference to the Late Arrest of Gen. Walker," *Louisville Courier*, January 12, 1858.

"The Central American Question – What Walker May Do," *New York Times*, January 1, 1856.

"A Serious Farce," *New York Times*, December 14, 1853.

1856–57 *New York Herald* Horace Greeley editorials

Harrison, Brady. *William Walker and the Imperial Self in American Literature.* University of Georgia Press, August 2, 2004. ISBN 0-8203-2544-9. ISBN 978-0-8203-2544-6.

Freehling, William H., *The Road to Disunion: Volume I: Secessionists at Bay, 1776-1854* Retrieved March 12, 2010

Hall, Richard, *On Afric's Shore: A History of Maryland in Liberia, 1834-1857*

Latrobe, John H. B., p.125, *Maryland in Liberia: a History of the Colony Planted By the Maryland State Colonization Society Under the Auspices of the State of Maryland, U. S. At Cape Palmas on the South - West Coast of Africa, 1833-1853* (1885). Retrieved Feb 16 2010

Sagarin, Mary, *John Brown Russwurm: The story of Freedom's journal, freedom's journey*, Lothrop, Lee & Shepard, 1970.

Tim Hetherington (2009). *Long Story Bit By Bit: Liberia Retold*. New York: Umbrage. ISBN 978-1-884167-73-7.

Graham Greene (1936). *Journey Without Maps*. Vintage. ISBN 978-0-09-928223-5.

Gabriel I. H. Williams (July 6, 2006). *Liberia: The Heart of Darkness*. Trafford Publishing. ISBN 1-55369-294-2.

Alan Huffman (2004). *Mississippi in Africa: The Saga of the Slaves of Prospect Hill Plantation and Their Legacy in Liberia Today*. Gotham Books. ISBN 978-1-59240-044-7.

John-Peter Pham (April 4, 2001). *Liberia: Portrait of a Failed State*. Reed Press. ISBN 1-59429-012-1.

Barbara Greene (March 5, 1991). *Too Late to Turn Back*. Penguin. ISBN 0-14-009594-2.

Weisman, Brent Richards. 1999. *Unconquered People*. Gainesville, Florida: University Press of Florida. ISBN 0-8130-1662-2.

Major John C. White, Jr., "American Military Strategy In The Second Seminole War", 1995, Global Security Website. Quote: "The greatest lesson of the Second Seminole War shows how a government can lose public support for a war that has simply lasted for too long. As the Army became more deeply involved in the conflict, as the government sent more troops into the theater, and as the public saw more money appropriated for the war, people began to lose their interest. Jesup's capture of

Osceola, and the treachery he used to get him, turned public sentiment against the Army. The use of blood hounds only created more hostility in the halls of Congress. It did not matter to the American people that some of Jesup's deceptive practices helped him achieve success militarily. The public viewed his actions so negatively that he had undermined the political goals of the government."

Letter Concerning the Outbreak of Hostilities in the Third Seminole War, 1856, from the State Library and Archives of Florida.

"Tour of the Florida Territory during the Seminole (Florida) Wars, 1792-1859", from Jacob K. Neff, *The Army and Navy of America*, Philadelphia: J.H. Pearsol and Co., 1845. "Quote: "The Florida war consisted in the killing of Indians, because they refused to leave their native home—to hunt them amid the forests and swamps, from which they frequently issued to attack the intruders. To go or not to go, that was the question. Many a brave man lost his life and now sleeps beneath the sod of Florida. And yet neither these nor the heroes who exposed themselves there to so many dangers and suffer[ings], could acquire any military glory in such a war."

"Seminole Wars", Tampa Bay History Center

Knetsch, Joe. 2003. *Florida's Seminole Wars: 1817-1858*. Charleston, South Carolina: Arcadia Publishing. ISBN 0-7385-2424-7.

The Cayuse War (Early Indian Wars of Oregon, Vol. One), by Frances Fuller Victor. Taxus Baccata: 2006.

Tiller, Veronica E. (1983). *The Jicarilla Apache Tribe: a history, 1846-1970*. University of Nebraska Press. ISBN 0-8032-4409-6.

Utley, Robert M. (1981). *Frontiersmen in blue: the United States Army and the Indian, 1848-1865*. University of Nebraska Press. ISBN 0-8032-9550-2.

Carter, Harvey L. (1990). *"Dear Old Kit": The Historical Christopher Carson*. University of Oklahoma Press. ISBN 0-8061-2253-6.

The Friend (1901). *The Friend Volume 74*.

Thompson, D. Jerry (2006). *Civil war to the bloody end: The life and times of Major General Samuel P. Heintzelman*. San Antonio, Texas: Texas A&M University Press. ISBN 1-58544-535-5.

Kroeber, L. Alfred; Clifton B. Kroeber (1994). *A Mohave War Reminiscence, 1854 - 1880*. Dover Publications. ISBN 0-486-28163-9.

Ray Hoard Glassley: *Indian Wars of the Pacific Northwest*, Binfords & Mort, Portland, Oregon 1972 ISBN 0-8323-0014-4

Denson, Jerry & The Ellis County Historical Society: The Battle of Little Robe Creek, 1858 - "Our Ellis County Heritage 1885-1979" - *AHGP/ALHN Independent Oklahoma Genealogy & History (OkGenNet)*

E.A. Schwartz, *The Rogue River indian War and Its aftermath, 1850-1980*. Norman, OK: University of Oklahoma Press, 1997.

Allen, James B.; Leonard, Glen M. (1976), *The Story of the Latter-day Saints*, Salt Lake City: Deseret Book Company, ISBN 0-87747-594-6

Abanes, Richard (2003), *One Nation Under Gods: A History of the Mormon Church*, Thunder's Mouth Press, ISBN 1-56858-283-8

Allen, James B. (Autumn 1966), "The Significance of Joseph Smith's "First Vision" in Mormon Thought", *Dialogue: A Journal of Mormon Thought* **1** (3): 29–46.

Avery, V.T.; Newell, L.K. (1980), "The Lion and the Lady: Brigham Young and Emma Smith", *Utah Historical Quarterly* **48** (1): 81–97.

Bergera, Gary James, ed. (1989), *Line Upon Line: Essays on Mormon Doctrine*, Salt Lake City: Signature Books, ISBN 0-941214-69-9.

Bloom, Harold (1992), *The American Religion: The Emergence of the Post-Christian Nation* (1st ed.), New York: Simon & Schuster, ISBN 978-0-671-67997-2.

Brodie, Fawn M. (1971), *No Man Knows My History: The Life of Joseph Smith* (2nd ed.), New York: Alfred A. Knopf, ISBN 0-394-46967-4.

Brooke, John L. (1994), *The Refiner's Fire: The Making of Mormon Cosmology, 1644–1844*, Cambridge: Cambridge University Press, ISBN 0-521-34545-6.

Bushman, Richard Lyman (2005), *Joseph Smith: Rough Stone Rolling*, New York: Alfred A. Knopf, ISBN 1-4000-4270-4.

Compton, Todd (1997), *In Sacred Loneliness: The Plural Wives of Joseph Smith*, Salt Lake City: Signature Books, ISBN 1-56085-085-X .

Foster, Lawrence (1981), *Religion and Sexuality: The Shakers, the Mormons, and the Oneida Community*, New York: Oxford University Press, ISBN 978-0-252-01119-1 .

Harris, Martin (1859), "Mormonism—No. II", *Tiffany's Monthly* **5** (4): 163–170 .

Hill, Donna (1977), *Joseph Smith: The first Mormon*, Garden City, New York: Doubleday & Co., ISBN 0-385-00804-X .

Hill, Marvin S. (1989), *Quest for Refuge: The Mormon Flight from American Pluralism*, Salt Lake City, Utah: Signature Books, ISBN 978-0-941214-70-4 .

Hodgins, Gordon Frank (1984). A comparison of the theology of salvation in the teachings of Martin Luther and Joseph Smith, Jr. (M.A. thesis). Wilfrid Laurier University.

Howe, Eber Dudley (1834), *Mormonism Unvailed: Or, A Faithful Account of that Singular Imposition and Delusion, from its Rise to the Present Time*, Painesville, Ohio: Telegraph Press, OCLC 10395314 .

Larson, Stan (1978), "The King Follett Discourse: A Newly Amalgamated Text", *BYU Studies* **18** (2): 193–208 .

Mack, Solomon (1811), *A Narraitve [sic] of the Life of Solomon Mack*, Windsor: Solomon Mack, OCLC 15568282 .

Marquardt, H. Michael; Walters, Wesley P (1994), *Inventing Mormonism*, Signature Books, ISBN 1-56085-108-2.

Marquardt, H. Michael (1999), *The Joseph Smith Revelations: Text and Commentary*, Signature Books, ISBN 978-1-56085-126-4.

Marquardt, H. Michael (2005), *The Rise of Mormonism: 1816–1844*, Grand Rapids, MI: Xulon Press, p. 632, ISBN 1-59781-470-9.

Neilson, Reid Larkin; Givens, Terryl, eds. (2008), *Joseph Smith Jr.: reappraisals after two centuries*, Oxford University Press, ISBN 0-19-536978-5.

Newell, Linda King; Avery, Valeen Tippetts (1994), *Mormon Enigma: Emma Hale Smith* (2nd ed.), University of Illinois Press, ISBN 0-252-06291-4.

Newell, Linda King; Avery, Valeen Tippetts (1994), *Mormon Enigma: Emma Hale Smith* (2nd ed.), University of Illinois Press, ISBN 0-252-06291-4.

Oaks, Dallin H.; Hill, Marvin S. (1975), *Carthage Conspiracy: The Trial of the Accused Assassins of Joseph Smith*, Urbana and Chicago, IL: University of Illinois Press, ISBN 0-252-00554-6.

Ostling, Richard; Ostling, Joan K. (1999), *Mormon America: The Power and the Promise*, San Francisco: HarperSanFrancisco, ISBN 0-06-066371-5.

Persuitte, David (2000), *Joseph Smith and the origins of the Book of Mormon*, Jefferson, North Carolina: McFarland & Co., ISBN 0-7864-0826-X.

Phelps, W.W., ed. (1833), *A Book of Commandments, for the Government of the Church of Christ*, Zion: William Wines Phelps & Co., OCLC 77918630.

Prince, Gregory A (1995), *Power From On High: The Development of Mormon Priesthood*, Salt Lake City: Signature Books, ISBN 1-56085-071-X.

Quinn, D. Michael (1994), *The Mormon Hierarchy: Origins of Power*, Salt Lake City: Signature Books, ISBN 1-56085-056-6.

Quinn, D. Michael (1998), *Early Mormonism and the Magic World View* (2nd ed.), Salt Lake City: Signature Books, ISBN 1-56085-089-2.

Remini, Robert V. (2002), *Joseph Smith: A Penguin Life*, New York: Penguin Group, ISBN 0-670-03083-X.

Roberts, B. H., ed. (1902), *History of the Church of Jesus Christ of Latter-day Saints* **1**, Salt Lake City: Deseret News, ISBN 0-87747-688-8.

Roberts, B. H., ed. (1904), *History of the Church of Jesus Christ of Latter-day Saints* **2**, Salt Lake City: Deseret News, ISBN 0-87747-688-8.

Roberts, B. H., ed. (1905), *History of the Church of Jesus Christ of Latter-day Saints* **3**, Salt Lake City: Deseret News, ISBN 0-87747-688-8.

Roberts, B. H., ed. (1909), *History of the Church of Jesus Christ of Latter-day Saints* **5**, Salt Lake City: Deseret News, ISBN 0-87747-688-8.

Roberts, B. H., ed. (1912), *History of the Church of Jesus Christ of Latter-day Saints* **6**, Salt Lake City: Deseret News, ISBN 0-87747-688-8.

Shipps, Jan (1985), *Mormonism: The Story of a New Religious Tradition*, Chicago: University of Illinois Press, ISBN 0-252-01417-0 .

Smith, George D. (1994), "Nauvoo Roots of Mormon Polygamy, 1841–46: A Preliminary Demographic Report", *Dialogue: A Journal of Mormon Thought* **27** (1): 1 .

Smith, George D (2008), *Nauvoo Polygamy: "... but we called it celestial marriage"*, Salt Lake City, Utah: Signature Books, ISBN 978-1-56085-201-8 .

Smith, Joseph, Jr. (1830), *The Book of Mormon: An Account Written by the Hand of Mormon, Upon Plates Taken from the Plates of Nephi*, Palmyra, New York: E. B. Grandin, OCLC 768123849 . See Book of Mormon.

Smith, Joseph, Jr. (1832), "History of the Life of Joseph Smith", in Jessee, Dean C, *Personal Writings of Joseph Smith*, Salt Lake City: Deseret Book (published 2002), ISBN 1-57345-787-6 .

Smith, Joseph, Jr.; Cowdery, Oliver; Rigdon, Sidney et al., eds. (1835), *Doctrine and Covenants of the Church of the Latter Day Saints: Carefully Selected from the Revelations of God*, Kirtland, Ohio: F. G. Williams & Co, OCLC 18137804 | displayeditors= suggested (help). See Doctrine and Covenants.

Smith, Joseph, Jr. (March 1, 1842), "Church History [Wentworth Letter]", *Times and Seasons* **3** (9): 706–10 . See Wentworth letter.

Smith, Lucy Mack (1853), *Biographical Sketches of Joseph Smith the Prophet, and His Progenitors for Many Generations*, Liverpool: S.W. Richards, OCLC 4922747 . See The History of Joseph Smith by His Mother

Van Wagoner, Richard S.; Walker, Steven C. (1982), "Joseph Smith: The Gift of Seeing", *Dialogue: A Journal of Mormon Thought* **15** (2): 48–68 .

Van Wagoner, Richard S. (1992), *Mormon Polygamy: A History* (2 ed.), Salt Lake City: Signature Books, ISBN 978-0-941214-79-7 .

Vogel, Dan (2004), *Joseph Smith: The Making of a Prophet*, Salt Lake City, UT: Signature Books, ISBN 1-56085-179-1 .

Widmer, Kurt (2000), *Mormonism and the Nature of God: A Theological Evolution, 1830–1915*, Jefferson, N.C.: McFarland, ISBN 978-0-7864-0776-7.

A Peculiar Place for the Peculiar Institution: Slavery and Sovereignty in Early Territorial Utah, Ricks, Nathaniel R., Master Thesis, *Brigham Young University*, 2007.

Lester E. Bush, Jr. and Armand L. Mauss, eds., *Neither White nor Black: Mormon Scholars Confront the Race Issue in a Universal Church*, Signature Books, 1984

Reeve, W. Paul (May 31, 2012), *The Wrong Side of White*, University of Chicago Divinity School

Bush, Lester E., Jr. (Spring 1973), "Mormonism's Negro Doctrine: An Historical Overview", *Dialogue: A Journal of Mormon Thought* **8** (1), retrieved 2012-11-01

Edward P. Spillane (1908). "Peter Hardeman Burnett". The Catholic Encyclopaedia, vol. III. Retrieved 2007-05-09.

California State Library. "Governor Peter Burnett of California". State of California. Retrieved 2007-05-09.

Hittell, Theodore Henry. *History of California* (4 vol 1898) old. detailed narrative; online edition

Brands, H.W. *The Age of Gold: The California Gold Rush and the New American Dream* (2003) excerpt and text search

Burns, John F. and Richard J. Orsi, eds; *Taming the Elephant: Politics, Government, and Law in Pioneer California* (2003) online edition

Cherny, Robert W., Richard Griswold del Castillo, and Gretchen Lemke-Santangelo. *Competing Visions: A History Of California* (2005), college textbook

Cleland, Robert Glass. *A History of California: The American Period* (1922) 512 pp. online edition

Pedersen, Kern, Makers of Minnesota: An Illustrated History of the Builders of Our State. St. Paul: Minnesota Territorial Centennial (1949)

Alexander Ramsey at the *Biographical Directory of the United States Congress*

"John Whiteaker". *Governors of Oregon*. Oregon State Library.

Myrtle M. McKittrick, *Vallejo, Son of California*, 1944 This book deals mainly with the Mexican period in General Vallejo's life.

Alan Rosenus, *General Vallejo and the Advent of the Americans*, 1995 ISBN 1-890771-21-X This book deals mainly with the American period in General Vallejo's life.

Madie Brown Emparan, *The Vallejos of California*, 1968 Contains twelve brief biographies of General Vallejo, his wife Benicia, and each of ten surviving children.

Theodore H. Hittell (1897) [1885]. *History of California, Vol IV*. San Francisco, CA: N.J. Stone & Company.

California State Library. "John Bigler". State of California.

Judson A. Grenier (2003). *Officialdom: California State Government, 1849-1879*.

Anderson, Margo J. *The American Census: A Social History*. Yale University Press, 1988. ISBN 0-300-04709-6

Cardoso, J. J. "Hinton Rowan Helper as a Racist in the Abolitionist Camp" *The Journal of Negro History*, Vol. 55, No. 4 (Oct., 1970), pp. 323–330 in JSTOR

Channing, Steven A. *Crisis of Fear: Secession in South Carolina* (1974) online pp 104-5

Fredrickson, George M. "Antislavery Racist: Hinton Rowan Helper," in Fredrickson, *The Arrogance of Race: Historical Perspectives on Slavery, Racism, and Social Inequality* (1988), pp 28–53 online excerpt

Battison, Edwin. (1960). "Eli Whitney and the Milling Machine." Smithsonian Journal of History I.

Cooper, Carolyn, & Lindsay, Merrill K. (1980). Eli Whitney and the Whitney Armory.

Whitneyville, CT: Eli Whitney Museum.

Dexter, Franklin B. (1911). "Eli Whitney." Yale Biographies and Annals, 1792–1805. New York, NY: Henry Holt & Company.

Hall, Karyl Lee Kibler, & Cooper, Carolyn. (1984). Windows on the Works: Industry on the Eli Whitney Site, 1798–1979.

Bulman, Joan (1956). *Jenny Lind: a biography*. London: Barrie. OCLC 252091695.

Kielty, Bernadine (1959). *Jenny Lind Sang Here*. Boston: Houghton Mifflin. OCLC 617750.

Kyle, Elisabeth (1964). *The Swedish Nightingale: Jenny Lind*. New York: Holt Rinehart and Winston. OCLC 884670.

Maude, Jenny M. C. (1926). *The life of Jenny Lind, briefly told by her daughter, Mrs. Raymond Maude, O. B. E.* London: Cassell. OCLC 403731797.

Southern, Eileen. *The Music of Black Americans: A History.* W. W. Norton & Company; 3rd edition. ISBN 0-393-97141-4

3 Hine, Darlene Clark. *Black Women in America: an historical Encyclopedia.* Brooklyn, NY: Carlson Publishing, 1993. pp 499–501.

Nathan, Hans. *Dan Emmett and the Rise of Early Negro Minstrelsy.* Norman: University of Oklahoma Press, 1962

Wierich, Jochen. *Grand Themes: Emanuel Leutze, "Washington Crossing the Delaware," and American History Painting* (Penn State University Press; 2012) 240 pages; Argues that the painting was a touchstone for debates over history painting at a time of intense sectionalism.

Hutton, Anne Hawkes (1975). *Portrait of Patriotism: Washington Crossing the Delaware.* Radnor, Pennsylvania: Chilton Book Company. ISBN 0-8019-6418-0.

Landow, George (1979). *William Holman Hunt and Typological Symbolism.* Yale University Press. ISBN 0-300-02196-8.

Maas, Jeremy (1984). *Holman Hunt and the Light of the World.* Ashgate. ISBN 978-0-85967-683-0.

Bronkhurst, Judith (2006). *William Holman Hunt: A Catalogue Raisonné.* Yale University Press. ISBN 978-0-300-10235-2.

Lochnan, Katharine (2008). *Holman Hunt and the Pre-Raphaelite Vision*. Art Gallery of Toronto. ISBN 978-1-894243-57-5.

Lindsay, Jack. *Gustave Courbet his life and art*. Publ. Jupiter Books (London) Limited 1977.

Masanès, Fabrice, *Gustave Courbet* (Cologne: Taschen, 2006) ISBN 3-8228-5683-5

Nochlin, Linda, *Courbet*, (London: Thames & Hudson, 2007) ISBN 978-0-500-28676-0

Nochlin, Linda, *Realism: Style and Civilization* (New York: Penguin, 1972).

Murphy, Alexandra R. *Jean-François Millet*. Museum of Fine Arts, Boston, 1984. ISBN 0-87846-237-6

Armstrong, Carol (1991). *Odd Man Out: Readings of the Work and Reputation of Edgar Degas*. Chicago and London: University of Chicago Press. ISBN 0-226-02695-7

Auden, W.H.; Kronenberger, Louis (1966), The Viking Book of Aphorisms, New York: Viking Press

Bade, Patrick; Degas, Edgar (1992). *Degas*. London: Studio Editions. ISBN 1-85170-845-6

Baumann, Felix; Karabelnik, Marianne, et al. (1994). *Degas Portraits*. London: Merrell Holberton. ISBN 1-85894-014-1

Benedek, Nelly S. "Chronology of the Artist's Life." Degas. 2004. 21 May 2004.

Benedek, Nelly S. "Degas's Artistic Style." Degas. 2004. 21 March 2004.

Bowness, Alan. ed. (1965) "Edgar Degas." *The Book of Art Volume 7*. New York: Grolier Incorporated: 41.

Brettell, Richard R.; McCullagh, Suzanne Folds (1984). *Degas in The Art Institute of Chicago*. New York: The Art Institute of Chicago and Harry N. Abrams, Inc. ISBN 0-86559-058-3

Brown, Marilyn (1994). *Degas and the Business of Art: a Cotton Office in New Orleans*. Pennsylvania State University Press. ISBN 0-271-00944-6

Canaday, John (1969). *The Lives of the Painters Volume 3*. New York: W.W. Norton and Company Inc.

Dorra, Henri. *Art in Perspective* New York: Harcourt Brace Jovanovich, Inc.:208

Dumas, Ann (1988). *Degas's Mlle. Fiocre in Context*. Brooklyn: The Brooklyn Museum. ISBN 0-87273-116-2

Dunlop, Ian (1979). *Degas*. New York, N.Y: Harper & Row. OCLC 5583005

"Edgar Degas, 1834–1917." *The Book of Art Volume III* (1976). New York: Grolier Incorporated:4.

Gordon, Robert; Forge, Andrew (1988). *Degas*. New York: Harry N. Abrams. ISBN 0-8109-1142-6

Growe, Bernd; Edgar Degas (1992). *Edgar Degas, 1834–1917*. Cologne: Benedikt Taschen. ISBN 3-8228-0560-2

Guillaud, Jaqueline; Guillaud, Maurice (editors) (1985). *Degas: Form and Space*. New York: Rizzoli. ISBN 0-8478-5407-8

Hartt, Frederick (1976). "Degas" *Art Volume 2*. Englewood Cliffs, NJ: Prentice-Hall Inc.: 365.

"Impressionism." *Praeger Encyclopedia of Art Volume 3* (1967). New York: Praeger Publishers: 952.

J. Paul Getty Trust "Walter Richard Sickert." 2003. 11 May 2004.

Kendall, Richard; Degas, Edgar; Druick, Douglas W.; Beale, Arthur (1998). *Degas and The Little Dancer*. New Haven: Yale University Press. ISBN 0-300-07497-2

Krämer, Felix (May 2007). "'Mon tableau de genre': Degas's 'Le Viol' and Gavarni's 'Lorette'". *The Burlington Magazine* **149** (1250).

Mannering, Douglas (1994). *The Life and Works of Degas*. Great Britain: Parragon Book Service Limited.

Muehlig, Linda D. (1979). *Degas and the Dance, 5–27 April May 1979*. Northampton, Mass.: Smith College Museum of Art.

Peugeot, Catherine, Sellier, Marie (2001). *A Trip to the Orsay Museum*. Paris: ADAGP: 39.

Reff, Theodore (1976). *Degas: the artist's mind*. [New York]: Metropolitan Museum of Art. ISBN 0-87099-146-9

Roskill, Mark W. (1983). "Edgar Degas." *Collier's Encyclopedia*.

Thomson, Richard (1988). *Degas: The Nudes*. London: Thames and Hudson Ltd. ISBN 0-500-23509-0

Tinterow, Gary (1988). *Degas*. New York: The Metropolitan Museum of Art and National Gallery of Canada.

Turner, J. (2000). *From Monet to Cézanne: late 19th-century French artists*. Grove Art. New York: St Martin's Press. ISBN 0-312-22971-2

Werner, Alfred (1969) *Degas Pastels*. New York: Watson-Guptill. ISBN 0-8230-1276-X

Jobert, Barthélémy, *Delacroix*, page 62. Princeton University Press, 1997. ISBN 0-691-00418-8

Clark, Kenneth (1991). *Landscape into Art*. New York: HarperCollins.

Leymarie, J. (1979). *Corot*. Discovering the nineteenth century. Geneva: Skira. ISBN 0-8478-0238-8

Tinterow, Gary; *et al.* (1996). *Corot*. New York: Metropolitan Museum of Art. Cite uses deprecated parameters (help)

Bills, Mark (2006). *William Powell Frith: Painting the Victorian Age*. Yale University Press. ISBN 0-300-12190-3

Wood, Christopher (2006). *William Powell Frith: A Painter and His World*. Sutton Publishing Ltd. ISBN 0-7509-3845-5

Bell, Adrienne Baxter (2003), *George Inness and the Visionary Landscape*, George Braziller, Inc., p. 151, ISBN 0-8076-1525-0

Dore Ashton, *Rosa Bonheur: A Life and a Legend*. Illustrations and Captions by Denise Browne Harethe. New York: A Studio Book/The Viking Press, 1981

Anderson, Nancy K. et al. *Albert Bierstadt, Art & Enterprise*, Hudson Hills Press, Inc.: New York, New York, 1990.

Hendricks, Gordon. *Albert Bierstadt, Painter of the American West*, Harrison House/Harry N. Abrams, Inc.: New York, New York 1988.

Prettejohn, Elizabeth: *Interpreting Sargent*, page 9. Stewart, Tabori & Chang, 1998.

Fairbrother, Trevor: *John Singer Sargent: The Sensualist* (2001), ISBN 0-300-08744-6, Page 139, Note 4.

Watson, Robert P., American First Ladies, Salem Press, Pasadena, CA, 2006

www.firstladies.org

Bennett, David J (2007). He *Almost Changed the World: The Life And Times Of Thomas Riley Marshall*. Freeman & Costello. ISBN 978-1-4259-6562-4.

Ferrell, Chiles Clifton (1899). *'The Daughter of the Confederacy' – Her Life, Character, and Writings*. Mississippi Historical Society.

W. U. Hensel, "The Christian Riot and The Treason Trials of 1851, An Historical Sketch" (tarlton.law.utexas.edu)]

William Parker, "The Freedman's Story - Parts I & II", *Atlantic Monthly*, Vol. XVII, March/February 1866

Jonathan Katz, *Resistance at Christiana: The Fugitive Slave Rebellion*, Cromwell, 1974

Thomas P. Slaughter, *Bloody Dawn - The Christiana Riot and Racial Violence in the Antebellum North*, Oxford University Press, 1981

William Parker and His Impact on the Christiana Resistance (millersville.edu)

Forbes, David, *A True Story of the Christiana Riot*, The Sun Printing House, 1898

Danson, Edwin. *Drawing the Line: How Mason and Dixon Surveyed the Most Famous Border in America*. Wiley. ISBN 0-471-38502-6

Ecenbarger, Bill. *Walkin' the Line: A Journey from Past to Present Along the Mason–Dixon*. M. Evans. ISBN 978-0-87131-962-3

Parker, Hershel (1996). *Herman Melville: A Biography. Volume I, 1819–1851*. Baltimore: Johns Hopkins University Press. ISBN 0-8018-5428-8.

Parker, Hershel (2005). *Herman Melville: A Biography. Volume II, 1851–1891*. Baltimore: The Johns Hopkins University Press. ISBN 0-8018-8186-2.

Gorman, Herbert (1929). *The Incredible Marquis, Alexandre Dumas*. New York: Farrar & Rinehart. OCLC 1370481.

Hemmings, F.W.J. (1979). *Alexandre Dumas, the King of Romance*. New York: Charles Scribner's Sons. ISBN 0-684-16391-8.

Reed, F. W. (Frank Wild) (1933). *A Bibliography of Alexandre Dumas, père*. Pinner Hill, Middlesex: J.A. Neuhuys. OCLC 1420223.

Ross, Michael (1981). *Alexandre Dumas*. Newton Abbot, London, North Pomfret (Vt): David & Charles. ISBN 0-7153-7758-2.

Schopp, Claude (1988). *Alexandre Dumas, Genius of Life.* trans. by A. J. Koch. New York, Toronto: Franklin Watts. ISBN 0-531-15093-3.

Spurr, Harry A. (October 1902). *The Life and Writings of Alexandre Dumas.* New York: Frederick A. Stokes, Company. OCLC 2999945.

Jones, Brian Jay. *Washington Irving: An American Original.* (Arcade, 2008). ISBN 978-1-55970-836-4

Warner, Charles Dudley. *Washington Irving.* (Riverside Press, 1881).

Williams, Stanley T. *The Life of Washington Irving.* 2 vols. (Oxford University Press, 1935). ISBN 0-7812-5291-1

Burstein, Andrew. *The Original Knickerbocker: The Life of Washington Irving.* (Basic Books, 2007). ISBN 978-0-465-00853-7

Bowers, Claude G. *The Spanish Adventures of Washington Irving.* (Riverside Press, 1940).

Hellman, George S. *Washington Irving, Esquire.* (Alfred A. Knopf, 1925).

Irving, Pierre M. *Life and Letters of Washington Irving.* 4 vols. (G.P. Putnam, 1862). Cited herein as PMI.

Irving, Washington. *The Complete Works of Washington Irving.* (Rust, *et al.*, editors). 30 vols. (University of Wisconsin/Twayne, 1969–1986). Cited herein as *Works.*

Maurois, Andre (1956). *Olympio: The Life of Victor Hugo*. New York: Harper & Brothers.

Maurois, Andre (1966). *Victor Hugo and His World*. London: Thames and Hudson. Out of print.

Robb, Graham (1997). *Victor Hugo: A Biography*. W.W. Norton & Company: 1999 paperback edition. ISBN 0-393-31899-0.

Craraft, James. *Two Shining Souls: Jane Addams, Leo Tolstoy, and the Quest for Global Peace* (Lanham: Lexington, 2012).

Ferguson, Robert (2001). *Henrik Ibsen: A New Biography*. New York: Dorset Press. ISBN 0760720940.

Meyer, Michael. *Ibsen*. History Press Ltd., Stroud, 2004.

Harding, Walter. *The Days of Henry Thoreau*. Princeton University Press, 1982

Hendrick, George. "The Influence of Thoreau's 'Civil Disobedience' on Gandhi's Satyagraha." *The New England Quarterly* 29, no. 4 (December 1956). 462–71.

Howarth, William. *The Book of Concord: Thoreau's Life as a Writer*. Viking Press, 1982

Myerson, Joel et al. *The Cambridge Companion to Henry David Thoreau*. Cambridge University Press. 1995

Nash, Roderick. *Henry David Thoreau, Philosopher*

McFarland, Philip. *Hawthorne in Concord*. New York: Grove Press, 2004. ISBN 0-8021-1776-7.

Mellow, James R. *Nathaniel Hawthorne in His Times*. Boston: Houghton Mifflin Company, 1980. ISBN 0-365-27602-0.

Miller, Edwin Haviland. *Salem Is My Dwelling Place: A Life of Nathaniel Hawthorne*. Iowa City: University of Iowa Press, 1991. ISBN 0-87745-332-2.

Porte, Joel. *The Romance in America: Studies in Cooper, Poe, Hawthorne, Melville, and James*. Middletown, Conn.: Wesleyan University Press, 1969.

Schreiner, Samuel A., Jr. *The Concord Quartet: Alcott, Emerson, Hawthorne, Thoreau, and the Friendship that Freed the American Mind*. Hoboken, NJ: John Wiley and Sons, 2006. ISBN 0-471-64663-6.

Wineapple, Brenda. *Hawthorne: A Life*. Random House: New York, 2003. ISBN 0-8129-7291-0.

Koch, Daniel R. (2012). *Ralph Waldo Emerson in Europe: Class, Race and Revolution in the making of an American Thinker*. London: I.B. Tauris.

McAleer, John (1984). *Ralph Waldo Emerson: Days of Encounter*. Boston: Little, Brown and Company. ISBN 0-316-55341-7.

Myerson, Joel (2000). *A Historical Guide to Ralph Waldo Emerson*. New York: Oxford University Press. ISBN 0-19-512094-9.

Brown, T. Allston (1903), *A History of the New York Stage, Volume I*, New York: Dodd, Mead and Co, p. 450.

Swanson, James (2006). *Manhunt: The 12-Day Chase for Lincoln's Killer*, New York: Harper Collins, pp. 42–43. ISBN 978-0-06-051849-3

Scott, John Albert (1927). *Fort Stanwix and Oriskany: The Romantic Story of the Repulse of St.Legers British Invasion of 1777*. Rome, NY: Rome Sentinel Company. OCLC 563963.

Watt, Gavin (1997). *The Burning of the Valleys: Daring Raids From Canada Against the New York Frontier in the Fall of 1780*. Toronto: Dundurn Press. ISBN 978-1-55002-271-1. OCLC 317810982.

Watt, Gavin K; Morrison, James F (2002). *Rebellion in the Mohawk Valley: The St. Leger Expedition of 1777*. Toronto: Dundurn Press. ISBN 978-1-55002-376-3. OCLC 49305965. Cite uses deprecated parameters (help)

Zenzen, Joan M (2008). *Fort Stanwix National Monument: reconstructing the past and partnering for the future*. Albany, NY: SUNY Press. ISBN 978-0-7914-7433-4. OCLC 163593261.

Dedicated

To

Elizabeth, Peter and Patricia Murphy

Acknowledgements

I'd like to thank all those who helped me labor through this writing. The most important of you know who you are. Those who read along the way, offered intellectual criticism and supported me to its completion. I'd even like to thank those that offered constructive criticism as well although I hated that part much more.

About the Author

None of your fucking business. Just kidding. But still none of your fucking business.

Made in the USA
Lexington, KY
11 October 2014